RICHARD BRATBY

FORWARD

RICHARD BRATBY

FORWARD

100 Years of the City of Birmingham Symphony Orchestra

Elliott&Thompson

First published 2019 by
Elliott and Thompson Limited
2 John Street, London WC1N 2ES
www.eandtbooks.com

ISBN: 978-1-78396-453-6

Picture Credits:
Images courtesy City of Birmingham Symphony Orchestra, with the following exceptions:

Front cover image: Trustees of the Congregation of the Most Holy Redeemer
Back cover image: Andrew Fox
Alamy Stock Photo: Phil Broom 59; Chronicle x; Lebrecht Music & Arts 14 top, 14 bottom left, 26–27, 93. ArenaPAL: Clive Barda 235. © BBC 133. Mat Beckett from River Rea Films 52. Bridgeman Images: Chris Christodoulou 218; Lebrecht Music Arts 160; Laurie Lewis 228; Godfrey MacDominic 126; Tully Potter 66. Alastair Carew Cox 246–47. CBSO: Architeky Vanek 44; E W Baldry 88; City Engineer's Dept., Birmingham 113, 174; Morland Braithwaite 101; Harold Holt 10; Geoffrey Gordon House ARPD 97; Christian Hunt 121; Simon Livingstone Studios 75, 116; John Whybrow Collection 5, 69, 72; Hans Wild 83; Reg Wilson 173; Crispian Woodgate 140. Benjamin Ealovega 248, 251. @AdamFradgley 176–77. Andrew Fox ii-iii, 61, 125, 178–79, 185, 207, 210–11, 260–61, 263. Getty Images: Erich Auerbach 164; Bettmann 9; Tony Buckingham/Redferns 220; Heritage Images/Hulton Archive 92; Hulton Deutsch 29; ullstein bild 231; Universal History Archive vii; Universal Images Group 111. Courtesy of the Ruth Gipps Archive 105. Frans Jansen 257. Mirrorpix 40, 98 top, 99, 100, 103, 129, 215. Camilla Jessel Panufnik FRPS 138, 217. Neil Pugh – DecisiveImaging 54–55, 63, 188–89, 240, 243. Revolver Records 85. Aaron Scott Richards 124. Eric Richmond, courtesy Lomonaco Artists 236. Topfoto/Woodmansterne 167. Wikipedia: CC0 14 bottom right; West Midlands Police, CC BY-SA 2.0 108–9. Alan Wood 84, 137, 151, 181, 192, 196, 205, 268.

Figures featured on the chapter openers are as follows: 1. Henry Wood; 2. Thomas Beecham; 3. Adrian Boult; 4. Leslie Heward; 5. George Weldon; 6. Rudolf Schwarz; 7. Louis Frémaux; 8. Simon Rattle; 9. Andris Nelsons; 10. Mirga Gražinytė-Tyla

9 8 7 6 5 4 3 2 1

A catalogue record for this book is available from the British Library.

Designer: Karin Fremer
Picture researcher: Jennifer Veall

Printed and bound in Italy by Printer Trento

To Annette

CONTENTS

Foreword and Acknowledgments

Over a century of history, the City of Birmingham Symphony Orchestra has been known by several names. For the first twenty-seven years of its existence it was officially the City of Birmingham Orchestra; but it was also referred to as the City Orchestra, the Civic Orchestra or the Municipal Orchestra. Even today, you'll sometimes encounter Brummies who, though aware and intensely proud of the CBSO, have never paused to consider what the initials stand for. And as the CBSO enters its second century, those four letters have long since ceased to refer to the ninety players of the orchestra alone. What is sometimes referred to as the 'CBSO family' also includes a full symphonic chorus, two youth choruses, a youth orchestra, CBSO Centre, a sizeable administrative team and a huge network of outreach projects – each of them, in its own way, among the finest in the world.

But throughout it all, the idea of the CBSO as Birmingham's orchestra – the musical embodiment of one of the world's great cities, in all its ambition, complexity and diversity – has been a constant. Birmingham has always prided itself on leading where other cities follow, and the CBSO's list of 'firsts' is striking: the first major orchestra to present children's concerts,

the first to appoint permanent education staff, a pioneer in its attitude to female musicians and board members, and a globally recognised example of the power of the arts to drive urban renewal. Before all of this, though, it was the first British orchestra to receive guaranteed regular funding from a city council – an unprecedented and enduring gesture of belief in the power of art to enrich lives. Throughout a hundred years of war, recession and social change, the CBSO has always been Birmingham's orchestra: rooted in and responsive to the community that founded it, and which it continues to serve.

In this centenary year, this is a short and (unavoidably) personal attempt to retell the story of an orchestra in its city, interspersed with reflections on some of the many different ideas and experiences that have shaped the CBSO's story. The life of the orchestra has always extended far beyond the concert platform. I've also tried to spotlight a few of the personalities who have played an important part in the CBSO's history – some familiar, some deserving of greater recognition. It's far from comprehensive. Any orchestra is a community of remarkable

OPPOSITE *27 August 1873: the world premiere of Sullivan's* The Light of the World *at the Birmingham Triennial Festival.*

personalities, and for every story that I've tried to retell here there have been at least twenty for which I haven't had room.

So this is primarily a story of music and musicians, with only minimal reference to the vast amount of work that has always gone on behind the scenes. Every member of the CBSO's administrative team is as vital as each musician, and the brief description of their present-day activities given in the final chapter is a very small gesture towards acknowledging a century of resourceful, loyal and untiring backstage service – sometimes at the expense of health, family life and financial security – to the orchestra and the city.

I have drawn extensively on the work of my distinguished former colleague Beresford King-Smith, who served the CBSO for half of its entire existence, who created its archive, and whose book *Crescendo!* remains the definitive history of the CBSO's first seventy-five years. This book would have been impossible without his generous advice and support: we that are young(ish) shall never see so much, nor live so long.

My thanks also go to Stephen Maddock and Abby Corfan for commissioning this book in the first place, to Maria Howes for her enthusiasm in bringing it to completion, to Adam Nagel for his good humour and heroic work on the digital performance archive, and to Helen Tabor for indulging me in my search for sources. The professionalism and patience of Corinna Rayner and her team of archivists at the Library of Birmingham went far beyond the call of duty. My thanks also to James Jolly of *Gramophone* and to Christopher Morley of the *Birmingham Post*.

One of the greatest pleasures of writing this book has been the way that it has served as a pretext for talking to those of my former CBSO colleagues, friends, fellow concertgoers and extended 'family' members who were willing to share their time and their memories (many of which are included here), and for whose generosity I owe sincere thanks: Alpesh Chauhan, Sheila Clarke, Maggie Cotton, Ben Dawson, Peter Donohoe, Peter Dyson, Wally Francis, Fiona Fraser, Sarah Gee, Mirga Gražinytė-Tyla, Alwyn Green, David Gregory, Simon Halsey, Rosemary Harby, Prue Hawthorne, Niki Longhurst, Bryony Morrison, Andris Nelsons, Annie Oakley, Sakari Oramo, Tommy Pearson, Mark Phillips, Sir Simon Rattle, Julian Robinson, David and Elaine Russell, Cathy Scott-Burt, Michael Seal, Gordon Sill, Ed Smith, Paul Smith, Stan Smith, James Strebing, Angela Swanson, Jackie Tyler and Richard Whitehouse.

A very special, personal thank you, too, to all the comrades-in-arms who aren't mentioned in these pages but who helped make my years at the CBSO a pleasure as well as a privilege – and particularly Gavin Allsop, Anna Ambrose, Claire Armour, Steven Barwell, Nikki Bawcutt, Galia Bouhayed, Heather Brannan, Natalie Bridge, Andrea Chalk, Baz Chapman, Joanna Clarke, Peter Clarke, Barrie Collier, Bekah Cork, Elen Elis, Sarah Ferguson, Mike Flower, Rachel Groves, Peter Harris, Richard Hawley, Seb Huckle, Amy Lauder, Katie Lucas, Lisa Mallett, Claire Marshall, Amy May, Sarah Melhuish, Christine Midgley, Alison Morrell, Jackie and Stephen Newbould, Ben Noakes, Joanne Norman, Madeleine Norris, Gill Powell, Zoe Poyser,

Melanie and Patrick Ryan, Dan Rowlinson, Keith Stubbs, Sian Wood and Richard York. None of you will need to be told why.

For encouragement, support and advice, my thanks go to Alexandra Coghlan, Martin Cullingford, Jessica Duchen, Tommy Pearson, Igor Toronyi-Lalic, Clare Stevens and the late James Hamilton Brown, known to his pupils as Minim. And, supremely, to my wife Dr Annette Rubery, who having already endured a decade of spoiled weekends and distracted dinners as a CBSO widow, tolerated a further twelve months with a fellow writer's sympathy and understanding, and to whom, with more love than I can ever say, this book is dedicated.

A Note on Titles

From 1920 to 1948, the official name of the orchestra was the City of Birmingham Orchestra (CBO); 'Symphony' was added (apparently at the whim of George Weldon) in 1948. For a brief period during the Second World War it was also known as the City of Birmingham (Emergency) Orchestra. I've tried, as far as possible, to use the title appropriate to the period under discussion – but there may be occasional overlaps.

Likewise the orchestra's main conductor has at various times been given the title of chief conductor, principal conductor, music director and musical director, without any great consistency. I have tried to use the appropriate title in each case, but ask for indulgence if inconsistencies have, on occasion, crept in.

A Note on Finance

Professional orchestras are intrinsically uneconomical, and at almost no point in the last hundred years could the CBSO have been considered financially secure. Most well-adjusted music-lovers find the subject demoralising, so to avoid drowning the story in numbers, and since the orchestra's finances from 1920 to 1995 have been extensively covered by Beresford King-Smith in *Crescendo!*, I have avoided discussing money except where necessary. As a rule of thumb, and unless stated otherwise, it should be assumed that at any given point in this history the orchestra is either barely breaking even or is facing a worrying financial shortfall. This is also likely to apply for the foreseeable future.

Prologue:
October 1912

'People who talk of the spread
of music in England and the
increasing love of it, rarely seem to
know where the growth of the art is
really strong and properly fostered:
some day the press will awake to
the fact, already known abroad
and to some few of us in England,
that the living centre of music
in Great Britain is not London, but
somewhere further north.'

EDWARD ELGAR

with

Sir Edward Elgar.

Founding fathers: as early as 1905, Sir Edward Elgar (left) predicted the need for
a permanent professional orchestra in Birmingham. After several false starts,
his colleague Granville Bantock (right) would help make it a reality in 1920.

For four days in October 1912, Birmingham was the centre of the musical world. On the morning of Tuesday 1 October, the first day of the 47th Birmingham Triennial Musical Festival, concertgoers could sense the significance of the occasion before even a note had been heard. Traffic was diverted, and the streets around the Town Hall filled with music-lovers of all stations – the women in a flurry of colours, the men in the more sombre formal wear of the Edwardian era. The previous day had been sunny, but rain had fallen overnight and the morning was overcast and blustery; canvas awnings had been stretched outside the Town Hall to protect the assembled elegance. Yet despite the clouds the company still managed to sparkle. Viscount Cobham, the Festival's president, had decamped for the week from his home at Hagley Hall to the Judges' Lodgings in Edgbaston, bringing with him a sizeable party of Worcestershire aristocracy.

The Lord Mayor of Birmingham, Alderman William Bowater, brought 200 guests, and across the square in the Council House, municipal gardeners were already placing flowers and potted palms up the grand staircase, while upstairs tables were being laid for a ceremonial civic luncheon, with particular attention being paid to the Lady Mayoress's Parlour – a retiring room for female guests. Some 120 instrumentalists and 351 choral singers were assembled on the platform of the Town Hall when the eleventh chime sounded from the clock tower in Chamberlain Square and the Festival's new principal conductor, Sir Henry Wood – lured from his annual series of promenade concerts in London to take on this immeasurably

more prestigious duty – lowered his baton to begin Mendelssohn's *Elijah*: the masterpiece created in 1846 for this city, this festival and this hall, and performed almost as an act of devotion at every Triennial Festival since.

Rehearsals had been under way for several days. Sir Edward and Lady Elgar had attended an early orchestral rehearsal at Queen's Hall in London, where Wood had convened the players from Manchester, London and Birmingham who made up the Festival Orchestra. Lady Elgar had been put out by Wood's breezy, no-nonsense rehearsal manner – 'quite unbearable, even shutting door noisily', she noted in her diary – and at the public dress rehearsal in Birmingham on Monday 30 September, the correspondent of the *Birmingham Daily Gazette* was startled to hear a roar of laughter from the choir in the middle of Bach's *St Matthew Passion*.

It seemed improper, and when the Finnish soprano Aino Ackté arrived in a striking black hat with a white feather and sang the final scene from Richard Strauss's *Salome* with one hand on her hip, it proved too much for one member of the Birmingham public. 'If that's Strauss ["She pronounced it Straws," noted the *Gazette*], I want no more of it,' she was heard to declare. But she was in a decided minority. For music-lovers across the UK and Europe, the stature of the Birmingham Festival rested on its new music.

With the annual genuflection to *Elijah* out of the way, it wasn't long in coming. The opening night's concert began with Beethoven's *Coriolan* overture and Bach's Brandenburg Concerto No. 3 before Moriz Rosenthal performed the First Piano Concerto by his teacher, Franz Liszt. But then

On an August afternoon in 1888, crowds spread out into Council House Square (the future Victoria Square) after a Triennial Festival concert in the Town Hall.

came something entirely new: Elgar's *The Music Makers*, conducted by the composer – his fourth commission for the Festival. The first had been *The Dream of Gerontius* in 1900, and if the Festival Chorus had been unprepared on that occasion, it was now thoroughly familiar with Elgar's style. Dora Penny (the 'Dorabella' of the *Enigma Variations*) 'had no words to describe' how beautifully the contralto Muriel Foster sang her solos.

Next came another novelty. Jean Sibelius had arrived from Helsinki a few days earlier, and was staying with his friend Granville Bantock, the principal of the Birmingham School of Music, at Broad Meadow, Bantock's country house just outside the city at Kings Norton. Bantock's son Angus watched in awe as the bald, taciturn and 'massively built' Finnish guest powered his way through the household's stocks of whisky. They conversed in French: Sibelius remarked that the pine trees in the garden were 'like my own dear Finland'. After rehearsing his Fourth Symphony (Bantock served as interpreter, and Henry Wood relayed the translated instructions to the orchestra from the side of the stage), he took Sunday 29 September off for a Shakespearean day trip to Stratford-upon-Avon (he was enchanted by the town's oak trees). The performance that he conducted on 1 October was only the second time the symphony had been heard – the first outside of Finland – and by the time it was finished it was well after 10 p.m.

The concert, however, still had three more items to run: solos from both Foster and Rosenthal, and to finish, Rossini's *William Tell* overture, by which time any hopes of the traditional Birmingham post-concert supper of tripe and onions at Joey's Restaurant had long since faded. Unsurprisingly, the following morning's *St Matthew Passion* struck critics as laboured, even with Felix Salmond playing cello continuo. The evening concert began with another premiere: *The Song of St Francis*, by the Shropshire-born Henry Walford Davies; and it seems as if the choir had got its wind back. The *Gazette* went into a rapture of superlatives: 'How many choirs, from Birmingham to the nebula of Orion, could have sung like the Birmingham choir last night? . . . we shall be surprised if they beat it before the year 2012.'

But the strain was starting to affect the orchestra, who, after accompanying Pablo Casals in Haydn's D major Cello Concerto, disintegrated altogether while Granville Bantock was conducting the first performance of his symphonic poem *Fifine at the Fair*. Bantock took

it on the chin, and turning to the audience, said, 'I crave your pardon, ladies and gentlemen', before starting the thirty-minute work all over again. By the time Casals returned to play Richard Strauss's *Don Quixote*, it was already past 10.30 p.m. – with a scene from Verdi's *Otello* and Wagner's *Tannhäuser* overture still to come. Casals' playing, according to the *Gazette*, was 'perfect'; the concert's timings 'well – extremely liberal'.

No one presumably gave much thought to the Town Hall staff (who'd been deluged with photographs of Sibelius from autograph-hunters), still less the orchestral musicians who, at eleven o'clock the following morning, were scheduled to give the traditional Festival performance of Handel's *Messiah*. 'Well indeed it was for Sir Henry that Handel was not in the Birmingham Town Hall yesterday – with a gun,' commented the *Gazette*. That evening's concert, however, was Verdi's *Requiem*, with a solo quartet that comprised Ackté and Foster as well as the Irish-born tenor (and future papal count) John McCormack and the American bass-baritone Clarence Whitehill. Wood described it, decades later, as 'the happiest and certainly the truest Italian rendering of Verdi's *Requiem* I ever directed'.

Not everyone agreed. The soloists were recuperating in the green room when the door swung open and a 'distinguished, soldierly-looking man' burst in, declaring, 'That is the worst performance of Verdi's *Requiem* I ever heard.' 'Who the hell is this major-general?' demanded McCormack, outraged. 'That's no general!' replied Whitehill. 'That's Sir Edward Elgar.' Ackté, whose intonation had wobbled, burst into tears, and McCormack didn't speak to Elgar again for two decades.

Wood, meanwhile, forged on with Frederick Delius' *Sea-Drift* – not a premiere exactly, but sufficiently unexpected for the composer himself to suspect some ulterior motive. 'Who is responsible for this friendly act?' Delius had written to Granville Bantock when news reached him at his home in Grez-sur-Loing, south of Paris, that Wood planned to revive the piece. Declining to conduct *Sea-Drift* himself, Delius had holed up in the anonymity of the massive Queen's Hotel on New Street, where he'd fallen in with a fellow festivalgoer and kindred spirit, the eighteen-year-old Philip Heseltine (the future composer Peter Warlock).

Emerging for the rehearsal of Sibelius' symphony – at which he was heard to mutter, 'Damn it, this is not conventional music' – Delius had despaired of Wednesday morning's *St Matthew Passion* ('Could not stand more than forty minutes of it,' he wrote to his wife Jelka; 'I have done forever with this old music. It says nothing whatever to me') and retreated to the hotel, where he and Heseltine found a piano and bashed through his own *In a Summer Garden*. He was cheered by the arrival of the composer Henry Balfour Gardiner in a fast car, just in time for *Sea-Drift*. They sped off together in the direction of Berkshire and were nearly killed when the steering failed near Oxford.

Back at the Town Hall, the concert continued with a Mozart aria and the entire final scene of Wagner's *Die Walküre*. Wood, however, had saved one final sensation for the last morning of the Festival: he followed Brahms's *German Requiem* with a Bach motet, Beethoven's Seventh Symphony and the closing scene of Richard Strauss's *Salome*, sung by Aino Ackté. The British premiere of Scriabin's *Prometheus* was supposed to have been the Festival's closing shock, but Scriabin, at this time increasingly absorbed in his doomed, apocalyptic *Mysterium* project, proved disappointingly worldly on the subject of travel expenses. He refused to attend, and Wood felt unable to rehearse *Prometheus* without him.

Salome wasn't new to Birmingham, but Ackté, in a bright blue turban, snarled and soared her way towards Strauss's bone-melting final dissonance with shattering communicative power. 'She heaved and oscillated, and in realisation of the scene she envisioned, showed her upper teeth in imitation of amatory savagery,' gasped the *Gazette*, pronouncing her 'the great fire-bringer to the Festival'. At least one audience member disagreed. Ludwig Wittgenstein – the future philosopher – had just returned from a trip to Iceland with his close friend, the young Birmingham lawyer David Pinsent.

They had arrived at New Street station at 7 a.m. on the sleeper train from Edinburgh, freshened up at the Pinsent family home in Harborne, and taken an omnibus to Five Ways, before ditching it in favour of a taxi and arriving at the Town Hall just in time for the Brahms, which Wittgenstein said he'd never enjoyed more. ('And he has heard it pretty often,' commented Pinsent to his diary.) But he refused to go back in after the interval for *Salome*, and stood outside in Paradise Street instead. Pinsent stuck it out, remarking that the Strauss was 'rot, but very clever and amusing in consequence'.

Programme

OF THE

IRMINGHAM TRIENNIAL MUSICAL FESTIVAL,

IN AID OF THE FUNDS OF

THE GENERAL HOSPITAL.

—— To be held in THE TOWN HALL, ——

ON

Tuesday, Wednesday, Thursday & Friday, Oct. 13, 14, 15 & 16, 1903

UNDER THE DISTINGUISHED PATRONAGE OF

HIS MAJESTY THE KING.   HER MAJESTY QUEEN ALEXANDRA.

H.R.H. THE PRINCE OF WALES.   H.R.H. THE PRINCESS OF WALES.

T.R.H. THE DUKE AND DUCHESS OF CONNAUGHT AND STRATHEARN.

T.R.H. THE PRINCE AND PRINCESS CHRISTIAN OF SCHLESWIG-HOLSTEIN.

H.R.H. THE PRINCESS LOUISE, DUCHESS OF ARGYLL.   H.R.H THE DUCHESS OF ALBANY.

H.R.H. THE PRINCESS BEATRICE, PRINCESS HENRY OF BATTENBERG.

ALLDAY LTD., TYPE., BIRM.

Jean Sibelius conducted his Fourth Symphony at the 1912 Triennial Festival, and returned to conduct his Third with the fledgling CBO in 1921, depleting the drinks cabinet of his friend Granville Bantock.
OPPOSITE *Programme book for the 1903 Triennial Festival. In 1912, too, the Festival was a major social occasion as well as a gargantuan feast of music.*

Throughout the week local newspapers had been printing the daily audience figures and door takings for each concert, and after the dress rehearsal earlier in the week, word about Ackté had clearly spread. Only Tuesday evening's Elgar and Sibelius premieres had attracted a larger crowd. Friday night's closing concert, on the other hand, was the most poorly attended of all. Just 963 people (the morning concert had drawn nearly 1,200) heard Sir Edward Elgar return to the platform to conduct *The Apostles*, the work he had composed for the 1903 Festival and which was already, it was rumoured, box-office poison.

No matter. Over four days Birmingham had witnessed eight large-scale concerts, including eight substantial choral works, premieres by Sibelius, Elgar, Bantock and Walford Davies, and challenging contemporary works by Strauss and Delius. Soloists such as Ackté, Rosenthal and Casals were names to conjure with. The hospitality had been brilliant; the choir, it was generally agreed, had sung superbly, and whatever the demands of such a packed schedule, the orchestra's principal players, at least, were (the *Gazette* felt) 'not surpassed by any in the world'.

'A marked improvement of manners must be noticed,' the *Gazette* added, approvingly, noting that 'the oratorios were not applauded till the close'. After 145 years the Triennial Festival was having a demonstrably civilising effect on the City of Iron. Everyone, surely, could agree that this had been an occasion in the great tradition of the Birmingham Triennial Musical Festival: something bigger than merely (as the Festival had been described in the 1904 edition of *Grove's Dictionary of Music and Musicians*) 'the most important "music meeting" in the Provinces'? It had been, as the correspondent of the *Musical Times* put it, 'a Gargantuan feast of music'. On Friday 4 October, as the final alleluias of Elgar's *The Apostles* swelled and faded into the autumn evening, no one could have known that it would be the last.

2

The Boa Constrictor
of North Bromwich

G argantuan feasts can lead to indigestion. On Friday 22 January 1886, addressing the annual dinner of the Clef Club of Birmingham, Sir Arthur Sullivan reached around for a simile to describe the musical life of the Second City. He came up with an image worthy of his collaborator W. S. Gilbert:

> Formerly it might have been said that Birmingham was a sort of boa constrictor, that it made a mighty meal on music once in every three years, and then relapsed into a state of coma in order to digest it.

It struck a chord. The assembled gentlemen laughed (according to the following morning's *Birmingham Daily Post*), though the chairman of the orchestra committee of the Triennial Festival would later remark that he found Sir Arthur's comment 'a somewhat cynical observation'.

Too late: Sullivan's boa constrictor had slithered into the Brummie imagination. A generation later, in 1919, the Halesowen-born novelist and composer Francis Brett Young repeated the idea in his novel *The Young Physician*, a thinly disguised memoir of life in the Midlands metropolis of 'North Bromwich' in the years before the Great War:

> Edwin discovered that North Bromwich, a city that takes its music as a boa constrictor takes food, in the triennial debauch of a festival and then goes to sleep again, supported – or rather failed to support – a society for the performance of orchestral music.

If the Festival was far from being the only musical activity in the city, it hardly needed restating that it was the most important – and that its dominance was not entirely healthy. True, Brett Young acknowledged that a remarkable amount escaped the boa constrictor's jaws in the first decade of the twentieth century:

> In this way they heard a great deal of good music: the nine symphonies of Beethoven, with the Leeds choir in the last; the usual orchestral extracts from the *Ring*, the *Meistersinger* overture and the *Siegfried Idyll*; the Fourth, Fifth and Sixth Symphonies of Tschaikovski [sic]; the tone-poems of Strauss and a small sprinkling of modern French music.

From the late eighteenth century until the First World War, the fact remained that orchestral music in Birmingham subsisted (or as Brett Young had noticed, failed to subsist) on the crumbs left over from that three-yearly blow-out. For the musical world at large – and much of the city itself – the Triennial Festivals *were* musical life in Birmingham. The event that had begun in 1767 as a three-day 'Music Meeting' in aid of the city's proposed General Hospital on Summer Lane, had evolved over the course of the nineteenth century from a highlight of the Warwickshire social calendar (the first musical director was the Coventry composer Capel Bond, and an annual ball, open to all classes of society, was a central part of the programme until 1855) into an occasion of international significance.

It was the buttonmaker Joseph Moore, the presiding genius of the Festival from 1802 to 1849, who led the campaign for Birmingham to build itself a town hall, and from the outset the new hall was intended as a home for the Festival, with the organ as a central feature of the architecture. The Town Hall was barely completed in time for the opening night of the Festival on 7 October 1834. Equipped with a world-class venue, Moore raised his artistic sights high, and for the 1837 Festival he brought Felix Mendelssohn to Birmingham. Mendelssohn conducted his oratorio St Paul and A Midsummer Night's Dream overture; improvised on the organ; appeared as soloist in the premiere of his Second Piano Concerto, and – just to round things off – gave a brief morning Bach recital on the organ before rushing to catch the Liverpool to London mail coach for the ten-and-a-half-hour trip back to the capital.

Mendelssohn was astonished by what he'd seen. In a letter to his mother dated 4 October 1837, he started something of a tradition (echoed by a parade of major composers) of being overwhelmed both by the grand scale on which things were done in 'Brummagem' (he'd obviously picked up a bit of the local dialect while staying with Moore) and by the uninhibited enthusiasm with which he'd been received. 'I cannot at this time attempt to describe the Birmingham Musical Festival,' he wrote.

It would require many sheets to do so, and whole evenings when we are once more together even cursorily to mention all the remarkable things crowded into

those days. One thing, however, I must tell you, because I know it will give you pleasure, which is, that I never had such brilliant success, and can never have any more unequivocal than at this festival. The applause and shouts at the least glimpse of me were incessant, and sometimes really made me laugh: for instance, they prevented my being able for long to sit down to the instrument to play a pianoforte concerto.

. . . I send you a complete programme of the Musical Festival. Imagine such a mass of music! and besides this prodigious pile, the various acquaintances who came flocking thither at that time; a man must be as cold-blooded as a fish to resist all this.

Mendelssohn was invited back in 1840, this time to conduct Lobgesang and play his First Piano Concerto. The London and Birmingham Railway, with its terminus at Curzon Street, had opened in September 1838 and Mendelssohn, clearly intrigued, doodled a series of sketches of the industrial city: a panorama of smoking chimneys, archways, and a steam locomotive (recognisable despite apparently having only two wheels) plus passenger carriage – as well as rather more accurate renderings of the Stork Hotel in Old Square and the Town Hall itself.

His reception was every bit as enthusiastic, and in 1845 the Festival commissioned a major new choral work for the following year. The premiere of Elijah under the composer's direction in Birmingham Town Hall on 26 August 1846 was the last great triumph of Mendelssohn's

Facsimile of a pen-and-ink sketch
by Mendelssohn in the possession of
Mr. Felix Moscheles, and reproduced
by his kind permission.

'A man must be as cold-blooded as
a fish to resist all this.' Starting in 1837
Felix Mendelssohn (ABOVE) participated in
three Birmingham Triennial Festivals, and the
premiere of his Elijah at the Town Hall in August
1846 influenced British music for the next
half-century. TOP Mendelssohn's own sketch of
Birmingham shows both the Town Hall and the
(now-demolished) Stork Hotel in Old Square.
LEFT Manuscript score of Elijah's
aria 'Lord God of Abraham'.

short life, and a far-reaching moment, not just in the history of the Triennial Festival but for the direction of British music for the rest of the nineteenth century. Not everyone saw that as a happy outcome (the music critic of the *Birmingham Daily Post*, Ernest Newman, would eventually joke that Sir Charles Hubert Parry was 'sickening for another oratorio'), but *Elijah* was a sublime moment in the history of the Triennial Festival, and – to judge from his letter to his brother Paul, the day after the premiere – Mendelssohn felt it too:

> No work of mine ever went so admirably the first time of execution, or was received with such enthusiasm, by both the musicians and the audience, as this oratorio! . . . During the whole two hours and a half that it lasted, the large hall, with its two thousand people, and the large orchestra, were all so fully intent on the one object in question, that not the slightest sound was to be heard among the whole audience, so that I could sway at pleasure the enormous orchestra and choir, and also the organ accompaniments.

Elijah was performed at every subsequent Triennial Festival, and a pattern was set. A Birmingham Festival commission carried Europe-wide prestige. The twenty-two-year-old Sullivan certainly heard Mendelssohn's footsteps behind him when his cantata *Kenilworth* was premiered at the September 1864 Festival. William Pountney, a chorus member, encountered him shortly beforehand, 'strolling round the picture galleries

of the Society of Artists all alone. I asked him how he was, and with a look of anxiety he replied that he was "very squeamish".'

Kenilworth had to compete only with Henry Smart's *The Bride of Dunkerron* and Michael Costa's *Naaman*. Subsequent Festival commissions would include works by Niels Gade, Max Bruch (*The Lay of the Bell*, 1879) and Camille Saint-Saëns (*La Lyre et la harpe*, 1879). Parry's First Symphony (1882) and *Judith* (1888), and Stanford's Requiem (1897) were Festival commissions, as were Sullivan's own *The Light of the World* (1873) and *Overture di Ballo* (1870). UK premieres included Wagner's *Das Liebesmahl der Apostel* (1876), Grieg's overture *In Autumn* (1888) and Anton Bruckner's *Te Deum* (1903). Perhaps it was merciful that the self-effacing Bruckner never got to read the *Daily Telegraph*'s verdict: 'It is noisy, simple enough for any choral society, and in a way effective, but scarcely good enough for a Birmingham Festival.'

Bruckner at least never endured anything like the ordeal suffered by Charles Gounod, who conducted the premiere of his 'sacred trilogy' *La Rédemption* on 30 August 1882. The response was ecstatic, and comparisons with *Elijah* didn't seem excessive. But the performance narrowly avoided disruption by Mrs Georgina Weldon, a former lover of Gounod, who (or so he'd been warned in an anonymous letter) was armed with a revolver. In fact she seems to have been carrying only pamphlets, and the Festival's ushers prevented her from entering the Town Hall. Already furious after discovering her hotel room double-booked, Mrs Weldon scented a conspiracy, and having attempted to sue the Festival for assault (it was eventually settled out of court), initiated a series of legal actions culminating in a successful libel suit against a bewildered Gounod in May 1885.

Gounod was sentenced to pay a 'monstrous' £10,000 in damages to Mrs Weldon. The musical world recoiled: his 1885 Birmingham commission *Mors et Vita* was premiered without him, and even an appeal in the name of Queen Victoria herself for Gounod to be permitted to conduct the London premiere proved fruitless. Mrs Weldon was resolute. Dismissing the request as 'impudence', she declared that 'if he attempts to set his foot in England, as matters now stand, I shall have him immediately arrested.' He never did.

As a devoted family man, Antonín Dvořák had no such worries. He rhapsodised, like Mendelssohn, over this 'immense industrial town where they make excellent knives, scissors, springs, files and I don't know what else – and besides these, music too. And how well!' The premiere of his cantata *The Spectre's Bride* on 27 August 1885 thrilled him. 'The choir and orchestra are first class,' he wrote home, and he returned on 9 October 1891 for the first performance of his *Requiem*, which he'd composed in lieu of a suggestion from the Festival committee that he might like to set Cardinal Newman's *The Dream of Gerontius*.

Newman's time would come on 3 October 1900, and from an unexpected quarter – the Worcester violin teacher Edward Elgar, who had played in the orchestra for the 1885 Festival, the year that the Austrian conductor Hans Richter had taken charge. Richter was an artist of international stature. A friend and champion of Brahms, Dvořák and Bruckner, he had been chosen by Richard Wagner himself to conduct the first complete *Ring* cycle at Bayreuth in 1877. He brought a Central European outlook to the Festival, introducing new music by Brahms, Tchaikovsky, Wagner and Richard Strauss, as well as nurturing an emerging British generation: Parry, Charles Villiers Stanford, Granville Bantock and Samuel Coleridge-Taylor.

If Elgar felt disappointed with the premiere of *The Dream of Gerontius* on 3 October 1900 (a recent change of chorus masters meant that the choir was underprepared), he was in a minority. The public cheered, and the *Yorkshire Post* was far from alone in reporting, 'This has been a great day, for it has witnessed the production of a remarkable work.' The final twelve years of the Triennial Festival, punctuated by major Elgar premieres – *The Apostles* (1903), *The Kingdom* (1906) and *The Music Makers* (1912) – look in retrospect like a high-water mark of musical life both in Birmingham and pre-war England itself. A copy of the programme book for the 1903 Festival, now in the CBSO archive, carries on a single page the autographs of the composers Elgar, Parry, Stanford and Frederic Cowen; the conductor Hans Richter, the chorus master R. H. Wilson, and the singers Clara Butt, Muriel Foster, David Ffrancgon-Davies, Robert Kennerley Rumford, Agnes Nicholls, Andrew Black and John Coates. It's practically a signing-in sheet for the British musical renaissance.

And the general consensus was that 1912 had been the most impressive Festival of the century so far. 'It would seem that the Festival was at the zenith of its success,' wrote the *Musical Times*, and few reporters failed to mention that, with the arrival of Sir Henry Wood, the Triennial Festival was now under the direction of an Englishman for the first time since 1849. The 1915 Festival was eagerly anticipated, and even after the outbreak of war in August 1914 there were many who felt that it should go ahead as planned. Nonetheless, in December 1914, the board of the General Hospital – still, after 147 years, the Festival's ultimate guarantors – announced its postponement, citing the declining financial performance of the previous two Festivals and the impact of the First World War:

> Having regard to the circumstances under which the Festival in 1915 would be held, to the absence of many of the chief supporters of the Festival on military duty or for other reasons, and to the loss of the social atmosphere which has contributed so largely to the success of past Festivals, the Board came to the conclusion with much regret that it would be too great a risk for a charitable institution to undertake.

There were protests: Stanford, in a letter to *The Times* on 11 December 1914, pointed out that the Festivals had continued throughout the Napoleonic Wars, 'when the Empire and Birmingham alike were much smaller and poorer than they are now'. He made the point that it meant a serious loss of income for freelance musicians, already struggling under wartime austerity.

The board was unmoved. Still, the precise moment at which it became obvious that this mighty institution – which had accompanied

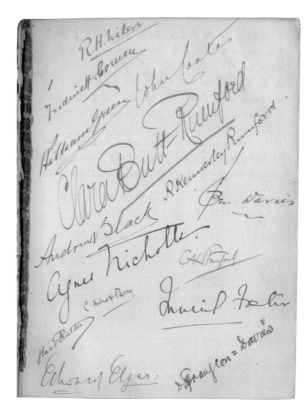

The owner of this 1903 Triennial Festival programme must have been a chorus member – or else they bought a backstage steward a pint. This single flyleaf contains the autographs of Elgar, Parry, Stanford and the conductor Hans Richter, as well as the composer Frederic Cowen, the chorusmaster R. H. Wilson and most of that year's vocal soloists.

Birmingham's growth from the Georgian market town of Matthew Boulton and James Watt into one of the world's greatest industrial cities – was not merely dormant, but defunct, is strangely hard to pinpoint. No plans were made for a Festival in 1918, and after the war, commentators in the Birmingham press were suggesting that the Triennial Festivals had served their purpose even while other regional

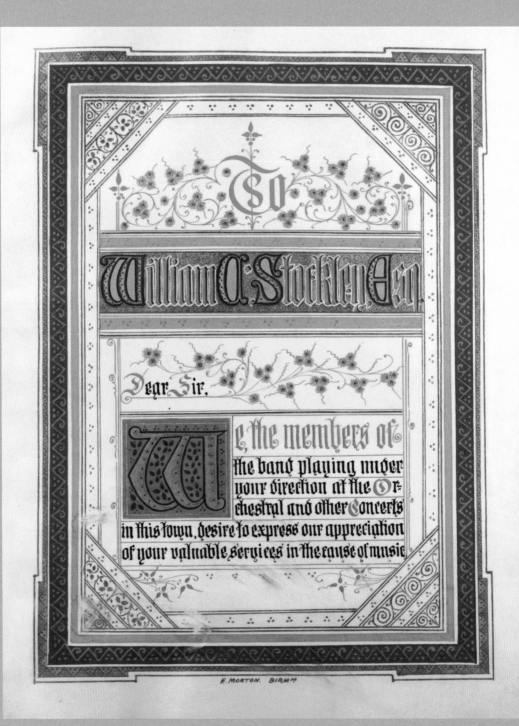

To

William C. Stockley Esq.

Dear Sir,

We, the members of the band playing under your direction at the Orchestral and other Concerts in this town, desire to express our appreciation of your valuable services in the cause of music

E. MORTON. BIRM.H

This illuminated address to William Stockley (see page 21) – presented by members of his 'band' in 1886 – shows the regard in which he was held by his musicians, including the young Edward Elgar.

festivals – Leeds, Norwich, the Three Choirs – were pulling themselves back onto their feet. By 1924 the *Birmingham Daily Gazette* felt able to pronounce the Birmingham Triennial Musical Festival 'dead through incompetence and mismanagement'.

That wasn't entirely fair. But Birmingham has never overindulged the British leaning towards nostalgia. When, in 1889, Queen Victoria conferred on Birmingham the dignity and status of a city, it chose to retain as its heraldic motto the single word 'Forward'. There was little

looking back. By the end of 1920, the city had already embarked on a completely new musical adventure.

Buying a New Orchestra

Sir Thomas Beecham knew exactly who deserved the credit for giving Birmingham a permanent orchestra: himself. In the middle of 1916 (as he recalled in his memoir *A Mingled Chime*):

> I received an invitation to attend a meeting in Birmingham summoned to consider the best way of forming a municipal orchestra. It was surprising that what had proved impossible in peace time should be regarded as feasible in the middle of a world war, but so many unexpected things had happened since 1914 that this perhaps was but one more to be added to the list. So I went and duly attended several gatherings, at which all the trite sentiments ever uttered upon such a subject anywhere since life began were rolled out by one speaker after another. How necessary it was for Birmingham to have an orchestra, what a valuable contribution to the city's culture it would be . . . But of any idea how to put it into practical operation there was little evidence; certainly no one seemed ready to spend any of their own money on it, and the Lord Mayor, Mr Neville Chamberlain, was very clear that the present was not the time to add one farthing to the rates in the interests of the fine arts.

Exasperated, Beecham put his contacts to work, drew once again on his family's pharmaceutical fortune (Beecham's Pills – a laxative – were as lucrative then as Beecham's cough medicines are today) and on 10 October 1917, the seventy-seven-player New Birmingham Orchestra was born. And on 1 August 1918 it died. The Town Hall, having been handed over to the city's Food Control Department for war work (consisting mostly, it seems, of the distribution of ration books and exhibitions of allotment vegetables), was officially declared to be unavailable for the next season's concerts. No politician – not even Chamberlain – felt inclined to intervene. Beecham had had enough, and suspended the orchestra indefinitely. 'The proposition was transparently clear: no hall, no music: no music, no orchestra; and that it was for Birmingham to decide if this was what it wanted.' But, he added:

> The effort was not entirely in vain. I had demonstrated that the thing could be done in a practical and fairly economical way, and a few years later the council came forward with a grant which brought about the establishment of an actual municipal orchestra.

Bravo, then, Sir Thomas. Or perhaps not. The symphony orchestra is a creation of eighteenth- and early nineteenth-century Europe, an era when musicians' wages were low and royal and aristocratic patrons maintained ensembles as a badge of prestige. Many of the great orchestras

'In 1889 Birmingham chose to retain as its heraldic motto the single word "Forward"'

of Central Europe originated in royal courts and their associated opera houses. Money was of little object, and performers were effectively salaried courtiers. Gustav Mahler's appointment as director of the Imperial and Royal Court Opera in Vienna was signed by Emperor Franz Joseph himself.

Royal patronage in Britain was rarely so extravagant, and the first significant orchestras in the UK were assembled and run by impresario-entrepreneurs such as Johann Salomon, the violinist who brought Haydn to London. By the mid nineteenth century, civic pride could sustain a semi-permanent ensemble in some growing industrial cities. But any orchestral concert promoter – whether a private music club such as the Royal Liverpool Philharmonic Society (founded in 1845) or an individual such as Sir Charles Hallé, who'd founded his orchestra in Manchester in 1858 – had to juggle donations from wealthy supporters and potential income from ticket sales against formidable and swelling fixed costs. By definition a symphony orchestra employs a large number of musicians, and that means a large wage bill.

By the early twentieth century the circle had become impossible to square. Even the buccaneering new London Symphony Orchestra, founded with dizzying ambition as a musicians' collective in 1904, was forced by 1917 to abandon its own concerts and operate as a band for hire. It was – and remains – the case that no permanent symphony orchestra with aspirations to perform the classical repertoire can survive without external subsidy; at least, not if it wishes to pay its musicians and staff a living wage, while charging ticket prices that the majority of the music-loving public can realistically afford. The captains and the kings have departed; they just don't make them like Ludwig II of Bavaria any more (and in Britain, they never did). Without guaranteed public funding, regular private donations, or (more usually) both, the blunt unalterable fact remains that a symphony orchestra cannot survive in the modern world. The sums don't add up, and even the pockets and charisma of a Beecham could stretch only so far.

That didn't stop people trying. Between 1873 and Beecham's final departure in the summer of 1918, numerous orchestras launched and crashed in Birmingham. In his definitive history of the CBSO, *Crescendo!*, Beresford King-Smith has traced the history of ten of these groups. He says that he could easily have chronicled at least ten more. George Halford's Orchestral Concerts (1897–1907) provided much of the varied diet enjoyed by Francis Brett Young's youthful music-lovers, and a Birmingham Symphony Orchestra (no relation to the later CBSO) and a Birmingham Philharmonic Society both operated with varying

success between 1906 and 1919. Beecham was involved with the Philharmonic Society prior to the Great War, and he went straight for the avant-garde jugular: one concert in February 1911 included both Strauss's *Ein Heldenleben* and the final scene of *Elektra*.

If any one of these orchestras deserves to be remembered as the ancestor of the CBSO, it's probably the freelance ensemble that was managed by William Cole Stockley. A piano salesman and organist with a goatee beard that made him resemble Charles Dickens, he had become chorus master and orchestral fixer of the Triennial Festival in 1855. In 1873, noticing that while choral singing in the Festivals was steadily improving, the orchestras were still distinctly scratchy, he recalled, 'I decided to inaugurate a series of orchestral concerts, and to give the gentlemen of the band the opportunity of gaining greater proficiency.'

Stockley's first concert lost him a hundred pounds. Still, he persevered and gave three or four concerts annually until financial pressures (and competition from younger, keener local promoters) forced him to retire in 1897. His eighty-strong orchestra – known as 'Mr Stockley's Band' – drew on the best players in the Midlands, including, from November 1882, the twenty-five-year-old Edward Elgar. On 13 December 1883, Stockley conducted the first professional performance anywhere of one of Elgar's orchestral works, *Intermezzo moresque*. 'Mr Elgar's modesty', he recalled,

> was of the kind that often accompanies great talent, for I could not persuade him

to conduct his *Intermezzo* or even listen to its performance from the auditorium, but he insisted on playing in his place in the orchestra, from whence he came to the front in response to a most cordial demand from the audience.

Elgar's gratitude was lifelong. He dedicated his next orchestral work, *Sevillana*, to Stockley and years later, in his 1905 Birmingham lectures, acknowledged his own creative debt to 'our revered chief, Mr Stockley'. The respect in which Stockley was held by his players appears to have been absolutely sincere. In May 1886, they presented him with a portrait by Henry Turner Munns, and an illuminated address listing every member of the orchestra (Elgar included) and thanking him for his services to music in Birmingham. When he finally retired in March 1897, Stockley returned the compliment. His final concert programme included a personal note of thanks to his supporters:

Mr Stockley begs to tender his most grateful thanks to the Subscribers to his Concerts and the public for the liberal and steadfast support they have accorded to him during the last twenty-four years, in his endeavours to establish a permanent Orchestra in Birmingham, and feels that on his retirement from professional work he may consider that his efforts have not been wholly unsuccessful . . .

Mr Stockley earnestly hopes that his Concerts may have engendered a love for this high branch of art in Birmingham,

and that this work may be continued with greater success in the time to come.

It was. The disappearance of the Triennial Festival and the near miss of Beecham's New Birmingham Orchestra in 1918 seem only to have fuelled a growing sentiment in Birmingham that orchestral music needed to be put on a permanent footing – and that the city itself should guarantee its financial security. Granville Bantock made cause with the music critic of the *Birmingham Daily Post*, Ernest Newman, in lobbying for a new orchestra, funded at least in part by the city, and they found an ally in Neville Chamberlain – who, whatever his wartime pragmatism (he was a politician, after all) was a sincere music-lover. (Chamberlain was an accomplished pianist, and had a special love of Beethoven's string quartets.)

After November 1918, in the euphoria of peace and victory, the political mood was right for optimistic, life-enhancing public projects. Chamberlain imagined a Birmingham in which, with the support of the City Council, 'every club and every big works should have its own orchestra and glee society', and was briefly convinced by a vast civic remodelling plan (always popular in Birmingham) devised by the architect William Haywood, which would have filled in the city centre canals, spread a huge piazza over the top of New Street station and replaced the Council House with a forty-storey neoclassical skyscraper.

Albert Speer hadn't yet given this sort of town planning a bad name. From the whole epic scheme, only Baskerville House and the adjacent Hall of Memory were ever built. But a central feature of Haywood's futuristic vision was a

SIR GRANVILLE BANTOCK (1868–1946)

Declaring that 'I would rather reign in Hell than serve in Heaven', Granville Bantock became principal of the Birmingham School of Music (now the Royal Birmingham Conservatoire) in 1900. For the next thirty-four years he was at the centre of musical life in the city: participating in the last Triennial Festivals, succeeding Elgar as Peyton Professor of Music at the University of Birmingham, and, in 1919, leading the drive to found the City of Birmingham Orchestra.

Even before he arrived in Birmingham, Bantock was one of the most dynamic forces in British music. He was a bohemian, larger-than-life figure. Visitors to his home in Edgbaston might bump into Gustav Holst, George Bernard Shaw or Sibelius – who dedicated his Third Symphony to Bantock. They all had to take their chances with the household menagerie, which at various times included marmosets, terriers and an aggressive parakeet called Scheherazade. Bantock even attempted to buy a mongoose, before realising that it would probably try to eat his baby son.

Musically, Bantock was a full-blooded Romantic, drawing inspiration from Celtic mythology in his symphonies, and Arabic poetry in his choral masterpiece *Omar Kháyyám* (1906–9). It would not have been Bantock's style to force his own music on the City Orchestra. Nonetheless, it was fitting that the CBO's first ever concert should begin with his overture *Saul*. After his death in 1946, his friend Havergal Brian predicted, 'Some day, when the far-away, receded tide returns, Bantock's orchestral and choral epics will be wanted. Birmingham should be ready to share that honour.'

huge circular concert hall in Lancaster Circus, called (with unwitting prescience) the Rotunda. A concert hall, of course, presupposed concerts, and an orchestra to give them.

Granville Bantock was an old hand at managing committees, and he worked quickly. Together with the piano manufacturer Gerald Forty and several former backers of Beecham's orchestra, he presented a new orchestral scheme to the new Lord Mayor, Sir David Brooks, on 17 March 1919. Donations from a group of wealthy guarantors were central to the plan, but so too – for the first time in the history of any British orchestra, and a quarter of a century before the founding of the Arts Council – would be a measure of public funding, provided by the City of Birmingham.

By 3 July 1919 (the earliest date in the earliest surviving minute book) an 'Executive Committee of the City Orchestra' was holding meetings, chaired by Bantock. They agreed that the new venture would be called the City of Birmingham Orchestra, possibly because most of the other potential names had been used up in the preceding two decades, but also because (even though the orchestra was to be self-governing) the city authorities were anxious to stamp their ownership on their new acquisition. This was, after all, Britain's first orchestra to be subsidised through the rates, and Birmingham's leadership in this, as in so many fields, was a source of justifiable civic pride, even if some found the idea of a municipal orchestra faintly vulgar. The North Bromwich solicitor Ernest Wilburn, in Francis Brett Young's novel *Portrait of Clare* (1927), summed up that particular attitude:

It seems that we are going to get some good orchestral music at last. Oldham [Brett Young's fictionalised version of Ernest Newman], the critic of the *Mail* is responsible. It's not that North Bromwich is musical; but Oldham has been pushing Leeds and Manchester down their throats, and North Bromwich people can't bear to think that anyone else is ahead of God's Own City, so they're buying a new orchestra, just as they'd buy a new sewage farm or fire brigade or a new Velázquez, to show the others what their money can do.

But, he adds, 'Humble people like myself and Oldham get the benefit of their stupid competitiveness.'

The benefit was recognised as real. Just as the massive Elan Valley water scheme had brought health to the citizens of Birmingham in the last decade of the nineteenth century, so the Corporation of what an American journalist had called 'the best-governed city in the world' was now about to give them music. 'In 1920, the notion of musicians receiving a "handout" from the taxpayer would have struck most people as either peculiar or outrageous,' writes Richard Morrison in his history of the London Symphony Orchestra. In Birmingham, however, a consensus had already emerged that it was nothing more than common sense.

By the end of 1919 it had been decided that the concerts would begin the following season. But who should direct them? 'Anyone but Beecham' seems to have been the general opinion, and on 5 January 1920 the committee

Appleby Matthews (in civvies, to the right of the bass drum) sits amid the members of his 'other' orchestra, the Birmingham Police Band – around 1920.

shortlisted four conductors: Edgar Bainton, Julius Harrison, Richard Wassell and Appleby Matthews. The thirty-five-year-old Matthews, the conductor of the city's Police Band who since 1916 had been presenting concerts with his own Appleby Matthews Orchestra, and whom A. J. Sheldon, the new music critic of the *Post* thought 'likely to become one of the leading conductors of the day', got the job, with Wassell appointed as his deputy.

Matthews immediately drew up plans for an inaugural concert season. For a fee of £1,000 for a one-year contract, he agreed to act as administrator as well as conductor, and by the summer of 1920, he had planned fourteen large-scale concerts at the Town Hall, and some thirty-eight 'Sunday Popular Concerts' with a smaller orchestra and more varied programmes. The first of these was set for Sunday 5 September 1920, at the Theatre Royal, New Street.

BIRMINGHAM TOWN HALL

To do great things, Leonard Bernstein is supposed to have said, two things are needed: a plan and not quite enough time. When, in December 1830, Birmingham's town clerks announced an architectural competition for a building 'to be used for the Music Festivals as well as for the general purposes of a Town Hall', competitors had only two months to submit their designs. The winner was Joseph Hansom – future patentee of the horse-drawn taxi cab – with a classical design based on the temple of Castor and Pollux in Rome.

Unfortunately the architects were required to guarantee the building work. As costs overran, Hansom's fledgling firm was bankrupted. Embittered by the experience, he turned to socialism. But the result, when the Town Hall finally opened in 1834 (actual completion took until 1851), was one of Britain's great Greek Revival buildings: 'completely satisfying from the outside, aloof and awe-inspiring', according to the architectural historian Nikolaus Pevsner.

The inside, apart from the lofty central concert hall, was trickier. Cramped corridors proved inconvenient for the performers at the Triennial Festivals, and indeed for the CBSO from 1920 to 1991 (even after the Second World War, musicians had to queue in Victoria Square to receive their pay packets through a ground-floor window). Substantially reconstructed in 1925–7 and 1996–2007, the Town Hall has also hosted political meetings (an anti-Boer War rally addressed by David Lloyd George in 1901 degenerated into a riot) as well as all-night jazz sessions, tea dances, rock concerts and weightlifting championships.

Birmingham Town Hall was less than a century old when this postcard was issued, some time before 1906. The colour tinting tactfully masks the blackening effect of Birmingham's coal smoke.

3

The Peacock and the Progressive

At 7 p.m. on Sunday 5 September 1920, Appleby Matthews stepped up to the podium at the Theatre Royal and gave the downbeat for Granville Bantock's symphonic overture *Saul*. In front of him was an orchestra of seventy-five players – rather more than he had suggested to the management committee would be the norm; but then, he was determined to make an impression. They were gathered from the professional bands that played in Birmingham's theatres and cinemas (Alex Cohen, the leader, served as director of music at the brand new Futurist Cinema on John Bright Street), and many were veterans of earlier Birmingham orchestras. Others were members of the City of Birmingham Police Band – Matthews' 'other' ensemble, a sixty-piece symphonic wind band that he had drilled to sparkling precision.

In fact, the City of Birmingham Orchestra had met as an ensemble for the first time at 9.30 a.m. the previous morning in the bandroom of Steelhouse Lane police station. Somehow, they had successfully rehearsed a programme that included, as well as Bantock's overture (an obvious courtesy to one of the orchestra's founders, 'of local connection, though of wider eminence', as the *Birmingham Daily Gazette* pointed out), the aria 'Donne mie, la fate a tanti' from Mozart's *Così fan tutte*, sung by the local baritone Herbert Simmonds, and Tchaikovsky's Fourth Symphony. Next came three extracts from Mendelssohn's *A Midsummer Night's Dream*, Elgar's *Serenade for Strings*, two Gilbert and Sullivan numbers from Simmonds, and to finish, Wagner's overture to *Tannhäuser*.

In an era before LPs or even broadcast music, long and varied concert programmes were expected, and by the standards of the Triennial Festival this was positively concise. But still, it was an impressive statement of intent: four Birmingham musical icons (Bantock, Elgar, Sullivan and Mendelssohn), alongside substantial works that gave notice of Matthews' determination to build a truly symphonic ensemble, without neglecting a civic orchestra's duty to entertain.

By all accounts, Matthews' new orchestra handled it with style. 'After last night, it was clear that Birmingham has a city orchestra of which it is going to be proud,' reported the *Gazette*. 'The finding of a very large public [the audience was around two thousand] was that the orchestra has justified the pains given to its creation,' it continued, noting that the Tchaikovsky, in particular, 'was a triumph for the orchestra'. The tone of the strings, moreover, 'was noticeably good throughout' – never a given on just one day's rehearsal, even with seasoned players.

It was an encouraging start: and six more 'popular' concerts followed at the Theatre Royal in September and October. But while these continued throughout the season, the centrepiece of Matthews' ambitions for the CBO lay at the far end of New Street, in the Town Hall – where a series of six 'Symphony Concerts' would present exclusively serious repertoire, with internationally known conductors and soloists. This was the flagship of the City Orchestra project, and for the very first symphony concert, on 10 November 1920, Sir Edward Elgar had been invited to conduct a programme of his own music. This was a proposition that could decently be laid before the cream of Birmingham society, and the management committee took the opportunity to make a public appeal for subscribers. They aimed straight at their readership's sense of civic pride, pointing out that:

1. Ours is the first City Orchestra to be established.
2. Birmingham's lead is of national importance, as is proved by the enquiries which pour in from all parts of the country.
3. Complete success is represented by a PERMANENT orchestra which is SELF-SUPPORTING.

. . .

6. The series is musically the finest which has ever been offered to Birmingham.

The last was a valid point. The roll-call of guest conductors makes impressive reading: Elgar, Hamilton Harty (then newly appointed to the Hallé Orchestra), Ralph Vaughan Williams (who would conduct his own *London Symphony*), Adrian Boult and Landon Ronald. In the middle of the list is the Brummie upstart, Matthews himself, who had assured the *Birmingham Post* that in March 1921 he would conduct the British premiere of Mahler's Eighth Symphony. It is tempting to wonder if he had actually seen the score – not that a city that had mustered nearly 500 players and singers for the 1912 Triennial Festival would have had much trouble assembling the forces required. Matthews probably intended to co-opt the Police Band too. But even in the first flush of enthusiasm, the idea that Matthews could have got a bill for eight soloists past the

management committee was pure cloud cuckoo land, and in the event he conducted Beethoven's Ninth Symphony instead.

For now, though, Elgar's visit was the priority, and the committee was determined to make it 'as public as possible'. The Lord Mayor, William Cadbury, held a civic reception; Bantock acted as host, and Matthews, in his capacity as orchestral manager, supplemented his Sunday-night forces by hiring a team of woodwind principals from Henry Wood's Queen's Hall Orchestra in London, including the oboist Leon Goossens and the horn-player Alfred Brain (the future uncle of the great horn virtuoso Dennis Brain). Elgar had chosen a challenging programme. Two substantial and virtuosic works that had flopped before the war – the Second Symphony and the 'symphonic study' *Falstaff* – sandwiched a practically unknown new piece, the Cello Concerto, which had been poorly received after an under-rehearsed premiere by the London Symphony Orchestra just over twelve months before.

That might be why, according to the *Gazette*, the programme 'did not attract a record audience', although the Cello Concerto was 'splendidly played' by Felix Salmond. But, it added, 'The London additions to the orchestra, and the vitalising effect of Sir Edward conducting his own pieces, gave a life and a force not otherwise to be obtained.' The hall might have been worryingly empty, but everyone present seems to have felt a sense of occasion. Salmond joined the cello section of the orchestra after the interval to play the symphony, and Elgar found his mind drifting back over four decades to his youthful days in Mr Stockley's Band.

'At the rehearsal this afternoon, there was only one vacant seat in the orchestra,' he told Robert Buckley, the music critic of the *Birmingham Post*. 'It was the one in which I used to sit. I almost expected to see myself come on with the fiddle.'

More than any other, this first symphony concert was the occasion that the orchestra would collectively remember as its founding moment – even if, far from being its first public performance, it was actually its ninth. Memories get blurred. For years, Matthews loyalists would write indignantly to the *Birmingham Post* whenever the CBSO accidentally referred to 10 November 1920 as the orchestra's first concert. Unquestionably, though, this was the date that marked the CBO's emergence on the national stage, and embodied Matthews' ambition to give Birmingham a symphonic ensemble of the stature of Manchester's Hallé Orchestra or Liverpool's Philharmonic. Symbols matter. Sixty years later, an audience member – a Mr Swann, who had travelled in from Stourport – told Beresford King-Smith how after the concert he had gone backstage to Elgar's dressing room, clutching a friend's autograph book. Knocking, and receiving no reply, he pushed the door open and saw Appleby Matthews kneeling at Elgar's feet, apparently in homage.

> Feeling that, if Mr Matthews knelt in the great man's presence, then this was certainly no place to be, he beat a hasty retreat and thereby missed the opportunity of getting Elgar's autograph. Only later did he realise that Matthews had been helping him undo his button-up boots!

Matthews was back on his feet a couple of days later, and barely off them again for the rest of the season. On 10 December he took a programme of Schubert, Nicolai, Sibelius and Weber to the Central Hall in Derby – the orchestra's first recorded 'out-of-town' date and as well as preparing a constant stream of repertoire for the Sunday 'popular' concerts, he continued to make a splash with his choice of guest conductors. And not only in the flagship symphony concerts: Matthews was quite happy to squeeze some of the biggest names in British – and indeed international – music onto the cramped stage of the Theatre Royal. Even before Elgar's concert, Gustav Holst had appeared on 10 October 1920 to conduct the first five movements of *The Planets* – their first performance outside of London, and only their third public performance anywhere. It was, pronounced the *Gazette*, 'a masterwork; strong, imaginative, sincere, original'.

The 1921–2 season featured Rutland Boughton and Arthur Bliss (then at the height of his bright-young-thing notoriety), who conducted his anarchic *Rout* twice in one concert, and Granville Bantock finally appeared, conducting extracts from his *Sappho*, in October 1922. But the biggest name to appear at a Sunday concert, on 20 February 1921, was Jean Sibelius – back in Birmingham for the first time since 1912. Bantock's fourteen-year-old daughter Myrrha remembered the wintry evening when he arrived at Tir-Nan-Og, the Bantock family home on Wheeley's Lane, Edgbaston. 'We rose to greet him,' she recalled, in her memoir *Granville Bantock: A Personal Portrait*:

6

FIRST CONCERT

Town Hall, Wednesday, Nov. 10th, 1920.

PROGRAMME.

PART I.

Symphonic Study "Falstaff" (Op. 68) ... *Elgar*

Concerto for Violoncello and Orchestra (Op. 85) *Elgar*

(First Performance in Birmingham.)

FELIX SALMOND.

An Interval of Fifteen Minutes.

PART II.

Symphony No. 2 in E Flat (Op. 63) ... *Elgar*

CONDUCTOR :

SIR EDWARD ELGAR, O.M.

ABOVE *The first Symphony Concert, conducted by Elgar, marked the CBO's debut as a full symphony orchestra. Every piece on the programme was less than ten years old.*

RIGHT 'To the members of the City of Birmingham Orchestra in token of gratitude for 22 March 1927.' Gustav Holst conducted the CBO more than any other living composer in the 1920s.

Although vain of his appearance, Sibelius was really an ugly man, but he was undeniably striking. The great domed head, which he kept shaved so that it should not be said of him that he was going grey or bald was the first thing one noticed . . . A thick, short neck and very strange, large ears with long lobes made me think at once of a Nordic troll. I must admit that I found him rather terrifying. He radiated force and power; without knowing why, you felt awed in his presence.

Appleby Matthews clearly didn't feel awed. Near the end of the rehearsal of *En Saga*, he rushed up to the podium and remonstrated with Sibelius. Possibly he was sharing his own experience of getting a good result from the Birmingham band on minimal preparation: in any case, on just one rehearsal Sibelius conducted *En Saga*, *Valse Triste*, *Valse Lyrique* (which was encored) and the Third Symphony. 'No wonder the people applauded,' reported the *Gazette*, and Sibelius was delighted. 'I conducted excellently – according to the musicians,' he wrote to his wife Aino. The following night Bantock accompanied Sibelius to a reception at Birmingham University. The great master was in an expansive mood; puffing on a cigar throughout, he gave autographs to anyone who asked.

If there is one eternal truth in the classical music business, it is that artistic success does not, of itself, lead to financial stability. True, the City Orchestra looked permanent: so much so that in January 1921 Clayton Cooper, a member of the management committee, proposed to

set up a new amateur choral society 'to work in conjunction with the orchestra conditional that this committee has no financial responsibility', and the City of Birmingham Choir gave its first concert with the orchestra on 28 November 1921, with Matthews conducting Rutland Boughton's *Bethlehem*. On 5 November 1923, under the baton of Joseph Lewis – since 1922, Matthews' official deputy conductor – it participated in the CBO's first concert to be broadcast by the BBC.

Yet none of this could alter the fact that they were not selling enough tickets. By the end of the 1920–21 season the budget already showed a deficit of over £2,000 against a projected annual income of £6,000. The city's £1,250 contribution to the orchestra's budget, important though it was in principle, was barely a sticking plaster. The management committee took an open-minded approach to the problem: expanding its own membership to include political opinion-formers such as the city's redoubtable Chief Constable Charles Rafter and Barry Jackson, the energetic founder of the Birmingham Repertory Theatre. Women had played in the orchestra from the outset, but by the end of the first season five women (including the soprano Zara Minadieu) also sat on the committee, and the former Mayoress Lady Brooks had set up a 'Ladies' Auxiliary Committee', which aimed to sell subscriptions via so-called 'Propaganda Parties'. ('Propaganda' was as overworked a marketing buzzword in the 1920s as 'viral' is today.)

A city-wide raffle to win 'A House for a Shilling!' was quickly organised, and just as quickly dropped when it was found to be illegal. Then there was the advert that the orchestra placed in the local press in April 1922, announcing its own imminent extinction. Even today, orchestras resort to similar measures when cashflow problems threaten to get out of hand: a press release warning of looming insolvency or threatening to axe a politically sensitive project (typically the education department) usually helps focus funders' minds. But there is a particularly passive-aggressive tone to this 'Appeal to All Who Are Interested in Music':

> In addition to the great educational value of the concerts for school children, the Orchestra has now established itself as one of the social amenities of the city . . . That this would be a calamity, both from the musical and social point of view, and also for the prestige of the city, is quite obvious.

The Sunday concert season was curtailed, and later moved to the Grand Theatre on Corporation Street (demolished in the early 1960s to make way for Priory Queensway) and the Futurist cinema on John Bright Street (which, after a stint as a Spearmint Rhino strip club, is currently a shisha lounge). Both these venues had the audience-friendly advantage of permitting smoking. In early 1922 Matthews experimented with a series of 'Suburban Concerts', in which a scaled-down orchestra played in city cinemas including the Gravelly Hill Picture House and the Waldorf Theatre, Sparkbrook. The forces for such concerts could number as few as a dozen players.

Matthews, meanwhile, continued to work like a Trojan. He personally brokered many of the

'If there is one eternal truth in the classical music business, it is that artistic success does not guarantee financial stability'

CBO's early relationships with venue managers and external promoters, and as conductor of the Police Band, he had a special relationship with Rafter. It helped that Rafter loved music: he kept a flute in his desk at the Council House and could often be heard tooting it for relaxation. To perform works such as *The Planets*, Matthews relied heavily on being able to 'borrow' extra players from the Police Band – an arrangement that led to friction with the Musicians' Union. Rafter offered what practical assistance he could, ensuring (among other things) that the Police Band was issued with instruments at the correct orchestral pitch. Meanwhile, as early as 21 February 1921 (the day after Sibelius' visit), Matthews had introduced an innovation that would have a far-reaching legacy: the CBO's first ever 'Children's Concert'.

Not everyone was convinced. Matthews got things done, but he got things done in his own way, and energetic fixers don't always make great performers. Opinions on his skills as a conductor

Appleby Matthews poses with the City of Birmingham Orchestra in 1921 – the earliest known photograph of the orchestra. Until 1925, the interior of the Town Hall was still much as Mendelssohn would have remembered it.

will remain divided: the three short 78s with the Birmingham Police Band that are his entire recorded legacy reveal his conducting to be just as smart and sparky as contemporary listeners described it. 'I knew both Appleby Matthews and Adrian Boult quite well in the 1920s,' said John Crowder, who sang in the Birmingham Festival Choral Society.

> Although Boult was a year or two younger than him, Matthews asked if he might have some conducting lessons from him. Adrian told me that when he started these, Matthews, though an excellent pianist, still couldn't read a score properly and was relying on gramophone records to learn the music. But, Adrian told me, 'I never met a quicker pupil.'

'He was rather like a little peacock,' remembered Leon Goossens. 'He always tried to walk a little taller than he was.' Crowder remembered that 'Matthews was very versatile but not a very acceptable character, really. It used to annoy the orchestra that, when there was a Town Hall date, Matthews would pop along to Eli Fletcher's pub nearby (which they were not allowed to do) in the middle of the rehearsal to get the latest racing news.' (Eli Fletcher's legendary boozer, the Hope and Anchor on Edmund Street, was a second home to many CBO and CBSO players until its demolition in 1965 to make way for Paradise Forum.) Others found him 'very sincere, and kind'.

In any case, Matthews' financial recklessness and habit of treating the CBO as his own private band started to irritate the management committee: at one point he hired the entire orchestra to a promoter in Cheltenham without informing the committee. Halfway through his second full season, in December 1921, the committee resolved, frostily, that 'the present Director and Conductor be relieved of all financial responsibilities and his programme for each season be presented to and approved by the Finance Committee'. Relations continued to cool. By July 1923 solicitors were involved; and on 27 October Matthews was formally given notice of termination. The committee was already considering two well-reviewed guest conductors, Eugene Goossens and Matthews' former teacher, Adrian Boult, as potential replacements.

Matthews went down fighting. He attempted to bill the CBO for use of his personal music library, but ended up being forced to sell his sheet music to the orchestra. (Orchestral parts stamped with his name still occasionally make it onstage at Symphony Hall.) Finally he spotted that his notice of termination contained an error – the dates were out by three days. He sued for wrongful dismissal, won, and was awarded a month's salary (£54) in damages. The CBO lawyered up and took it to the Court of Appeal. On 20 November 1924, entirely unsurprisingly, they lost again, and this time Matthews was awarded £600. The whole tawdry, ruinously expensive episode was thoroughly – and for the CBO, humiliatingly – covered in the Birmingham press.

By then Matthews had long since given his final concert with the CBO: at the Futurist Theatre on 30 March 1924, where he had conducted Mozart's Symphony No.40 before finishing with Wagner's *Meistersinger* prelude. Although he lived in Birmingham until his death in 1948, he would conduct the orchestra he founded on only one more occasion: on 12 September 1944, when he hired the orchestra to play the work that had first made his name three decades earlier, Elgar's *The Spirit of England*. At one point in the 1930s he was reduced to playing in the cafeteria in Lewis's department store. Yet without his determination it is unlikely that a city orchestra would ever have proved viable. In 1921 he was a worthy first recipient of the Gold Medal of the Birmingham Civic Society. By 1923 he was seen, rightly or wrongly, as a liability. Cometh the hour, cometh the man: the tragedy of Appleby Matthews' career, perhaps, was that his hour proved so brief.

A Musical Mussolini of the British People

It was during this winter season in Birmingham [1923–4] that it became clear that all was not well there, and I very soon sensed that the direction of the orchestra might be offered to me. I didn't need to think it over: about fifty concerts in the six winter months with nothing to do in the summer except prepare for next season was a plan which suited me perfectly.

Sir Adrian Boult, writing in his 1973 memoir *My Own Trumpet*, makes it all sound so simple, and (those faint background rumblings aside) so pleasant. Matthews had been generous to Boult, inviting him to guest-conduct in 1921

and again in 1923, and Boult was too decent to dwell on Matthews' plight. In 1923 he had taken over from Sir Henry Wood as the conductor of the Birmingham Festival Choral Society – the Triennial Festival's former chorus, now surviving (as it still does) as an amateur choral society. On 8 September 1924 Boult was appointed director and conductor on an annual salary of £800.

Immediately the air seemed to clear. It wasn't that the CBO's financial problems had gone away: in July the Midland Bank had written to the management committee noting that the orchestra appeared to have 'become permanently overdrawn'. But after the loose cannon Matthews, the CBO now had a thirty-five-year-old conductor with a growing reputation who knew exactly where he stood with the management, and appeared to be perfectly happy with that arrangement. Boult's contract stipulated that he should live in Birmingham; so he cheerfully moved into a house in Edgbaston. Granville Bantock wrote him a 'very kind letter of welcome' and invited him to dinner at Tir-Nan-Og – where the family had over-ordered on asparagus and expected Boult to handle the surplus.

Boult quickly discovered the advantages of working in Birmingham – 'a cheerful, bracing climate – how I noticed this on returning at 9 p.m. from my weekly day at the Royal College of Music – and a wonderful group of city fathers' – and declared the city 'in every way a happy place to work in'. He took an office (at his own expense) on the corner of Colmore Row and Bennetts Hill, and would walk into work each morning, sometimes meeting Gerald Forty of

APPLEBY MATTHEWS (1884–1948)

The CBO's first principal conductor made his own luck. Born in Tamworth, Thomas Appleby Matthews trained at Birmingham School of Music. By 1920 he had served as organist at St Philip's Cathedral, founded the Appleby Matthews Orchestra and Chorus (they gave the first complete performance of Elgar's *The Spirit of England* in October 1917) and had transformed Birmingham's Police Band, with which, in October 1921, he conducted the first commercial recordings ever made by a Birmingham-based ensemble. Appropriately enough, they included *In a Persian Market* by the Aston-born Albert W. Ketèlbey.

It's easy to see why Matthews inspired confidence. He got things done, and had a knack for making useful contacts. It was Matthews who conducted Rutland Boughton's opera *The Immortal Hour* at the Birmingham Repertory Theatre in June 1921 before taking it to the West End, where its long, successful run would be commemorated in John Betjeman's poem 'The Flight From Bootle'.

In 1922, meanwhile, Matthews guest-conducted both the Berlin Philharmonic and Paris's Lamoureux Orchestra, and it is hard to avoid the conclusion that his acrimonious departure from the CBO blighted his career. Apart from a single concert in September 1944, he never conducted the orchestra again, though he spent the rest of his life in Birmingham and served as wartime music director at St Philip's – where in 1944, still musically curious, he gave the Birmingham premiere of Tippett's First Piano Sonata. He was, recalled the CBO's first secretary H. S. Goodwin years later, 'a strange creature, though certainly in part a genius'.

the management committee for a pre-breakfast swim in Cannon Hill Park. On 7 October 1924, his first concert at the Town Hall – Wagner's *Flying Dutchman* overture, Strauss's *Don Juan*, *A Vision of Night* by Cecil Armstrong-Gibbs and Brahms's First Symphony – was broadcast live by the BBC.

Much of the 1924–5 season had already been decided but, to his delight, Boult was able to take an active role in shaping future programmes. 'Those six seasons were to be the only time in my life that I have been responsible for my own programmes,' he recalled in 1973. 'Looking back, I think they covered the ground reasonably well.' It's a classic Boult understatement. He invited leading European conductors to Birmingham: Bruno Walter directed Schubert's 'Great' C major Symphony in November 1926 and Ernest Ansermet conducted Honegger and Stravinsky (the CBO's first encounter with *The Firebird*) in February 1928. A planned visit from the great Czech maestro Václav Talich in 1926 regrettably had to be cancelled, and a printed slip in the programme explained why:

> M. Václav Talich has an engagement to conduct in Stockholm on February 28th. Under the impression there were 31 days in February he accepted the Birmingham engagement, which he now finds impossible to fulfil.

Ernst von Dohnányi appeared in 1929 as composer, pianist and conductor, and the *Birmingham Mail* was suitably impressed: 'Mr Dohnányi throughout the evening seemed very pleased with the City Orchestra,' it noted. 'Even the horns – often the *enfants terribles* of the orchestra – were on their best behaviour.' Dame Ethel Smyth conducted her own music and was delighted with the orchestra's sound: 'an energy, a keenness, and above all a warmth'. Boult also invited distinguished and emerging British conductors – Malcolm Sargent, Eugene Goossens (who conducted Bantock's *Hebridean Symphony*), Leslie Heward – and Sir Thomas Beecham was finally invited back, in January 1929. Confronted with a Sunday programme (Mozart and Bizet, mixed with a few 'lollipops') in the West End Cinema, Sir Thomas pronounced the acoustic 'worst ever!', and didn't return until 1935.

Boult even took it in good sort when, in late October 1925, the Town Hall's ceiling collapsed. He'd seen it coming: 'A friend of mine in the Festival Choral Society said he used to come with an umbrella, and he had it under the seat, as so much of the plaster was hanging from the ceiling.' Emergency repair work turned into a complete rebuild costing £37,000. In the process the Town Hall gained the curving balconies and oddly cramped stage configuration that it would retain until the CBSO finally left for Symphony Hall in 1991. The acoustic never recovered, and Neville Chamberlain assured Boult that he would have a brand new purpose-built concert hall 'before you leave Birmingham'. Meanwhile, until the Town Hall reopened in April 1927, the CBO's symphony concerts shifted to the Central Hall on Corporation Street. This redbrick Victorian Gothic pile hosted some of Birmingham's most significant musical premieres.

New music was Boult's real passion – whether it was Ravel's *Tzigane* or Medtner's

First Piano Concerto – and he understood the importance of getting his public on side. (Boult conducted the UK premiere of the Medtner concerto with Medtner's student, the Birmingham-born Edna Iles, as soloist, on 16 February 1930.) One evening in 1925, Boult got chatting to Sydney Grew, an organist and teacher at the Birmingham School of Music. What was needed, they agreed, was a forum for local musical news. Boult agreed to put up the cash and just five weeks later Grew published the first edition of the *Midland Musician*. Before long, concertgoers were using its pages to grill Boult on his plans, with one reader in February 1926 asking when Birmingham might get to hear 'a Mahler or Bruckner symphony'.

'These works are almost too long and elaborate for any of our programmes,' replied Boult. 'But there is no reason why one or two movements should not be played, and the matter will be considered for next season.' Local schoolchildren wrote that it was 'ripping to have nice seats' for the now regular children's concerts.

Grew was never in the pocket of the CBO, however, and after Joseph Lewis took offence at Grew's review of his performance of Schubert's 'Unfinished' Symphony, the orchestra officially dissociated itself from the magazine. Grew was always happy to offer a personal perspective, particularly over Bartók's *Dance Suite* – which received its first Birmingham performance on 2 March 1926. 'The Béla Bartók *Dance Suite* can hardly be said to have left audiences with mixed feelings, for the audience as a body seem to have felt annoyance that such a man as Bartók should

have done such a thing as write this music,' wrote Grew.

There have actually been riots in European concert halls during the past ten years over 'new' music . . . In Birmingham we do not hiss or fight. We merely express our annoyance, first by strong remarks concerning what we haven't liked, and then by declaring our intention of walking out of the concert hall the next time the wretched piece is played.

Boult picked up the gauntlet, and announced a second performance later that month. The CBO audience seems to have risen to the implied challenge, and in the next edition, Grew conceded defeat:

There was a magnificent audience at the final symphony concert, on March 23rd, and only ten or a dozen people left the Town Hall before the suite began. As a rule, far more than this number leave before the last item, having trains to catch; and so the Bartók, it seems, must actually have inspired many people to stay longer than usual . . . Birmingham showed itself wise in discovering at once that Bartók is a humourist . . . Other towns seem to have made the mistake of taking the music all in the grand serious way, which is the mistake people made a hundred years ago over Beethoven's Eighth Symphony.

The following season Boult kept his word and gave Birmingham its first taste of Bruckner's

Sixth Symphony – playing the *Scherzo* as a novelty item in a Sunday 'popular' concert at the West End Cinema on 30 January 1927. It must have sounded curious alongside Rossini's *Barber of Seville* overture, Borodin's Second Symphony and a selection of Elizabethan madrigals. The *Gazette*'s review didn't even mention it. Four days later at Central Hall came the Birmingham premiere of Mahler's Fourth Symphony, with the soprano Dorothy Silk as soloist. 'The works of this highly original composer are scarcely known in England,' wrote the critic of the *Gazette*, who was 'reminded constantly of Wagner and Schubert, while the shade of Berlioz flits more than once across the orchestra'. 'The result is a certain lack of coherence,' he concluded.

That didn't bother the Birmingham public. Boult organised a poll of the new works he'd introduced, with the most popular to receive a further performance in a forthcoming season. The winner, beating Bax's First Symphony, Bliss's *Colour Symphony*, Strauss's *Don Quixote* and (again) the Bartók *Dance Suite*, was the Mahler, which was duly performed again on 7 March 1929. Encouraged, Boult programmed *Das Lied von der Erde* on 13 February 1930: only the third performance in the UK and (commented the *Gazette*) 'the most significant concert of the series – for those who are prepared to do a little thinking about their music'. Astra Desmond and Steuart Wilson were the soloists, and the response from the audience was enthusiastic. True to form, the *Gazette* reported that 'the orchestration was not without fault, but Mr Boult, nevertheless, brought out a great deal of the beauty of the work'.

Throughout Boult's six years in Birmingham, there's an impression of foundations being laid and new doors being opened. In the winter of 1924–5 the CBO joined forces with the BBC's brand new, thirty-seven-strong Wireless Orchestra to perform a series of concerts at Covent Garden: Ernest Ansermet, Pierre Monteux and Bruno Walter conducted. In October 1926 Boult took forty-two players to Bristol for a three-week opera season at the Theatre Royal, which included the first professional staging of Dame Ethel Smyth's comic opera *Entente Cordiale*. Dame Ethel herself conducted.

The musicians seem to have had a high old time. Immediately after the final rehearsal the violinists Victor Fleming and Charles Bye and the timpanist Ernest Parsons piled into Fleming's car and drove through the night to visit Parsons' fiancée in Aberystwyth. They ran out of petrol, and were nearly killed after skidding on ice near Plynlimon: incredibly, recalled Fleming, they made it back the next day just before curtain-up – 'with half an hour to spare!' Two Holst celebrations in Cheltenham in March 1927 and March 1928 were less chaotic. Holst had now conducted the CBO on several occasions, and he described their March 1927 performance of *The Planets* as 'the most overwhelming event of my life'. In 1928 he conducted the European premiere of his *Egdon Heath*, while Boult, at Holst's suggestion, conducted Schubert's 'Great' C major Symphony. ('It has so many good tunes, and I like it!' wrote Holst.)

Boult understood the importance of maintaining political relationships and building an organisation that could weather problems

SIR ADRIAN BOULT CH (1889–1983)

Adrian Boult, recalled his friend and colleague Harold Gray, was 'first of all a gentleman; and secondly, very devoted to the cause'. It's true that Boult was courteous in his manner and meticulous in his approach to his work. But as the second principal conductor of the CBO in the 1920s, he was also an energetic orchestra-builder, a communicator, and a champion of new European music who introduced Mahler, Bruckner and Bartók to Birmingham.

When 'Dr Boult' first came to Birmingham, he was thirty-five years old and anything but a grand old man. Born in Chester and educated at Westminster School and Christ Church Oxford – where he was an outstanding athlete – he studied conducting at Leipzig Conservatoire, and gave his first ever concert in February 1914

with a scratch orchestra in his home town of West Kirby, Wirral. The programme included the world premiere of Butterworth's *The Banks of Green Willow*. In 1918 he gave the first performance of Holst's *The Planets*. Composer and conductor became lifelong friends.

Boult launched the BBC Symphony Orchestra in 1930, and was knighted in 1937. But he continued to cherish his relationship with Birmingham, and in 1959, when Andrzej Panufnik left earlier than expected, the seventy-year-old Boult agreed to act as caretaker for a single season. 'Only a carpet-bagger,' he joked. 'A sort of elderly umbrella to keep, if possible, some of the rain and snow off.' To date, he remains the only individual to have served twice as chief conductor of the CBSO.

such as the Town Hall closure and his own illness in late 1927. He hired a young music assistant – Harold Gray – for his new office in the Bull Ring, and nurtured that all-important relationship with Rafter and his Police Band. Boult told Beresford King-Smith about an occasion when a London-based contrabassoonist failed to arrive.

> He rang Rafter from the Town Hall. A quick check revealed that the appropriate bandsman was on point duty in Victoria Square, immediately outside, and Rafter told Boult to pop out and fetch him in straight away.

Financial worries never let up, and an official publication, printed in 1928, listed the Corporation's priorities (in order) as 'Cemeteries; Sewage disposal; Mental defectives; City of Birmingham Orchestra'. But Boult inspired confidence. At the end of his first season, the City Council doubled the orchestra's annual grant to £2,500. By the start of his last, the books showed a modest surplus, and the players now had a pension fund. His own reputation, too, had soared. For the first time (but certainly not the last) Birmingham had taken a gifted but inexperienced conductor and helped them emerge as an artist of international stature. Now (and also not for the last time) wealthier cities were casting covetous eyes. When the BBC announced plans for a new 100-piece symphony orchestra, Boult was the obvious choice.

Boult gave notice in the summer of 1929 and honoured his commitment to see out the 1929–30 season. At his farewell concert on 27 March 1930, he was presented with a score of *Das Lied von der Erde* – the CBO cellist Gwen Berry noticed that his successor designate, Leslie Heward, 'was dying to have a look at it'. As it turned out, this would not be the end of Adrian Boult's relationship with Birmingham. For now, though, the University of Birmingham, presenting Boult with an honorary degree, hailed him as 'a musical Mussolini of the British people'. Not all compliments date well. But the rest of the citation perfectly captures the mood of that moment:

> Birmingham . . . looked for much more than a skilled and inspiring conductor of an orchestra in its cradle. We needed a humanist technician to teach us that music of the right kind is an essential element in a true and progressive citizenship – as essential as good books in our Public Library, good pictures in our Art Gallery, or good buildings in our streets. We found that teacher in Mr Boult. And then the British Broadcasting Corporation decided that the nation needed the lessons that Birmingham had learned . . .

Mr Boult's translation to this exalted sphere only proves the profound truth that what Birmingham played and listened to a year ago, the nation will play and enjoy tomorrow. Already in the programmes of the BBC we can detect the iron hand in the artist's glove which directed our Municipal Orchestra and our Children's Concerts. Today we can cordially wish Mr Boult God-speed in his mighty task.

'AIN'T THOSE FIDDLES CLINKIN'?'

I f Appleby Matthews was to be believed – and he was never slow to advance his claims – the modern idea of the symphony orchestra as an educational resource was invented by him and the City of Birmingham Orchestra on the afternoon of Saturday 21 February 1921. Birmingham Town Hall was filled 'to its utmost capacity'. The audience was aged from nine to fourteen years, drawn from schools across Birmingham. Matthews conducted, and Sydney Grew gave spoken introductions, explaining the different instruments and urging the young audience to listen out for them in performances of Mendelssohn's *Spring Song*, Nicolai's *The Merry Wives of Windsor* overture, the *Pizzicato* from Delibes' *Sylvia*, and selections from Grieg's *Peer Gynt* and Elgar's *The Wand of Youth*.

Skip forward to Sunday 26 April 2015 and we find the CBSO, conductor Jamie Phillips and presenter Tom Redmond presenting a 'Bite-Size Classics' afternoon concert. It's aimed at the whole family, and the venue is Symphony Hall. But the idea remains the same: to introduce young people to the orchestra and its world through lively presentation, short, tuneful pieces, and the sheer thrill of hearing Birmingham's orchestra going full tilt. On the programme: *The Wild Bears* from Elgar's *The Wand of Youth* and *In the Hall of the Mountain King* from Grieg's *Peer Gynt*.

True, Matthews might have been startled by John Williams' *Theme from ET* and Britten's *Simple Symphony* but he would have recognised and appreciated exactly what was going on. That first children's concert was the product of Matthews' own personal missionary zeal to build a future audience, to knot his orchestra inextricably into the fabric of Birmingham life – and, one suspects, his desire to stand on a stage pontificating. 'It will mean, in five years' time, that the City Orchestra will need no subsidy or guarantors,' he predicted, inaugurating a century of over-optimistic claims for the social and economic potential of music education.

With one eye on the balance sheet, the management committee, too, was more than willing to try and tap a vast, self-replenishing new public for orchestral concerts – one, moreover, that reinforced the CBO's status as a civic amenity. So from 1921 onwards, not a single season of the CBSO's history has gone by without a programme of concerts and events aimed at reaching new audiences and performers. Education has been a fundamental principle, and condition, of the CBSO's existence for its entire history, and the relationship has benefited both the city and its orchestra.

In 1944, education work would be the decisive factor in transforming the part-time CBO into a permanent ensemble: more than 50 per cent of the city's grant to the new full-time orchestra would come from the city's education department. In 1992, the CBSO became the first UK symphony orchestra to appoint a specialist education manager, and as of 2020, three of the CBSO's four charitable objectives – effectively the 'constitution' of the CBSO – aim 'to promote, maintain or improve musical education'. Meanwhile, Appleby Matthews' vision has become universal. Almost every major orchestra in the world now has educational concerts and an outreach programme.

But in 1921 the idea was still novel enough to generate curiosity. Matthews set his young audience members a task – offering a prize of a guinea for the best essay on 'My Impressions of the Orchestral Concert'. We have no record of the winner, although Matthews' *amour propre* seems to have been particularly tickled by the little girl who wrote that 'The *Spring Song* was very good, and the man with the little cane, who waved his arms about, was a very good dancer, though he did not have much room.' By the start of the 1921–2 season – which incorporated five children's concerts, described as 'entirely unique in this country' – Matthews was rejoicing in 'the children's extraordinary keenness'. He was receiving enquiries about the scheme, he said, from as far afield as Belfast.

In a few years' time, he predicted, 'the question would not be "Is Birmingham musical?" but "Is there anywhere in the world so enthusiastically musical a city as this?"' Intrigued, the *Gazette* sent a reporter to the October 1921 children's concert. It was sold out, and once inside, the reporter noticed that:

> this child-audience's appreciation of the programme was not appreciably different from the appreciation of the usual adult audience. The attention was as earnest and the applause as warm. Only lack of interest was shown in a different way. Thus it was that in the sudden lulls of the orchestra one heard no intimate revelations of why Martha, the maid, was sacked, but, instead, the truth of why Emily, the dunce, was slapped. And, instead of uninterested grown men looking at the ceiling and waving their programme, uninterested little boys looked at the ceiling and chewed toffee.

The idea that music education can have near-magical effects on its recipients has always been a popular theme with the press. In February 1928, the *Gazette* returned to a schools concert conducted by Adrian Boult, and noted:

> They are children from the poorer districts chiefly, and it may be that in the grimy courtyards and the mean streets where they have their homes these children hum or sing snatches of the immortal music they have heard. They may dream of playing it some day, perhaps even of writing it. Certain it is they love it. We asked one tousle-headed boy from the Ladywood district what he thought of it, as they were all trooping out of the Town Hall, and he replied: 'We don't 'arf like it! Ain't those fiddles clinkin'?'
>
> 'Clinking' is a new word in the vocabulary of musical appreciation, but it seemed sufficient – the enthusiasm was there.

For the most part, though, work with schools is such an integral part of the orchestra's life that it can almost seem invisible – except to those performing, listening or participating, for whom it might be an encounter that defines the course of a lifetime. At present, the programme reaches some 20,000 participants per year, and the number of children who must have

CITY OF BIRMINGHAM ORCHESTRA.

Director and Conductor - - APPLEBY MATTHEWS.

CONCERT *for*
SCHOOL CHILDREN

FOURTH CONCERT:

**SATURDAY, MARCH 1st, 1924, at 2.30, at the
TOWN HALL, BIRMINGHAM.**

1	Shepherd's Hey	.. ..	..	*Grainger*
2	Scherzo *from* Symphony No. 4	.. ..	..	*Tschaikowsky*
3	Songs	(*a*) " Let me wander not unseen "	..	*Handel*
		(*b*) " The Organ Man "	..	*Schubert*
		(*c*) " Farmyard Song "	..	*Grieg*
		MISS EMILY BROUGHTON		
4	Overture	.. .. " Oberon "	..	*Weber*
5	Praeludium	.. ..	..	*Jarnefelt*
6	Songs	.. " The Lark in the morning "	*Collected and arranged*	
		" The Turkish Lady "	*by Vaughan Williams*	
		MISS EMILY BROUGHTON.		
7	Nell Gwynn Dances	.. .. ..	..	*German*

**Last Concert of the Season, Saturday, March 29th, at 2.30 p.m.
Plan may be seen and seats booked after March 10th.**

*Applications by Post should be addressed to THE SECRETARY, City of
Birmingham Orchestra, 159, Corporation St., Birmingham.*

encountered the orchestra in some form since 1921 is incalculable. After 1944, when a set number of days of education work (initially fifty per year) was made a permanent condition of the orchestra's grant from the city, visits to city schools with a scaled-down orchestra were built into every season, and an element of formula, and indeed routine, started to creep in. Percussionist Maggie Cotton, in her colourful memoir *Wrong Sex, Wrong Instrument* describes how in the late 1950s:

> the orchestra split into five sections and each of these covered four junior schools every day for at least one week in May . . . Initially I found that I was playing in section A, in other words a small light orchestra (Harold [Gray] at the helm), with section B being a string orchestra . . . separate brass and woodwind groups travelled around in their own cars and a solo violinist was also sent to four schools a day . . .
>
> Some schools resented this intrusion of a bunch of musicians disturbing their timetable. This was made patently obvious by the fact that there would be no one there to greet us, we had to find the hall ourselves and our platform staff had to request chairs for the players. Children were marched in in rigid silence, and as soon as the programme ended they trooped out again . . .

OPPOSITE *The CBO's Children's Concerts were one of Appleby Matthews' most far-reaching innovations. But to the young audience he was merely 'the man with the little cane who waved his arms about'.*

From a twenty-first-century perspective, it's not always easy to see the educational benefits of some of these occasions – under-rehearsed, presented by whichever player happened to lead a given ensemble, and constantly at risk of hijacking from principal players who saw these events as glorified rehearsals for their own recitals. (Cotton, on piano, recalls the viola-player Sammy Spinak forcing her to sight-read a Hindemith sonata on an out-of-tune school upright, in front of a baffled pre-teen audience.) After some 20,000 school visits, the City Council finally released the CBSO from the treadmill in 1970. Yet Beresford King-Smith remembered that 'the gains far outweighed any losses', and the end of this 'artistically stultifying' routine freed the CBSO's future education work to be more flexible, more responsive to changing times and communities, and – crucially – to be player-led.

That was the idea behind the 'Adopt-a-Player' scheme: launched in the 1984–5 season with the enthusiastic support of Simon Rattle and a substantial body of players. A school would build a close relationship with an individual CBSO player, who would serve as a personal contact point with the world of the music. In 2018, cellist Jacqueline Tyler would be awarded an MBE for her services to music education, but in 1984 she was a pioneer. 'It was groundbreaking,' she recalls.

> No one was doing anything like that. I think there was a real feeling among the players that we wanted to get out there. There wasn't really any training. And basically we were attached to a primary class for a term's worth of work. We went in, introduced

the kids to a piece of music. I think *The Planets* was the first one, and then we did *The Firebird, Petrushka*, the *Lemminkäinen Legends* – they loved the gory stories! And then they came to a proper concert. We prepared them as well as we could, in a creative sense, and they did lots of art work and dressing up. It was great fun actually.

The late 1980s was an adventurous time in orchestral education, and the animateur Richard McNicol helped train CBSO players. In 1992, the CBSO appointed a full-time education manager, Ann Tennant – the first UK symphony orchestra to create such a post. 'She was quite extraordinary,' remembers Tyler.

She encouraged an ethos of player-led project work – which is how it all started. She was very good at enabling people – seeing their strengths and nurturing them. Which, I think, has been very important for us as musicians here.

It's an ethos that isn't always visible from the outside, but for an increasing number of CBSO players, education work is a crucial element of a modern orchestral career – breaking up the routine of orchestral playing, and allowing musicians to develop their artistry in new, sometimes revelatory ways. Under Ann Tennant's successors Nancy Evans, Keith Stubbs and Lucy Galliard, the Learning and Participation

Spreading vitamins: principal cor anglais Rachael Pankhurst works with schoolchildren on a Music and Ability project in 2018.

department has grown into a vital part of the organisation: generating the statistics and the social-benefit stories that keep political funders happy, but – more importantly – finding ever more inventive and mutually rewarding ways to put the city orchestra's musicians and resources into the lives of the city's young people.

Some players have simply got an enormous buzz from assembling their own ensembles and putting on a show. In 1995, seeing the expansion in education work, six players – violinist Michael Seal, clarinettist Mark O'Brien, trumpeter Jon Quirk, timpanist Peter Hill, bass-player Tom Millar and violinist (moonlighting on keyboard) Wendy Quirk formed an 'orchestra in miniature'. With short, lively arrangements of popular classics and a ready supply of humour, the Little Big Time Band would be the forerunner of a whole stable of CBSO educational ensembles, visiting schools (and proving surprisingly popular with adult audiences too) throughout the 1990s and 2000s as part of what would later be called the 'Roadshow' programme.

For Seal, it proved an endlessly entertaining adjunct to his orchestral work:

> I remember a kid in Sparkhill: he was nine years old, and he just helped himself to an instrument. I said, 'You're not having that tambourine', so he said, 'F*** off.' But you do hear some lovely things when you're sitting six feet away from a row of primary school kids. You hear some lovely reactions when you play, and some lovely responses to questions, just under their breath.

It's not only about schools, either: musicians who prefer to work with older students can coach the undergraduate-level players of the CBSO Youth Orchestra, or (since 1991) mentor students of the Royal Birmingham Conservatoire as part of the long-running Orchestral Training Scheme. But CBSO players have played in retirement homes, hospitals and worked with community groups. As Composer in Association in 1996, Judith Weir, plus CBSO bass trombonist Alwyn Green and a team of CBSO colleagues, worked closely with Alveley Village Band – a community ensemble in a Shropshire mining village, whose members, ranging in age from seven to seventy-two, played flutes, clarinets, violins, electric guitars, accordions and no fewer than five tubas.

'For me, the best project that we're doing at the moment is the dementia project. That is blowing my mind,' says Jackie Tyler.

> We're working in partnership with the ExtraCare charity, working alongside support staff with dementia sufferers. We make music with them, and we try and get them to lead the sessions in a way – perhaps someone might have chosen a drum to play and they come up with a rhythm. We take that rhythm on board and create a piece with it – or support that rhythm, lift it.

OVERLEAF *The CBSO's annual Christmas concerts are occasions for the whole CBSO family. In December 2017, Simon Halsey leads an audience singalong – supported by the orchestra, Chorus (in black), Youth Chorus (in purple) and Children's Chorus (in pink).*

So, in that moment, they're actually able to do something that is not about memory. It's not about trying to do everyday tasks, which they can't remember. It's actually about being involved with something really enjoyable in that moment. And what we've learned is that when they leave that room, they might forget that they've been there, but that feeling of mattering – and having an important part to play, and of enjoying themselves – goes with them through the day.

There can't be many better illustrations of the way orchestral education work affects the musicians, as well as the people with whom they interact – or any activity that so comprehensively demolishes the boundaries between performer and listener. In modern music education, no one plays a passive role, and in a city such as Birmingham, the artistic rewards for the orchestra are every bit as great as for the wider community. Education work has been part of the CBSO's contribution to city life for a century now, and from October 2018, with the CBSO announcing its collaboration in a new specialist music school in Sandwell, the depth and scope of that commitment looks likely only to grow. It's certain that there'll be no shortage of musicians eager to get involved.

'What we're trying to do is spread vitamins,' said Simon Rattle to Beresford King-Smith in 1995. 'If we're not in the business of changing people's lives, I don't know what business we are in.' But it goes both ways. 'I mean, I love all the work that I've done,' says Jackie Tyler.

I really have loved it all, and it's made me think about music differently. If you've got to find a way of creating something that's inspired by a piece of music, you've simply got to think about that music in a new way. So it just constantly expands your musicianship. I think it's something we don't shout about enough.

Musical Youth

CBSO chorus director Simon Halsey's roots are in community music. He'd been saying for several years that he wanted to set up a youth chorus for the CBSO, when shortly after the CBSO had moved into Symphony Hall in 1991, he received a phone call from chief executive Edward Smith to say, 'This is the time.' He didn't need to say much more. 'It seemed to me that we were being asked to do Mahler Three, all the time – and now we had the hall to do Mahler Eight,' recalls Halsey.

We'd been using school choirs from the area – each Christmas, Beresford and I would go around primary schools in Aston and Lozells to find choirs who could hardly sing. And I realised that it just wasn't good enough – and also, where were we going to get the next generation of singers for the CBSO Chorus? So we put an advertisement in the *Birmingham Post* and the *Birmingham Mail*. It said, 'Your child can sing with Simon Rattle.' And they queued up round the block, like they were auditioning for *Annie*. More than 700 children tried.

So, at a stroke, the CBSO doubled its family of choruses. Or rather trebled it, since the two halves of the new choir – Senior (later known simply as the Youth Chorus), for girls aged twelve to eighteen, and Junior (later the Children's Chorus) for girls and boys with unbroken voices aged eight to twelve – could, and did, function as separate ensembles. While Shirley Court conducted the younger singers, Adrian Partington – later to become director of music at Gloucester Cathedral – directed the older ones, and the CBSYC made its debut in spectacular style on 11 May 1995, in Carl Orff's *Carmina Burana*.

It all sounds so straightforward. In fact, like the adult CBSO Chorus before it, the Youth Chorus rapidly found itself pulled into the heart of the CBSO's work. The wordless female choruses in Debussy's *Nocturnes* and Holst's *The Planets* became the Youth Chorus's exclusive possession: rehearsing weekly in CBSO Centre (where, because both youth choirs are so big, one half for many years rehearsed in the bar), late-working staff and players got used to hearing Holst's unearthly harmonies floating up through the building. The Youth Chorus has found itself singing Mahler's Eighth with Simon Rattle, Britten's *War Requiem* with both Sakari Oramo and Andris Nelsons; providing street urchins for Oramo's *Carmen* in 2005 and doubling as a startlingly large brood of noble orphans in Nelsons' 2014 *Der Rosenkavalier*.

A strong reputation travels quickly, and the Youth Chorus has consistently been in demand even without its parent orchestra. When Claudio Abbado brought the Berlin Philharmonic to

London in 1999 for Mahler's Third Symphony, it was the CBSO Youth Chorus he requested (the performance was recorded by Deutsche Grammophon). In 2007, the Gothenburg Symphony Orchestra flew the youngsters to Sweden to perform Anders Eliasson's *Canto del Vagabondo* – one of the few youth choruses in Europe capable of tackling a score of such complexity.

Members of the Youth Chorus are, overwhelmingly, Birmingham schoolchildren. That they've premiered works such as Per Nørgård's *Will-o'-the-Wisps in Town* (2005), Jonathan Harvey's colossal *Weltethos* (2012) and Jonathan Dove's *There Was a Child* (2011) merely illustrates the truth that the higher the standard you set for young musicians, the more determinedly they rise to the challenge. The secret has been to aim for – and insist upon – the highest possible standards. With young musicians, of course, that depends on finding coaches and conductors with very specific skills, and Court's and Partington's successors, Marc Hall, Ula Weber and Julian Wilkins, have all been outstanding communicators as well as musicians.

Halsey's vision was always that the CBSO Youth Chorus should cause ripples. The pool of expertise that the CBSO's chorus team has accrued with young people and non-professional musicians has been applied to a range of other projects: a choir for boys with changing voices; SO Vocal, a 200-strong adult community choir based in Selly Oak, and from 1999 to 2016, the City of Birmingham Young Voices – a non-auditioned pop choir. Since 2012 the CBSO Youth Chorus has formed the core of the BBC Proms

Youth Choir – a 400-strong chorus drawn from all over the UK to perform each summer at the Royal Albert Hall. Halsey isn't entirely surprised by its snowballing impact.

'We must have had thousands of children through our choruses,' he observes.

If only 1 per cent of them felt transformed, imagine what we've done for the musical life of this country. And at the same time, we were the trendsetters: we showed everyone else how to do it. The Hallé came next; I advised because, of course, Mark Elder had been our principal guest conductor in Birmingham. I went and set up the Royal Northern Sinfonia's programme, and so on and so on.

We've even advised the Melbourne Symphony on how to do it. It spread throughout Australia and New Zealand; and very many American orchestras came to watch us and followed suit. I established a similar programme at the opera in Antwerp, and helped a number of Dutch orchestras get started with youth choruses. Then Simon Rattle and I started something similar in Berlin, which was subsequently copied by practically every town in Germany. So, from the CBSO Youth Chorus, we can truly claim to have sorted out the choral education of at least five countries.

The long-term value of youth ensembles was a lesson that the CBSO hardly needed to learn. The Midland Youth Orchestra (MYO), launched by the CBSO's then general manager Blyth Major

in 1955 but run as an independent organisation, sent a steady stream of players through to the CBSO during its forty-eight-year history, including the clarinettist Martyn Davies, the timpanist Peter Hill, violinist David Gregory and cellist Ian Ludford. Birmingham's own schools music service ran (and continues to run) one of the largest networks of school-age ensembles in Europe, headed by a Schools Symphony Orchestra capable of tackling *The Rite of Spring*.

So the idea that the CBSO should run its own youth orchestra seemed both unnecessary and possibly counterproductive until, in 2004, Stephen Williams and Anthony Bradbury of the Midland Youth Orchestra – faced with a heathy bank-balance but falling attendance – persuaded their committee that the best way to carry forward the MYO's legacy would be a complete relaunch, and a reunion with the CBSO. The CBSO's director of education, Keith Stubbs, agreed that the new CBSO Youth Orchestra would be run by the CBSO education department, coached by CBSO players, and, with the age range set at fourteen to twenty-one, would bring together school-age and Conservatoire-level players to create an orchestra that would, it was hoped, become a sort of National Youth Orchestra of the Midlands. The MYO's bank balance would be used to subsidise membership fees. The only obstacles to admission would be musical ability and commitment.

OPPOSITE *The CBSO Youth Orchestra works with the same conductors as the CBSO itself. Principal guest conductor Edward Gardner shares the applause after a performance of Mahler's First Symphony at Symphony Hall in February 2015.*

It's not every April morning that you arrive at work and are instructed to form a new symphony orchestra – one, moreover, whose first concert date has already been fixed – just six months away on 31 October 2004. Sakari Oramo and Anthony Bradbury had agreed to share the inaugural concert, so one artistic principle was fixed: from then on the CBSO Youth Orchestra would work only with conductors and soloists who had already worked with the CBSO itself. My own early experience of the Royal Liverpool Philharmonic's Merseyside Youth Orchestra – the early training ground of Simon Rattle, but also of CBSO deputy leader Jackie Hartley, percussionist Annie Oakley, clarinettist Jo Patton and former chief executive Ed Smith – supplied the rest of the ethos.

In return for near-professional levels of commitment, members would play the same repertoire, in the same halls, with the same artists and with the same levels of support as the CBSO itself. Vital to that aim was the active involvement of the CBSO players, as artistic advisers, coaches and audition panels. Associate conductor Michael Seal acted as orchestra trainer, creating a full, polished, string sound, and the idea of orchestral coaching at a high level turned out to appeal even to players who hadn't previously seen themselves as the 'education' type – the more so since the new orchestra was to carry the CBSO name.

The ambition of the project (the first two concerts included Sibelius' Second Symphony, Shostakovich's Sixth Symphony and Peter Maxwell Davies' Five Klee Pictures) unnerved some. A music department head at one higher education establishment in the city quietly briefed his contacts in the CBSO that the Youth Orchestra was overreaching and that students would be scared off by the difficulty – unaware that earlier that day, two of his own pupils had been in touch pleading for the chance to play ultra-taxing solo woodwind parts. (A more candid admission came later: 'We don't dare programme this stuff with our own students. You're embarrassing us.')

A rising tide, though, floats all boats. The Royal Birmingham Conservatoire and Birmingham's schools music service would become enthusiastic supporters of the CBSO Youth Orchestra, to mutual advantage. Meanwhile the CBSO Youth Orchestra played The Firebird with Sakari Oramo (2006), and Pictures at an Exhibition under Andris Nelsons (2009). Alexander Vedernikov, formerly of the Bolshoi, took the combined Youth Orchestra and Children's Chorus through the whole of Tchaikovsky's The Nutcracker (youthful jaws dropped when he walked on stage at Symphony Hall without a score). Michael Seal put out a call to friends, college mates and ex-members and packed Symphony Hall's Level 5 bar with thirty-two offstage horns, trumpets and trombones for Richard Strauss's Alpensinfonie. In Vaughan Williams' Sixth Symphony, John Wilson transformed the young musicians' sound: coaxing them to use portamento and softening edges until they could have been mistaken for the CBO under Leslie Heward.

Mirga Gražinytė-Tyla plucked the Youth Orchestra out of its usual thrice-yearly slots and put it at the centre of her March 2018 Debussy

The Birmingham teenagers who make up the CBSO Youth Chorus have sung with the Vienna and Berlin Philharmonics, and with conductors including Simon Rattle, Claudio Abbado and Charles Dutoit.

Festival, with a bravura performance of Debussy's *Images*. Katarina Karnéus sang Mahler's *Rückert-Lieder* and Tasmin Little played Korngold's Violin Concerto. There have been premieres, too. Tansy Davies' *Streamlines* (2007) was followed by commissions from Luke Bedford, Ben Foskett and Daniel Kidane as well as Charlotte Bray, a Birmingham Conservatoire alumna who had attended CBSO Youth Orchestra concerts as an undergraduate. Mark-Anthony Turnage's *Passchendaele* was a co-commission for the Youth Orchestra's tenth anniversary, in November 2014. Turnage spoke to the orchestra at the general rehearsal and came off the stage in tears: 'They're not just playing the notes – they're playing the music.'

The conductor that day was the twenty-four-year-old Ben Gernon – who'd had his first taste of orchestral music in 2006 as the CBSO Youth Orchestra's tuba-player. Currently principal guest

conductor of the BBC Philharmonic, he conducted an orchestra for the first time during the summer 2007 CBSO Youth Orchestra Academy. This summer course, under the direction of a CBSO associate conductor, selects a fifty-piece chamber orchestra and performs the sort of music that the 110-piece full youth orchestra is too big to play – anything from Beethoven symphonies to Rameau's *Les Boréades* or Magnus Lindberg's *Aventures*, receiving its second UK performance.

But it also allows for experiments – including an annual conductors' workshop in which, under Seal's tuition, any member can have a go at conducting the orchestra. As well as Gernon, early beneficiaries included trumpeter Jamie Phillips – later appointed associate conductor of the Hallé Orchestra – and cellist Alpesh Chauhan. 'It was the beginning of really fulfilling my musical passions,' he recalls. In 2014 Chauhan would become the first participant in the CBSO's

Violinists of the CBSO Youth Orchestra rehearse at CBSO Centre. The members range in age from fourteen to twenty-one, and are drawn from across the Midlands and beyond.

new Assistant Conductor scheme – a sort of working traineeship, mentored by the CBSO's music director. The scheme continues: Jonathan Bloxham (2016) and Jaume Santonja Espinós (2018) have each had the opportunity to develop their careers amid the daily operations of a major symphony orchestra.

Still, it is probably too early to judge the impact of the CBSO Youth Orchestra – though its earliest members are already making themselves heard. None have had quite the international impact of Laura Mvula, who played the violin in the CBSO Youth Orchestra under Sakari Oramo and went on to work as the CBSO's receptionist before landing the record deal that would lead

her to MOBO and Ivor Novello awards. But CBSO Youth Orchestra alumni are currently playing in the English Symphony Orchestra, at Longborough Festival Opera, in the orchestra of Welsh National Opera, at Covent Garden, and in the CBSO itself.

Youth music – though universally acknowledged to be a Very Important Thing – tends to fly below the critical radar. That's frustrating, but ultimately unimportant: the sound of young people from the full, gloriously diverse spectrum of Birmingham's schools and colleges performing Mahler, Messiaen and Jonathan Harvey with the likes of Oramo, Abbado and Rattle speaks eloquently for itself. And when that old, wrongheaded song about the death of classical music strikes up again (Charles Rosen called it classical music's 'oldest continuing tradition'), there are few more inspiring correctives than a performance by any of the CBSO's youth ensembles.

'You know, you can flog them, and push them and ask them for more, and they still keep giving because they just want to play,' says Michael Seal.

> One thing I will say about the Youth Orchestra is that there's a moment in every concert I've ever done with them where they sound like the Berlin Phil. It can be one chord, or it could be ten minutes. And then you'll hear somebody who is seventeen

or eighteen play a solo and you'll think, 'You've got one hell of a future ahead of you.' Sometimes they'll become a doctor, or a teacher or whatever, but they're still stunningly wonderful and now they've had that experience. You feel it's a privilege to work with them.

As one audience member emailed the morning after the CBSO Youth Orchestra played Mahler's Fifth Symphony under Andrew Litton, '¡El Sistema de Birmingham función muy bien!'

Michael Seal rehearses the CBSO Youth Orchestra in Sibelius' Fifth Symphony at CBSO Centre, October 2013. Although run on similar lines to the 'big' CBSO, the Youth Orchestra is actually considerably bigger.

MIDLAND YOUTH ORCHESTRA
1956–2004

When, in the autumn of 1955, the CBSO's General Manager Blyth Major advertised for young musicians to form a new Midland Youth Orchestra, he was quite clear that he was looking to the future. 'We expect to unearth a lot of talent in this venture – which will benefit orchestras all over the country,' he told the *Birmingham Daily Gazette*.

Major was astonished to receive over ninety applicants, aged between thirteen and twenty-one – so many, in fact, that the inaugural concert of the seventy-three-strong orchestra was delayed until 12 January 1957 to accommodate all the auditions and preliminary rehearsals. Major conducted Dvořák's Eighth Symphony and the Birmingham Post declared it 'a shiningly hopeful event'.

Major's project was independent of the CBSO, and the MYO remained autonomous throughout its 48-year history. But under a series of music directors – James Langley, Stephen Williams and Anthony Bradbury – it fulfilled Major's vision of a nursery of talent. Members included the future composer Brian Ferneyhough and the early-music pioneer David Munrow. The clarinettist Martyn Davies was one of the MYO's first intake. He went straight into the CBSO, where he played for over four decades.

In the twenty-first century, with changing patterns of education and leisure, it grew increasingly difficult to maintain a weekly orchestra, and in 2004 the MYO's committee proposed that its management be taken over by the CBSO. The MYO gave its final concert at the Adrian Boult Hall on 11 July 2004. Four months later it was relaunched under CBSO management as the CBSO Youth Orchestra.

CBSO violinist and general manager Blyth Major (rear) with string players from his Midland Youth Orchestra in the late 1950s. In 2004 the MYO would be reborn as the CBSO Youth Orchestra.

The Quiet
Yorkshireman

For the first time in the story, we can hear music. It's an old melody, described by its arranger Percy Grainger as *Irish Tune from County Derry*, but better known as 'The Londonderry Air' – and better still as 'Danny Boy'. This being wartime, the conductor Leslie Heward has dispensed with the two horns that Grainger suggests as optional extras, and is working only with the strings of the City of Birmingham Orchestra, of which he has now been conductor for just under eleven years. It's Valentine's Day 1941, we're in Birmingham Town Hall, and although there's been snow, the intensity of the playing generates its own warmth.

Heward doesn't pull the melody about: the phrasing is firm and eloquent, and while the players' vibrato is rich, it's unsentimental. They follow the melody's contours, and when Alfred Cave, the orchestra's leader, has a solo line, the texture delicately clears. Heward guides the music to a glowing climax and as the last phrases fall away, he holds firmly onto the final notes – as if, aged just forty-three, he senses how little time he has left.

Leslie Heward was the first conductor who really defined the City of Birmingham Orchestra. He stayed with the orchestra for over a decade, building a partnership whose reputation stretched far beyond the English Midlands, before his death of tuberculosis in May 1943. Today, he hovers just beyond living memory, with only the bare outlines of his extraordinary musicianship preserved on mono recordings. Only a tiny handful of those, in turn, feature the orchestra to which he devoted the best years of his short career.

But they're sufficient to hint at what it must have been like to hear him and the CBO in full flight during the last years of peace: why, while Heward was still a schoolboy, Stanford and Parry called him 'an amazing youth', and why after his death the composer and critic Cecil Gray felt that 'his position should have been that of a Toscanini, a Beecham, a Furtwängler or a Mengelberg'. Malcolm Arnold, who as a trumpeter in the LPO played under Heward in the early 1940s, put it more bluntly: 'He even used to make you realise that the 1812 was a piece of music and not just a damned noise.'

Heward had conducted the CBO only once before when in November 1929 he was invited to conduct a Sunday concert that everyone present knew was effectively an unofficial audition. The monster programme, at the West End cinema, included Schubert's 'Great' C major Symphony, a Mozart violin concerto, Berlioz's *Roman Carnival* overture, a Bach aria and orchestral excerpts from *Die Meistersinger*. Heward impressed both orchestra and audience, and rumours of his success were so widespread that he was forced to issue an official denial that he'd been offered the job.

His appointment was announced from the Town Hall stage at Adrian Boult's farewell concert on 27 March 1930, and the *Gazette* ran his picture on the front page the next morning, announcing his arrival with the headline 'From Infant Prodigy to Fame as Conductor'. George

OPPOSITE *Leslie Heward during the 1930s. 'I have never known a man more sensitive to beauty,' said the record producer Walter Legge.*

Cunningham, the city organist, was backstage with Boult and Heward that day. Next to the self-confident Boult, Heward seemed reticent – outwardly at least:

> 'Leslie, you'll have to conduct something,' said Sir Adrian. 'Which will you do?'
>
> 'Oh, what you like – anything,' he replied with a smile and a shrug.
>
> It sounded at the time like indifference, but I was soon to discover that it summed up two of his greatest qualities: his superb ability to deal with any musical problem, however difficult, and his modest diffidence, which shrank from all publicity and showmanship.

In the event, on Sunday 13 April 1930 Heward conducted Tchaikovsky's *1812 Overture* – a concert in aid of the CBO's Pension Fund, for which, along with Boult, he gave his services free of charge (a tradition continued today in the annual CBSO Benevolent Fund concert). Delayed in London, he conducted it without rehearsal: completely unaware that in the coda, the entire Birmingham Police Band was about to burst in. 'It's a wonder we didn't crack the nice clean roof of the Town Hall,' confided the cellist Gwen Berry to her diary, adding, 'Mr Heward conducted and, by Jove, he is fine.'

He *was* fine, too. Heward's modest personal manner concealed an uncompromising determination to shape the CBO into a taut, responsive ensemble, and an enthusiasm for new music that rivalled Boult's. He got down to business at the Town Hall on 9 October 1930,

> *'"There is no doubt that the music-loving public of Birmingham wants really good stuff," said Heward to the Gazette'*

with a programme that paired Handel's Concerto grosso Op. 6 No. 3 with Dohnányi's virtuosic Suite in F sharp. Over the decade that followed, Birmingham audiences would discover such novelties as Stravinsky's *Petrushka*, Hindemith's *Neues vom Tage* overture, Sibelius' *Tapiola*, Kodály's *Háry János* and Vaughan Williams' *Job*. Heward hired Philip Heseltine (better known as the composer Peter Warlock) to write programme notes; meanwhile he cultivated composers including Arthur Bliss, the Finn Uuno Klami, the German modernist Boris Blacher and Ernest Bloch, then widely regarded as one of the world's foremost living composers.

'There is no doubt that the music-loving public of Birmingham wants really good stuff,' said Heward to the *Gazette*, and even the Sunday 'popular' concerts at the West End cinema received a makeover. As in Appleby Matthews' time, they were still marathons – punctuated with parlour songs and solo instrumental numbers – but under Heward's direction the Sunday orchestra was expanded to forty-five players, and programmes might feature a Glazunov symphony, Walton's *Façade* suite, John Foulds' *Dynamic Triptych* or, in 1931, Elgar's brand new *Nursery Suite*.

Heward's most startling addition to the Birmingham repertoire, however, was probably Anton Webern's super-concentrated Symphony Op. 21: so startling, indeed, that Harold Gray – who had been appointed deputy conductor in June 1932 – always maintained that the performance on 16 February 1933 had been authorised by the management committee only because they thought there had been a typo and that the piece was actually by Weber. The audience reacted, according to a clearly disappointed *Gazette*, with 'the usual giggles and whispers, followed by a feeble flapping of hands. Nobody hissed or threw things at Mr Leslie Heward. I am glad for the latter's sake, but sorry for the sake of Birmingham's artistic vitality.' As to the piece itself: 'Without wishing to insult the animal kingdom, I can only compare Webern's progressions with the last convulsive wriggles of a half-drowned spider.'

It can't have done much to reassure the management committee. Birmingham's huge diversity of employers and growing motor car

Leslie Heward (left) and Harold Gray (right) stop for a picnic en route to an out-of-town concert in the 1930s. Heward never underestimated the importance of taking regular refreshment.

LESLIE HEWARD (1897–1943)

Leslie Hays Heward was a composer, a prodigy and a Yorkshireman. His father was a porter at Liversedge on the Lancashire and Yorkshire Railway and at the age of eight Leslie played the organ in Handel's *Messiah* in Bradford. By the age of sixteen he'd composed an opera, *Hamlet*, and hearing Hans Richter conduct the Hallé Orchestra, he exclaimed, 'Shouldn't I like to conduct that band some day!' He studied with Adrian Boult and Herbert Howells at the Royal College of Music, where Hubert Parry called him 'the kind of phenomenon that appears once in a generation', and Heward won his first major conducting post – in Cape Town, South Africa – in 1924.

Heward's unshowy, earnest podium manner masked a profound sensitivity. The record producer Walter Legge remembered,

Many a time during recording sessions I have seen his kind, light eyes moist and over-bright from some expressive piece of phrasing. And he would turn his back on the orchestra, brush his eyes with his sleeve like a child and say, 'Damn this music! I wish it didn't get me like this!'

Heward suffered throughout his life from asthma and contracted tuberculosis in Africa. His poor health was exacerbated by years of heavy smoking and hard drinking. (At the CBO's favourite pub, the Hope and Anchor on Edmund Street, Heward famously refused to order doubles – only trebles.) When he died in May 1943, he'd already accepted the job of his childhood dreams at the Hallé Orchestra, but in Birmingham the loss felt no less raw.

industry protected it against the very worst of the Great Depression, but another shortfall had opened up in the orchestra's budget. At the October 1932 general meeting the committee had urged Heward to devise 'lighter' programmes for the Sunday series. His reply was forthright, and it was duly reported in the *Birmingham Post*:

> I have heard it said that lighter music would pay better, but there is nothing lighter than we do that is at the same time good, and surely it is not the function of a subsidised orchestra to perform trash. I do not think the City Fathers would like to feel they were helping to finance a tripe shop.

But these were still difficult times in which to build a first-class ensemble. The CBO was at this time a freelance orchestra. Since 1920, players had been hired as required from October to March each year, rather than being permanent employees of a 'contract orchestra', like most UK symphony orchestras outside London today. In the summer, they simply dispersed across the country to find work (often at seaside resorts). It was cost effective, but it meant that Heward effectively had to retrain his orchestra from scratch at the start of each season. It also depended on the existence of a sizeable pool of excellent freelance musicians in Birmingham. Since the arrival of the talking pictures in 1929, and the disbandment of most of Birmingham's fifty-plus cinema orchestras, this was becoming tricky.

A full-time contract orchestra was financially impossible, so Heward and the management

'*Heward never referred to the orchestra as "you" and himself as "I": it was always "we"*'

committee entered discussions with the BBC, whose director of music in Birmingham, helpfully enough, was the composer Victor Hely-Hutchinson – an old friend of Heward from his time conducting the Cape Town Orchestra in the 1920s. From the 1934–5 season, the BBC set up a Midland Orchestra, guaranteeing year-round work to a core of thirty-five musicians, while leaving them free to play in the CBO during the winter season. Heward was put in charge, meaning that he could now work with his principal players all year round.

Increasingly, too, there was local competition. A series of 'International Celebrity Subscription Concerts' at the Town Hall brought some major stars to the city. The 1935–6 season alone featured the violinist Fritz Kreisler, the great African-American bass Paul Robeson, the Viennese heart-throb tenor Richard Tauber and the full Berlin Philharmonic Orchestra ('100 players', boasted the adverts) conducted by Wilhelm Furtwängler. In a city built on new money, a section of the concertgoing public has always been impressed by star power and glamorous names. The *Gazette* detected an attitude of 'it's only the City Orchestra' as early as 1920, and even in the twenty-first century there is still a modest but noticeable difference in Birmingham between the audience for 'international' concerts (very free with standing ovations) and the more discriminating – if less demonstrative – CBSO regulars.

Heward responded by trying to improve conditions at the Town Hall. Big Brum, the bell in the Council House clock tower, could not be prevented from striking the hour mid-concert, and nor could massive (and astonishingly noisy) flocks of chattering starlings be stopped from wheeling in each evening to perch on the Town Hall roof. But Heward could and did engage soloists such as Benno Moiseiwitsch, Myra Hess, Lionel Tertis and Solomon. Egon Petri was the soloist in Busoni's colossal Piano Concerto, while guest conductors included Beecham, Ansermet, the Russian Nikolai Malko – who conducted Shostakovich's First Symphony – and Liszt's former pupil, Felix Weingartner. When Harold Gray told him that Mendelssohn had performed at the Town Hall, Weingartner pressed his hands to the walls and muttered, in a thick Viennese accent, 'This, then, is holy ground!' His concert sold out.

Sir Edward Elgar, meanwhile, conducted the orchestra for the second and last time in October 1932 – a performance of his cantata *King Olaf*, in the Potteries town of Hanley, where it had been premiered thirty-six years before. The CBO's status as the Midlands' flagship ensemble was by now well established, and on 24 April that year Heward had conducted the inaugural concert

at the new Shakespeare Memorial Theatre in Stratford-upon-Avon – opening (naturally) with Mendelssohn's *A Midsummer Night's Dream* overture and ending with the *Enigma Variations*. The hope had been that the composer would conduct, but Elgar took one glance at the modernist architecture of the new theatre and refused to step inside 'that distressing, vulgar and abominable building'.

But even while conducting some forty programmes a year Heward, too, could deliver some truly unforgettable occasions. One was the second complete performance of Walton's First Symphony on 22 November 1935. 'They really went all out for this and pulled it off,' wrote Walton's publisher Hubert Foss afterwards. 'The tears were rolling down my cheeks during the Epilogue', and the Town Hall crowd rose in a standing ovation. Heward gave the world premiere of Ernest Moeran's Symphony in G minor in London in January 1938, and brought it to Birmingham the following December – a performance, wrote the *Gazette*, that was 'lit up with flashes of sunlight brilliance'. Heward's red-blooded 1942 recording of the symphony is still unsurpassed.

That recording, however, was made with the Hallé Orchestra. Once again, success in Birmingham had drawn interest elsewhere. But darker forces were also in play. Heward was never particularly healthy, and by the late 1930s he was succumbing with repeated frequency to the tuberculosis that he had contracted in South Africa during the previous decade. His massive workload didn't help; nor (although contemporary accounts were too polite to say

HAROLD GRAY OBE (1903–91)

From the day when Adrian Boult hired him as his assistant in 1924, to his final CBSO concert in March 1982, no conductor gave longer or more devoted service to the orchestra than Harold Gray. While working for Boult he quietly took conducting lessons with Malcolm Sargent, and in June 1932, Leslie Heward appointed him deputy conductor. Although the title later changed to associate conductor, Gray held the post (with a brief break during the Second World War) until his official retirement in July 1979.

'I owe far more to Birmingham than ever it does to me,' said Gray, with typical self-deprecation. For fifty years, he was organist at Holy Trinity Church, Sutton Coldfield, and he also conducted the Birmingham Choral Union. But to the CBSO, he was indispensable: deputising for indisposed guest conductors, and conducting (literally) hundreds of summer Proms, schools concerts and out-of-town dates. 'If I needed a conductor at short notice I'd get hold of Harold Gray. He'd know the work and get on without any fuss,' said Sir Thomas Beecham.

'We called him Harold,' remembers violinist Stan Smith. 'He was sincere, and he loved music.' Gray's own programmes embraced William Alwyn, Ernest Bloch and the young Peter Maxwell Davies, and between 1957 and 1969 he became the first British conductor to perform all six of Nielsen's symphonies. He died in 1991, a fortnight before the CBSO moved into Symphony Hall. In tribute, Simon Rattle concluded his final CBSO concert in Birmingham Town Hall with Delius' *The Walk to the Paradise Garden*.

Heward and the CBO in the Town Hall, around 1931. Note the suspended microphone
and the elegant lyre-shaped music stands, which survived into the late 1940s.

so) did his heavy dependence on cigarettes and alcohol. Heward's capacity for drink was famous: Arthur Bliss, inviting him to visit in 1933, wrote that 'I have a bottle of brandy open ready for you.' As the City Orchestra faced the Second World War Heward spent extended periods at Romsley Hill Sanatorium, near Clent.

Heward still managed to fulfil one long-held ambition. In December 1940 and February 1941, during a brief bomb-free respite in the Birmingham blitz, he conducted the CBO in its first commercial recordings, for HMV and Columbia. Malcolm Sargent recommended a Harley Street lung specialist, but to no avail. Heward continued to work in Birmingham for as long as his health allowed. He was confident of recovery: on Boxing Day 1942 he accepted the music directorship of the Hallé Orchestra, and gave notice that his current season with the CBO would be his last.

And so, tragically, it proved. After conducting Sibelius' *Tapiola* and Beethoven's Fifth Symphony on 14 February 1943 he almost collapsed, and his wife Lenore pleaded with him to rest. He practically passed out during rehearsals for his next concert, on 7 March, and was forced to cancel. Worried concertgoers sent good wishes, and a group of fans clubbed together to buy him (at Lenore's suggestion) a set of *Grove's Dictionary of Music and Musicians*. He died at his home at 44 Harborne Road on 3 May 1943, aged forty-five.

Walter Legge, writing in *Gramophone*, did his best to sum up what had been lost. 'The outstanding qualities of all his work were its untarnished musicianship, its touching sensitiveness of line, and its clarity and beauty of texture,' he wrote.

> He did not want to impose his own personality on music and he did not try to make it more effective. I have never known a man more sensitive to beauty. He loved it in music, in poetry, in prose, in painting, in women and in flowers and it brought him often to the edge of tears.

A book of tributes to Heward, edited by Eric Blom, the music critic of the *Birmingham Post*, brims over with unfeigned affection. Norris Stanley, the leader of the orchestra from 1942 to 1958, put the players' perspective:

> Leslie Heward had the rare gift of coaxing from each of his players a little more than his best. He knew the highest standard of playing each individual player was capable of giving and expected that standard to be reached in every performance.
>
> When rehearsing he never referred to the orchestra as 'you' and himself as 'I': it was always 'we'. He never lost his temper . . . He was beloved by each member of his orchestra, and he also loved each one of them.

Heward's CBO career had begun with Schubert's Ninth. In an obituary notice, his friend Victor Hely-Hutchinson quoted the famous epitaph on Schubert's grave: 'Music has buried here a great treasure, but still greater hopes.'

RECORDING THE BIRMINGHAM SOUND

'I do believe that there are certain things – such as human discourse, friendship and music – that are meant to be live,' said Simon Rattle to the *Daily Telegraph* in 1999, a year after leaving the CBSO. 'To be limited to recordings is like choosing snapshots of your children over the children themselves. The point is the real, live thing.' His words raised eyebrows even then. Some record collectors, and even some artists, see recordings as the pinnacle of an orchestra's and a conductor's career – an attempt to create a single, definitive interpretation of a work and preserve it, like a butterfly pinned to a board, between layers of shellac or the bytes of a digital file. Why else would the CBSO have released some 225 recordings (many more remain unreleased) between 1940 and 2020?

The real motivation, as often with orchestras, has ranged from the idealistic to the utterly prosaic. For the performers, it's a matter of personal and professional artistic pride: the sense that when something special has been achieved, it deserves to be documented. Plus, recordings do make wonderful calling cards for an orchestra. A commercial release is heard, reviewed and enjoyed across the world. There's no doubt that Louis Frémaux's CBSO recordings in the 1970s – like Simon Rattle's in the 1980s and Andris Nelsons' in the twenty-first century – raised the international profile and reputation of orchestra and conductor alike. This is why some orchestras – though not the CBSO – maintain loss-making in-house record labels, it having become depressingly clear that classical recordings rarely make anything resembling a profit in the twenty-first century.

This wasn't always the case, though, and the CBO's earliest recordings were money-spinners. They certainly didn't do much for the orchestra's reputation, since – due to a spaghetti-like contractual tangle – none of Leslie Heward's recordings with the CBO actually named the orchestra. Worse, the very first – a mechanical recording of Bantock's *Hebridean Symphony*, conducted by Adrian Boult in the premises of Riley and Sons, piano manufacturers of Constitution Hill, on 28 January 1925 – was never issued. Just months after it was made, the label, Columbia, adopted electrical recording, and it was deemed unsuitable for release. The masters appear to have been lost.

So it was Heward who conducted the CBO's first commercial recordings, in the winter of 1940–41 – the winter of the Birmingham blitz. The producer Walter Legge explained the rationale in a letter to Thomas Beecham in January 1941: surveying the wartime state of Britain's orchestras, he concluded that 'the LSO is not better, or better off than of yore'. As for the BBC Symphony Orchestra,

> the slovenliness of the playing has to be heard to be believed. The only occasions on which this band plays with passable intonation, accuracy and style are when they are in [the] charge of Leslie Heward, who is working extremely well. His own band in Birmingham has been sadly depleted by the predatory moves of the BBC . . .

Birmingham it was, then, although those wartime depredations limited the options to music for small orchestras – Mozart, Tchaikovsky's *Andante cantabile* and Sibelius' *Rakastava* (a Heward speciality) – and a series of operatic arias, credited variously to 'The Leslie Heward String Orchestra' or simply 'Orchestra conducted by Leslie Heward'. Sessions started on 21 December 1940 in a freezing Birmingham Town Hall with Mozart's *Eine kleine Nachtmusik* – proceeded by a blast from a hooter on the roof of the building to scare away the flocks of starlings, whose chattering was clearly audible. There had been snow as well as bombs, and the following day the soprano Gwen Catley remembered:

> arriving at 9.45 a.m. to find windows blown out of your Town Hall. We all performed in our overcoats and the flautist for [Henry Bishop's] 'Lo, Hear the Gentle Lark' played the obbligato with his hat on!! The draught was so strong it upset him. I had not met Mr Heward before but we had a quick rehearsal – one take of each item – and that was that! All done in about two hours or less! No tea, no coffee, in fact no liquids of any kind . . .

Heward's February 1941 disc of Puccini's 'Un bel di' with the young soprano Joan Hammond became a wartime bestseller. Legge later recalled that Heward 'maintained a rather resentful dislike of Puccini, whose work he regarded as insincere and bogus.' If that's true, there's no trace of it here. Heward's health prevented any further recording after February 1941. So there's no recording of him in a large-scale orchestral work with the full CBO, though Constant Lambert

was called in later in the year to conduct an ardent performance of Tchaikovsky's *Romeo and Juliet*, and Basil Cameron conducted the CBO's first recorded concerto – Franck's *Symphonic Variations*, with Myra Hess as soloist – in Wolverhampton Civic Hall that summer.

As regional Entertainments National Service Association (ENSA) organiser, Legge had a close relationship with the CBO throughout the war years. He certainly saw the potential of the crack new full-time orchestra after George Weldon's appointment as music director in 1944 and in March 1945 recordings resumed in Dudley Town Hall – a venue free, as Weldon put it, of 'buses, trams, birds or clock-strikings'. Walton recorded his own *Sinfonia Concertante* with the pianist Phyllis Sellick, while Weldon laid down works ranging from Dohnányi's *Wedding Waltz* to what might be the world premiere recording of Dvořák's Fifth Symphony (in F major), all charged with Weldon's signature tautness and panache.

But the relationship cooled, principally because in the absence of adequate orchestras in the capital, Legge had now founded his own London 'super-orchestra', the Philharmonia. The Wolverhampton-born soprano Maggie Teyte, however, thought that his frostiness stemmed from an incident when he had attempted to conduct the CBO in a rehearsal for an ENSA concert. He showed up wearing a Russian blouse, and promptly broke his baton. 'Second time he took up the baton. PAM. PAM . . . the orchestra walked off.' In any case, after June 1946 the CBSO was not to record again for nearly two decades.

Long-players

The CBSO made its first LP in January 1966 for Lyrita. The conductor was Hugo Rignold and the main work was Arthur Bliss's *Meditations on a Theme by John Blow* – the piece he'd written for the CBSO as the first ever Feeney Trust commission in 1955. Bliss attended the sessions, at Kingsway Hall, London, and professed himself delighted. The angry young man of Appleby Matthews' day was now Master of the Queen's Music: the percussionist Maggie Cotton said that 'he always seemed to me to be a quaint cross between Peter Rabbit and Queen Victoria'.

Since 1970, CBSO recordings have come in an unbroken stream. Some are wonderfully vivid documents of a particular moment – the veteran military bandmaster Sir Vivian Dunn conducting Sullivan orchestral suites, Reginald Kilbey in Eric Coates (Richard Weigall's oboe

> *'Louis Frémaux's recordings began a wider transformation of the orchestra's reputation'*

solo in *Elizabeth of Glamis* is exquisite) or Malcolm Arnold conducting his own Fifth Symphony. But Louis Frémaux's eighteen recordings for EMI / HMV laid the foundations of the modern CBSO discography, and began a wider transformation of the orchestra's reputation.

That meant French music, of course, from bonbons by Massenet, Offenbach and Saint-Saëns to more substantial works by Frémaux's close friends Poulenc and Ibert. But not just that: Walton was delighted with Frémaux's recording of his Gloria and Te Deum and thanked him personally for 'the splendid results', while the CBSO–Frémaux recording of John McCabe's *Notturni ed Alba* documents a modern British masterpiece that the orchestra had premiered in 1970.

The grand projects made the biggest splash. Saint-Saëns' 'Organ' Symphony, recorded in quadrophonic sound in the cathedral-like Great Hall of Birmingham University, was immediately hailed as a landmark. 'Vital and affectionate,' commented *Gramophone*, noting the 'sumptuously recorded' sound. Next came a stunning set of Berlioz's monumental *Grande Messe des morts*, recorded in April 1975 in the same venue – the first large-scale recording by Frémaux's brand-new, hand-picked CBSO Chorus. Intensely proud of their joint achievement, Frémaux chose it as one of his Desert Island Discs. 'It is very alive in the beautiful resonance of the Great Hall of the University,' he declared. And there was very nearly a Britten *War Requiem* with many of the same players who had performed in the world premiere. The plans disintegrated after Frémaux's sudden departure in March 1978.

Hugo Rignold conducts the recording of Bliss's Meditations on a Theme by John Blow – the first
of the CBSO's Feeney Trust commissions – at Kingsway Hall, London, in January 1966.

Simon Rattle, though, has never hidden his ambivalence about the recording process. 'For me, the most important thing about recordings is that they are the most effective way to make the orchestra play better,' he said in 1986. 'None of these recordings I'm making now is my last will and testament.' And yet he came of musical age in the digital era. 'There's never been any other conductor in my life who's taken such an interest in the recording process as Simon,' says violinist David Gregory. 'He was always in the box, when he wasn't on the rostrum – listening to everything, balancing, discussing things with the producer . . . we've never had anyone with such interest, or technical knowledge.'

'We try now to do more and more straight performances in the recording studio, with as few retakes as possible,' Rattle told Nicholas Kenyon during the recording of Mahler's 'Resurrection' Symphony in 1986. Later, he would come to prefer recordings based almost entirely on live performances: 'You need to hear the rough edges,' he says. That had its perils. A live concert recording of Mahler's Seventh Symphony at Snape Maltings in Suffolk in 1991 found the vital euphonium player indisposed, and CBSO bass trombonist Alwyn Green – the obvious stand-in – without a suitable instrument. A phone call to Green's retired parents in Norwich, the rescue of a dusty childhood euphonium from the attic, and a high-speed drive south saved the day.

February 1983: Simon Rattle conducts massed forces in the Great Hall of Birmingham University during the recording of Britten's War Requiem.

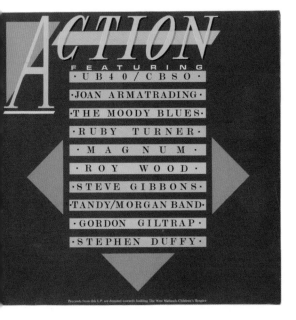

Not every CBSO recording makes it into
Gramophone. In 1986, the orchestra
collaborated with UB40 on Orchestral
Dub – a charity crossover project in aid of
the West Midlands Children's Hospice.

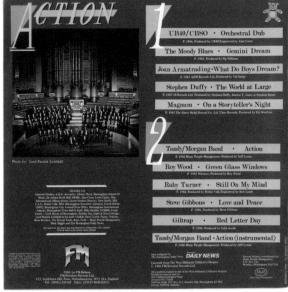

Rattle's seventy-plus Birmingham recordings
– from Janáček's *Glagolitic Mass* in 1981 to
Szymanowski's *Songs of a Fairy Tale Princess* in
2006 – chart his entire journey with the CBSO.
There's Sibelius, Stravinsky, Britten and the
Second Viennese School; Turnage, Henze, Adams
and Adès; Haydn, Grainger, Duke Ellington and
Messiaen ('What a great Mars Bar of a piece!'
exclaimed Rattle at the *Turangalîla-Symphonie*
sessions in 1986).

Both Rattle and Ed Smith deny that Rattle
refused to renew his contract with EMI until the
label agreed to record Nicholas Maw's colossal
Odyssey in the Town Hall in 1990, but he certainly
applied some leverage. And of course there was
Mahler. Rattle's 'Resurrection' Symphony won
the CBSO's first *Gramophone* award in 1988:
recognition at the highest critical level that this
was now a partnership of international stature.
'We are dealing here with conducting akin to

genius,' declared the magazine, 'with insights and instincts that cannot be measured with any old yardstick.'

As the CD boom of the 1980s and 1990s ebbed, and the RLPO, LSO, LPO and Hallé all took their first steps into 'own-label' recording (the industry has generally been too tactful to call it vanity publishing), the CBSO decided against starting its own record label. Instead, it sought to build partnerships with major labels in a very fluid market. 'If we can find an established record label that can fulfil the prime function of a recording – which is to get your work out there to the widest possible audience – we prefer to do that,' says chief executive Stephen Maddock.

> For the orchestras who do run record labels, it's mostly about control, and about there being something rather than there being nothing. We've been lucky. We've worked with conductors and artists where there's always been the possibility of there being something. So then it's a question of whether control is the most important thing or not. By and large we've been able to have recording partnerships that have mirrored the characteristics of our music directors.

The one venture into self-publishing (so far, at any rate) came in 2007, when Sakari Oramo's revelatory interpretation of Elgar's *The Dream of Gerontius* seemed too good not to immortalise. With beautiful cover artwork by Norman Perryman, it was rush-released that June to coincide with celebrations of Elgar's 150th birthday, and sold 3,000 copies within a year: good enough to make the venture worthwhile, if not sufficient to justify launching a label. Instead, the CBSO's collaborative, flexible approach to major labels looked increasingly like a shrewd policy. There were some casualties: Andris Nelsons refused to allow the release of a complete, live Beethoven symphony cycle recorded in Symphony Hall during the 2012–13 season, and Sakari Oramo's luminous live accounts of Elgar's *The Apostles* and *The Kingdom* still await an enterprising label.

They were outweighed by some striking successes – complete Sibelius symphony and Rachmaninoff concerto cycles with Sakari Oramo, two pioneering discs of John Foulds that effectively restored his music to the repertoire, and spectacular, sumptuous recordings of Strauss, Shostakovich, Stravinsky and Tchaikovsky with Andris Nelsons, plus a DVD of 2012's fiftieth anniversary performance of Britten's *War Requiem* in Coventry Cathedral. A 2008 album of songs made famous by the Bollywood singer Mohammed Rafi, conducted by Michael Seal and sung by Indian movie vocalist Sonu Nigam, led to two nationwide concert tours, a Sony telecast and a spike in CBSO record sales in the Indian subcontinent.

As principal guest conductor, Edward Gardner recorded a joyous complete Mendelssohn symphony cycle in Birmingham Town Hall – standing on the very spot where Mendelssohn himself conducted *Lobgesang*. And a recording in Dudley Town Hall of rare piano concertos by Sauer and Scharwenka, with Stephen Hough as soloist, won Hyperion and the CBSO another

Gramophone award in 1996. That achievement was topped in 2002, when Oramo's and Hough's complete Saint-Saëns piano concerto cycle won Gramophone's Record of the Year – and then, in 2008, was voted the best classical recording of the past thirty years by Gramophone readers.

> '*In eighty years of recording, the CBSO has created a catalogue full of engrossing byways and truly magnificent peaks*'

There were splutters of astonishment from some quarters, as established UK critics struggled with the notion that fresh, inspired readings of life-affirming (if unfamiliar) repertoire could speak – and indeed, had spoken – for themselves.

Birmingham audiences didn't need telling twice and, indeed, to music-lovers across a digitally connected world, the perspective from within the M25 was beginning to look increasingly parochial. In February 2019, Mirga Gražinytė-Tyla was signed by Deutsche Grammophon – the fabled 'Yellow Label' of Karajan, Kleiber and Abbado – with a remit to record neglected repertoire with the CBSO,

beginning with Mieczysław Weinberg's colossal Symphony No.21. But the enduring value of recordings is that they allow listeners to explore – and in eighty years of recording, the CBSO has created a catalogue that is full of engrossing byways, as well as some truly magnificent peaks. The orchestra's followers will all have their own personal favourites. (Mine include the American mezzo Susan Graham's 2001 disc of rare French operetta arias, the first full orchestral album to be recorded at CBSO Centre. The record label, Erato, bought orchestra and staff champagne after the final take.)

There's no space here to discuss Sir Michael Tippett's own recording of A Child of Our Time, Rattle's championing of Berthold Goldschmidt or Mark Elder's uproarious rediscovery of Shostakovich's Hypothetically Murdered; still less film star Anthony Hopkins' self-penned compositions (one of his waltzes was taken up by André Rieu), or Walter Weller's controversial 1988 premiere recording of Barry Cooper's completion of Beethoven's 'Tenth Symphony'. We can probably agree, too, to pass tactfully over Orchestral Dub: the 1986 charity crossover LP with Birmingham reggae legends UB40 (Louis Clark of Electric Light Orchestra did the orchestrations, and the orchestra wears sunglasses on the album sleeve). It's worth adding, though, that in May 2018, after its soloist, the cellist Sheku Kanneh-Mason, played at the wedding of Prince Harry and Meghan Markle, Mirga Gražinytė-Tyla's first disc with the CBSO entered the US Billboard Emerging Artists chart – a pop chart – at Number One.

Conflict and Rebirth

Neville Chamberlain's career took him from Birmingham Council House to the most powerful elected office in the United Kingdom – which, on 30 September 1938, effectively meant the world. When he stood on the apron at Heston Aerodrome, having brought back from his meeting with Hitler in Munich the document that, he later insisted, guaranteed 'peace for our time', Birmingham responded with elation. Newsreels in city cinemas hailed the CBO's founder as 'Chamberlain the Peacemaker' – 'Birmingham's greatest living citizen, who by his courage and steadfastness averted a world catastrophe!'

This was more than just local pride. For a brief period, Chamberlain was an international hero. Cheering crowds mobbed his car in London, and along with more than 20,000 letters and telegrams of congratulations, he was deluged with gifts – a cross from the Pope, wines from the Rhineland, flowers from Hungary and 6,000 flower bulbs from Holland. His passion for gardening was well known, and so too was his love of music. To thank him for preserving the peace, the piano manufacturer Blüthner of Leipzig sent him a gift of a brand new concert grand.

When, less than twelve months later, Chamberlain's policy failed, and on the morning of Sunday 3 September he told the nation that 'this country is at war with Germany', his beloved Birmingham orchestra was almost one of the first things to go. The government issued emergency regulations closing all theatres, concert halls and cinemas for the duration of the war. The intention was practical – it was assumed that enemy bombing would begin almost immediately – and the management committee responded in the only possible way: by cancelling the 1939–40 season.

'On the administrative side, however, the nucleus of an organisation has been retained so that should the ban on public assemblies be raised or modified, it will be possible to proceed with the elaboration of a programme suited to the needs and limitations of the times,' reported the *Birmingham Daily Post* on 12 September. By this time, however, the City Council had already cancelled all the CBO's Town Hall bookings in case the hall should be needed for 'clerical purposes'.

As the first month of the war passed and no bombs fell, the situation seemed increasingly absurd. The BBC dissolved its Midland Orchestra: Birmingham's orchestral musicians now faced a season without paid work. Meanwhile public and press demanded to know why, in this time of communal crisis, they were deprived of entertainment. One correspondent to the *Birmingham Post* expressed concern that the city would use the war as a pretext to stop funding the orchestra, and added, provocatively, that 'the regime we seek to destroy in Germany has seen the cultural importance and true entertainment power of good music'. 'As a stimulus to public morale concerts as before would have an inestimable value,' wrote another. 'Let the City Orchestra lead the way. If Mr Leslie Heward is compelled by A.R.P. [Air Raid Precautions] to bring his players before us in the afternoon instead of the evening, we shall not object.'

Sure enough, on 29 September the City Council relented and authorised four orchestral matinee concerts between late October and

Christmas 1939. Heward returned to the UK from a tour of the USA the following day, but immediately fell seriously ill. He spent the next eight months in Romsley Sanatorium, and when the first wartime concert was given by the reconstituted 'City of Birmingham (Emergency) Orchestra' on 28 October 1939 in the Large Hall of the Midland Institute, it was conducted by his friend Victor Hely-Hutchinson. Such was the demand for tickets that between two and three hundred would-be concertgoers had to be turned away on the door.

There could be no possible doubt that the orchestra was now operating in a violently changed world. The Town Hall was surrounded with sandbags; auxiliary water tanks for firefighting had been set up in Victoria Square, and buses and trams – vital for carrying night workers to the massive aircraft and armaments factories at Castle Bromwich, Longbridge, Washwood Heath and Marston Green – had their smart Corporation liveries painted over with grey blackout camouflage. Home Guard detachments cruised the canal network in motor launches, Edgbaston Reservoir was drained in order to offer less of a landmark for enemy bombers, and the manager of the Express Café on Moor Street was fined £2 for serving an over-generous helping of eggs and bacon to a customer who turned out to be a government food inspector.

So concertgoers wouldn't have been surprised to find their programme books reduced to a single sheet of printed paper, sold for a penny – though frustratingly, since there was no room for an orchestra list, we can't now know the exact composition of the early wartime CB(E)O.

The notice to audiences printed on each sheet, however, gives a startling reality to the notion of keeping calm and carrying on:

> In the case of an Air Raid Warning the performance will continue. Patrons who wish to leave are asked to do so as quietly as possible. The nearest way to the Basement Shelter is by means of the Exit door adjoining the platform.

Hely-Hutchinson, along with Harold Gray, conducted most of the concerts in that first wartime season, and before long he was effectively running the musical side of the CBO. He refused to accept a fee for any of his work with the CBO, but his efforts (he was also serving as professor of music at Birmingham University, volunteering as an ARP warden, studying part-time for a doctorate at Oxford and commanding the University cadet force) were tireless. Gerald Forty of the management committee was astonished by his competence and energy:

> The problem of finding another conductor at short notice and of maintaining a full complement of players with War staring us in the face was one of extreme perplexity; but Victor solved it by the apparently simple expedient of doing the entire job himself – including the compiling of programmes, rehearsing the orchestra (which he did anonymously and gratuitously for many years), conducting the concerts and dealing efficiently and decisively with the innumerable emergencies . . .

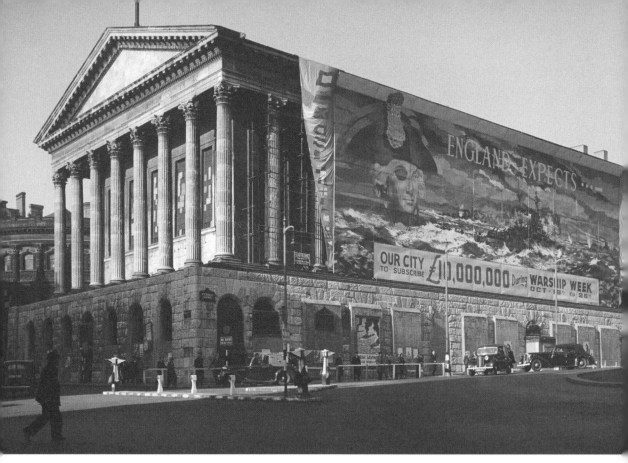

Warship Week, October 1942. The huge posters at least helped with the blackout; meanwhile Victor Hely-Hutchinson and George Weldon took regular overnight turns on the Town Hall's fire-watch.

As the so-called 'bore war' (the term 'phoney war' came later) continued, so too did the concerts. Audiences swelled. In January 1940 the Emergency Orchestra reverted to being the plain old CBO, and moved into the more capacious West End cinema. For the 1940–41 season, with Heward temporarily restored to health and back on the podium, the orchestra returned to the Town Hall. This had its own problems: such huge windows were not easily blacked out. The solution was to play without lighting, and Beryl Lawrence, a concertgoer, told Beresford King-Smith how she witnessed 'the orchestra playing on Sunday afternoons with bicycle lamps on their

music stands, which were switched on as the afternoons got darker'.

Later in the war, giant propaganda posters on the side of the Town Hall would help solve the blackout problem. A partial – if grim – resolution came when the long-feared Birmingham blitz finally began in August 1940. The Luftwaffe's priorities were to attack Birmingham's industries, but navigation and bomb-aiming were imprecise, and on the night of 24 September the bombers subjected the city centre to what the CBO management committee, in its annual report, called 'certain unwelcome attentions'. The explosions blew out 200 panes of glass in the

VICTOR HELY-HUTCHINSON (1901–47)

Best known today as the composer of the *Carol Symphony* (1927) – the theme tune to the BBC's *The Box of Delights* – Victor Hely-Hutchinson was one of the quiet heroes of the CBSO story. Born in Cape Town, and a pupil of Stanford, he became the BBC's Regional Director of Music in Birmingham in 1933. There seems to have been little that he wouldn't do for the orchestra – as programme-note writer, pre-concert speaker, or pianist.

In autumn 1940, while serving as an ARP warden, he performed a complete cycle of Beethoven piano sonatas in aid of CBO funds. While Leslie Heward fought the tuberculosis that would kill him in May 1943, Hely-Hutchinson conducted numerous concerts during the war years, appearing as soloist on fourteen occasions. 'His quiet confidence was most reassuring,' remembered the CBO's chairman Gerald Forty.

I see him in my mind's eye, sitting at my desk. He knocks out a half-smoked pipe, his inseparable companion ... while my ashtrays were being filled, his mind was concentrated on the matter at hand, and with a remarkable economy of words, he stated his views and recommended a solution.

Hely-Hutchinson never held an official post with the CBO, but it's doubtful whether the orchestra would have survived the war without him. He left for London in 1945 and died of pneumonia in March 1947, aged just forty-five. The CBO paid its own tribute three weeks later, when George Weldon conducted the premiere of his *Symphony for Small Orchestra*. An incomplete recording survives in the CBSO archive.

Town Hall's windows, as well as damaging the Council House and New Street station.

That made for cold conditions when Heward and the CBO made their first – and only – gramophone recordings together in the Town Hall in December 1940 and February 1941. Still, the very fact that such a project was thought possible demonstrates a shift in attitude from the emergency mindset of September 1939 to the 'can-do' spirit we attribute, with hindsight, to the war years. Recording sessions would continue throughout the war, under Basil Cameron, Constant Lambert and George Weldon, though the challenges never abated. Harold Gray was one of many CBO stalwarts who enlisted (he ended up as chief music adviser to Western Command), and at the end of the 1940–41 season the management committee noted:

> Since the outbreak of war no less than 30 members of the Sunday Orchestra have been lost to us, some to take up National Service of one kind or another, some to fill posts in BBC Orchestras in other locations. Fortunately the process has been a gradual one, otherwise the artistic results must have been disastrous. Owing to the transport risks of engaging players from a distance during the winter months, replacements had to be found from local sources, a matter of no small difficulty.

The orchestra made its contribution to the war effort in ways that ranged from children's concerts and midweek summer concerts (the first time players had ever been kept on during the summer months) to ENSA concerts for factory workers and a 'Pageant of the Allies' at Birmingham Town Hall in September 1941, in which Heward and the CBO accompanied a chorus of 250 female munitions workers. John Gielgud gave an oration, and exiled politicians from the nations of occupied Europe made patriotic speeches, as did a twenty-one-year-old aircraft factory technician described by the *Evening Despatch* as 'pretty, dark-eyed Mrs Elsie Lewis'.

This was no time for radical artistic experimentation, beyond the arrival of piano concertos by Prokofiev, Khachaturian and Shostakovich in the City Orchestra's repertoire. Other than this modest uptick of interest in music by Allied composers, and unlike during the First World War (when anti-German sentiment saw Wagner being dropped briefly from concert programmes and London's Bechstein Hall renamed the Wigmore Hall), there seems to have been little or no political element to the choice of music played. Hadn't Chamberlain himself said that Britain had 'no quarrel with the German people'? Hely-Hutchinson conducted Richard Strauss's *Le bourgeois Gentilhomme* suite in the first weeks of the war. Sibelius continued to be the most performed living composer, notwithstanding Finland's alliance of convenience with the Axis powers, and Wagner, Brahms and Beethoven remained as popular as ever.

Soloists, meanwhile, included the pianists Eileen Joyce, Cyril Smith, Moura Lympany and Clifford Curzon (in Delius' Piano Concerto), the violinists Eda Kersey, Max Rostal and Albert Sammons, and the great soprano Maggie Teyte.

Bomb damage on Bennetts Hill in April 1941. Opposite, on New Street, is the Theatre Royal – venue of the CBO's first ever concert in September 1920. Having survived the Luftwaffe, it was demolished in 1956.

The daughter of a Wolverhampton pub landlord, Teyte had been coached by Debussy himself to sing the role of Mélisande in his opera *Pelléas et Mélisande*, and is commemorated today on a mural at Wolverhampton railway station. (She later married Alfred Cave, the CBO's leader from 1933 to 1942, whom she described as 'looking just like an orang-utan'.) Sometimes Hely-Hutchinson would pitch in as piano soloist too, or join forces with Walter Stanton, the BBC's head of music in the Midlands, for a double concerto by Mozart or Bach.

War affected every aspect of life in Birmingham, in Britain and in Europe: bombing alone caused 9,000 casualties and some 2,241 deaths in Birmingham. At this distance it seems almost frivolous to remark that the CBO would end the war considerably stronger than it entered it, and on a footing of which Matthews, Boult and Heward could only have dreamed.

Yet those protests in September 1939 had revealed that, for many of Birmingham's residents, the idea of facing the war without their city's orchestra and what it represented had become unthinkable. Leslie Heward's early death was a personal and artistic tragedy for the orchestra, but not an existential threat. No one disputed that the music would – must

– continue, even if that meant the new chief conductor, George Weldon, shouldering his share of a weekly overnight fire-watch on the roof of the Town Hall.

Sometimes it was simply a matter of make do and mend. In his memoir *Around the Horn*, the horn-player Frank Downes recalls how in December 1940 he was summoned to the CBO office:

> and asked if I would go to Mr Heward's house in Harborne Road. I was to take the fourth horn part of a Sibelius symphony [the Second] as he wanted to cue certain tuba parts into the fourth horn copy which I was to play the following day. Apparently the tuba-player had been called to the forces and they had been unsuccessful in getting a replacement . . . I shall never forget how ill he looked that morning, propped up in bed. He took the part and as I gave him the score he copied in pencil the relevant tuba part without looking at it.

It's a minor detail of a single concert. But the simple fact that in a city under aerial bombardment, in the middle of the greatest conflict in human history, two musicians – one already dying – should go to such pains in order that their fellow citizens might, despite everything, hear the best possible performance of a Sibelius symphony, gives some inkling of how a city and a civilisation fought and endured.

Fast Forward

George Weldon was a conductor with his foot on the accelerator. Before the war, and in between concerts as assistant conductor of the Hastings Municipal Orchestra, he'd made a name on the motor-racing circuit. He loved speed, and owned a series of high-performance cars, which he raced at Brooklands, Goodwood and Silverstone. He was an official test-driver for Atalanta, in one of whose brand new roadsters he won the sports-car class in the September 1937 Lewes Speed Trials. Listen to his 1946 CBO recording of Glinka's *Ruslan and Ludmila* overture and that comes as no surprise. The orchestra rockets off the starting line with breathtaking élan: a performance of such energy and verve that it completely overturns casual assumptions about an underfunded regional band struggling through post-war austerity. As you listen, you can picture Weldon, as the pianist Phyllis Sellick described him, enthusiastically demonstrating 'how well his Aston Martin could corner at high speed – always with one eye on the rear mirror, in case of police cars'. It's still one of the fastest Ruslans on record.

Weldon's tenure as principal conductor in Birmingham was neither the longest nor the shortest, but it saw two major transformations – one utterly fundamental to the orchestra's future; one far more superficial but just as enduring. Under Weldon's conductorship, and at his express wish (though no one seems sure quite why he was so insistent) the City of Birmingham Orchestra was renamed the City of Birmingham Symphony Orchestra in February 1948 – halfway through the concert season.

Very straight up and down. George Weldon cut a dash on the podium, and few
CBSO conductors before Simon Rattle were more frequently photographed.

LEFT *Backroom boys. Clarinettist James Matthewson (left) doubled as orchestral librarian. General manager Denzil Walker (right) had been an aide-de-camp to the Viceroy of India and was addressed as 'Major'.*

BELOW *George Weldon with Harold Gray (right) and Norris Stanley (left). Stanley became leader of the orchestra in 1942 but would later clash with Andrzej Panufnik.*

And at the start of the 1944–5 season, Weldon and the orchestra's management succeeded where Beecham, Bantock, Matthews, Boult and Heward had all failed, and persuaded the city to fund the orchestra on a permanent basis, with players contracted for twelve months of the year. There would be no more fudged timeshares with the BBC, and no more would the ensemble be disbanded each summer, and its musicians obliged to seek summer jobs in seaside resorts or theatres.

This was the real foundation of the modern CBSO: a permanent, year-round orchestra in which the musicians are salaried full-time employees. With it came a bolder outlook. Anticipating busy seasons ahead, the orchestra hired Arthur Knight, a former horn-player, as its first 'roadie' to help shift and set up equipment. (The term at the time was the more genteel 'porter'; today they're called 'platform managers'.) A Benevolent Fund was established, in the spirit of the Beveridge Report, to help musicians with healthcare and hardship, and the orchestra's first logo – a roundel containing the letters CBO – was introduced. So perhaps Weldon earned his right to tinker with the name, despite scorn from John Waterhouse, the music critic of the *Birmingham Post*, who wrote, 'I find the adjectival "Symphony" an even more tiresome and meaningless convention than "Philharmonic".' No conductor – not Matthews, not Heward, not Rattle – presided over a more significant change in the orchestra's status than George Weldon.

Weldon had actually been the CBO's second choice. Heward had handed in his notice some

A short ride in a fast machine. George Weldon (right) shows off his new Triumph Roadster to the orchestra's leader, Norris Stanley.

months before his death, so the management committee had already lined up a series of guest conductors 'on spec'. Weldon was one; Muir Mathieson – the Scottish conductor and composer, best remembered for conducting the soundtracks of such classic wartime films as *Henry V* and *In Which We Serve* – was another. The front-runner, though – and far more of a 'name' than either of them – was Boyd Neel, whose virtuoso string orchestra (known to musicians, inevitably, as the 'Boiled Veal Orchestra') had lit up the scene in the late 1930s.

Still, Weldon had impressed at his first (and at that time, only) concert with the CBO on 4 April 1943, when he'd conducted Tchaikovsky's

'Pathétique' Symphony. Eric Blom of the *Birmingham Post* had written, 'I knew almost nothing about him, but I shall not be in the least surprised if he turns out to be the next permanent conductor for the Birmingham Orchestra. He is unquestionably the real thing.' The management committee resented being seen to take instructions from a mere critic, and Hely-Hutchinson – at that point effectively acting as an unpaid music director and still mourning the death of his friend Heward – had misgivings. They resolved to offer the post to Neel before, for unknown reasons, changing their mind and inviting Weldon to conduct the 1943–4 Sunday series. In June 1944 he was confirmed in post as musical director and conductor on a salary of £2,000 per year.

By then – the month of D-Day – the orchestra was once again operating in a changed world: this time for the better. The many destabilising blows that the CBO had suffered since the last summer of peace, combined with the huge wartime public appetite for concerts, had convinced the management committee that the time had come to try to secure the orchestra's foundations once and for all. The long-serving chairman Gerald Forty knew his city well, and at the orchestra's September 1943 general meeting, he issued a ringing appeal to civic pride, quickly reported in the press:

Weldon's concerts attracted a fashionable crowd and it was observed that seats in the choirstalls were often snapped up en bloc by young female concertgoers – the better to appreciate his film star good looks.

Weldon poses with his new full-time orchestra, some time after August 1944. Players include cellist Gwen Berry, veteran timpanist Ernest Parsons, and the oboist-composers Mary Chandler and Ruth Gipps.

It is essential to our very existence that we should engage a permanent orchestra on a full-time basis, and I say emphatically that unless we do, we shall be eclipsed by other orchestras, and we shall remain – as I am sorry to say we are at present – in a subordinate position in the musical world. That is a position this city has never complacently occupied in any other respect, and we are all determined that Birmingham shall occupy a position in the musical world consistent with her dignity.

Forty had already held discreet conversations with the necessary politicians, and the orchestra's newly appointed secretary, Ulric Brunner, set about devising the necessary administrative, legal and (crucially) financial plans for a full-time professional orchestra. Brunner completed the task, single-handed, in less than a year – whereupon, unsurprisingly, he resigned on grounds of ill health; not the last CBSO administrator to be made ill by the demands of the job. (He was succeeded by Major Denzil Walker, a former aide to the Viceroy of India.) Essentially, the City Council would increase the annual grant to £7,000, and the city's education committee would make a further grant of £7,500 in return for fifty days per year of education work. Taken together, by the start of the 1944–5 season, a permanent orchestra was finally viable.

Meanwhile, Weldon was lighting up the Town Hall. Audiences had queued across Victoria Square for his first concert, on 3 October 1943: he began with Walton's *Spitfire Prelude and Fugue*. 'The fire and the enthusiasm were there, but more than that there was that tightness of grip on the playing that speaks volumes,' reported the *Birmingham Mail*. Hely-Hutchinson, always generous, wrote to Forty early in 1944 admitting his mistake: 'I want to tell you how right I think you were about George Weldon – and by the same token, I was wrong – eighteen months ago.' As he left Birmingham for London, he predicted that 'in about three years . . . the whole show will be on top of the world'.

But things were still fairly ad hoc that season. 'Most of us worked in munitions factories, and George Weldon had to get permission from our bosses for us to get time off to play,' remembered the violinist Stan Murphy. One critic pointed out that it did no good at all to pretend that all was faultless, and that 'the strings consisted of an amalgam of Menuhins, Tertises, Piattis and Bottesinis, that our woodwind outshone any combination of Amadios, Leon Goossenses, Drapers and Camdens, and that the Brains had nothing on our horns'. Weldon didn't need to be told: 'I hope EB [Blom] will have a crack at the 1st violins, they deserve it,' he wrote to Brunner after a concert in January 1944. 'I wonder how many had looked at their part beforehand?! I am determined to raise the standard if I can.' He would soon have an unprecedented opportunity to do so.

In June 1944, Weldon had the privilege – rare for any conductor – of auditioning his new full-time orchestra from scratch. Naturally, Heward's orchestra formed the core. Weldon hung on to such veterans as timpanist Ernest Parsons – the orchestra's longest-serving member, recruited by Appleby Matthews – the principal bass Kenneth Burston and the leader Norris Stanley. But he started to introduce new players too – notably his close friend, the oboist, composer and conductor Ruth Gipps – and over the next few years, as a generation of young musicians (including Gipps' husband, the clarinettist Robert Baker, and the violinists Barrs Partridge and Blyth Major) demobbed, an orchestra that offered a permanent position and a good living wage found little trouble recruiting. The average age dropped markedly; fourteen of the sixty-one players were women. Birmingham finally had the permanent orchestra of Matthews' dreams.

Now it was a matter of sustaining it, and the problem, as post-war optimism shaded into a seemingly endless austerity, was turning energy and enthusiasm into a steady income. There was the bread-and-butter work of schools concerts, local choral societies and – for a while longer, anyway – ENSA concerts. But how to expand that? From the summer of 1945 onwards the CBO ran a series of popular Proms concerts in the Town Hall. In 1949, Ruth Gipps launched and edited *Play On*, the CBSO's first supporters' magazine. It was a glossy publication. A typical issue might include cartoons by members of the orchestra, an article about music in the USSR by Ernest Newman, and a photo of Weldon in helmet and goggles driving his new Hispano-Suiza. It was

GEORGE WELDON (1908–63)

George Weldon was born in Chichester. Refusing to wear callipers for a withered leg, he was excused games at Sherborne School and instead poured his spare time and energy into music. He was an excellent pianist. 'I am frequently asked why I took up conducting,' he told an interviewer in 1951, 'to which I usually reply, "I was no good at anything else."'

Weldon's humour was one facet of an intensely energetic personality. At thirty-six he cut a dashing figure in tails, and it was observed that the choirstalls for his concerts at Birmingham Town Hall were regularly snapped up en masse by young female fans. In Birmingham he drove a powder-blue Armstrong Siddeley, which he called 'The Boudoir', and the composer Ruth Gipps recalled him routinely hitting 100 mph on public roads. On one occasion, having dropped the pianist Denis Matthews off at Paddington station, Weldon raced the train back to Birmingham and greeted an astonished Matthews on the concourse at Snow Hill.

Weldon's personal life in Birmingham was a source of colourful rumours, and his sudden, involuntary departure prompted strong reactions. John Barbirolli, at the Hallé Orchestra, was so appalled that he immediately offered Weldon the post of assistant in Manchester. Weldon died, suddenly, while in South Africa to conduct the Cape Town Orchestra. He had taken an overdose of the painkillers that helped him cope with his deformed leg – whether intentionally or not remains unclear.

axed after a mere six issues, as financial realities grew increasingly stringent.

Mostly, though, the orchestra played many more concerts. In the 1944–5 season – the first of the new full-time establishment – the CBO gave at least 183 concerts and undertook 49 recording sessions. The following season, there were over 250 concerts, overwhelmingly conducted by Weldon, and it was rapidly becoming clear that merely to stand still financially the orchestra would have to work almost incessantly. Weldon had a Stakhanovite work ethic: between 1944 and 1951, he is known to have conducted some 1,330 concerts in the UK – an average of one every two days (for context, Simon Rattle conducted 934 concerts over his eighteen-year tenure). Happily, audiences in Birmingham took to him, and with a carnation in his buttonhole and a charismatic podium manner, he became a local celebrity. One young concertgoer, Ethel Hatton, compiled a scrapbook of all his activities, as if he was a matinee idol. Regulars in the stalls at the Town Hall thrived on his vitality: they called him 'Whacker Weldon'.

The press, however, criticised Weldon for repetition of repertoire – unsurprisingly, given the orchestra's workload and the amount of rehearsal time available. Performances could take on an air of the production line. 'He was very straight up and down, was George,' recalls violinist Stan Smith, who played under Weldon as a guest conductor in the 1950s. And with reason: between 1943 and 1951 Weldon and the CBSO performed Rachmaninoff's Second Piano Concerto on at least sixty occasions and Wagner's *Meistersinger* prelude fifty-three times.

It's no wonder that Weldon chain-smoked in rehearsals (he used a chamber pot as a super-size ashtray). Vaughan Williams' *Fantasia on Greensleeves* became so routine that Blom suggested that the orchestra could probably play it backwards. Weldon took him at his word and asked the orchestra's principal bassoon, Vaughan Allin, to write the piece out in reverse: it was premiered at a July 1946 Town Hall prom as *Enërg Essëlv* by the (allegedly) Turkish composer 'Nila Naguav', who appeared on stage to take his bow in a fez.

Yet their recordings show that under the right conditions Weldon and his new permanent orchestra could be electrifying: superbly drilled, audibly energised and capable of some gloriously stylish playing. Weldon's own interests were far ranging. He conducted twenty-three British and world premieres, including Ruth Gipps' First and Second Symphonies and Piano Concerto, John Veale's First Symphony and works by Mary Chandler, Graham Whettam, the (genuine) Turkish composer Ahmet Adnan Saygun and the Slovenian composer Lucijen Škerjanc.

He championed Medtner's piano concertos with Medtner's own protégée, the Birmingham-born Edna Iles, as soloist, even performing the First Concerto at an ENSA concert. ('The poor war workers,' commented Gwen Berry.) He gave Birmingham premieres of Stravinsky's *Capriccio*, Rubbra's Third Symphony, Vaughan Williams' Fifth and Sixth Symphonies, and Shostakovich's brand-new Ninth, and gave twenty-four separate performances of Britten's *The Young Person's Guide to the Orchestra*.

RUTH GIPPS MBE (1921–99)

Ruth 'Wid' Gipps joined the CBO as second oboe in the summer of 1944 – an early appointment to the new full-time orchestra. The fact that she was a close friend of George Weldon did not endear her to her new colleagues. 'They did not resent all the women in the orchestra or anything silly like that,' she recalled. 'Dorothy Hemmings, the strikingly beautiful first violin No. 3 was very popular, and several of the others were well-liked but . . . I, B. Mus, was plainly regarded by some as a little know-all and moreover a friend of the management.'

Gipps was already finding her voice as a composer and conductor, and Weldon offered her numerous opportunities. On 25 March 1945 she played in the orchestra in Rimsky-Korsakov's *Capriccio espagnol*, appeared as soloist in Glazunov's First Piano Concerto, and finally played cor *anglais* in the premiere of her own First Symphony. 'How often does musical history show a case of so remarkable a symphony written by a girl of twenty-one – or for that matter, by a boy?' asked the *Birmingham Post*.

But orchestral musicians can display a toxic pack mentality. It was whispered that Gipps and Weldon were lovers, and gossip continued after she left the orchestra that spring – and even after her husband Robert Baker joined the orchestra as first clarinet. Weldon continued to champion her music, and Gipps went on to found the London Repertoire Orchestra and to compose a further four symphonies. In 1949, meanwhile, she launched and edited *Play On* – the CBSO's first in-house magazine.

Weldon booked soloists ranging from the soprano Elisabeth Schumann to the pianist Benno Moiseiwitsch and the violinists Yfrah Neaman and Alfredo Campoli, and invited Neel, Mathieson and Adrian Boult to guest-conduct, as well as Harold Gray. In October 1948, Arthur Bliss conducted the premiere of his *Adam Zero* suite, and in September 1946 Samuel Barber conducted his own First Symphony and *Adagio for Strings*. 'He squeezed the last ounce of drama and eloquence out of the strings in the *Adagio* and even made two back desks look as though they were about to burst a blood vessel,' wrote the *Gazette*, before concluding that 'the orchestra obviously needed more rehearsals'.

That was one problem. Another was symbolised by the man in a muffler and cloth cap who wandered in off the street during a rehearsal in Nottingham in November 1949. The horn player Frank Downes documented the incident in *Around the Horn*:

> At the final chord he called out to the conductor, 'Oi! I say, what was that called?'
>
> A surprised George Weldon turned to face him. 'That was the Piano Concerto by Škerjanc.'
>
> 'Bloody awful, wasn't it?' came the critical reply, as he walked out into the street.

Weldon was caught in the eternal trap of the artistic director. To cover its costs, the CBSO needed regular and frequent full houses, which meant a near-continual diet of familiar music. Yet when Weldon introduced rare and contemporary repertoire, the box office promptly dipped, and he was reprimanded by the management committee. His energy never seems to have waned, and incredibly, amid all this urgent activity and against a background of deepening financial crisis, he even persuaded the committee to let him increase the string section by two more players from the 1949–50 season, bringing the orchestra's strength to sixty-three. Some players, however, still found alternative means of supplementing their income. Vaughan Allin drove in regularly from Norfolk, and had equipped his bassoon case with a double-barrelled shotgun, so he could bag something for dinner on the way into work.

But when the executive chairman Gerald Forty died in October 1950 – having served and steered the CBO since even before Appleby Matthews – Weldon lost his strongest ally. The new chairman, Stephen Lloyd, was Neville Chamberlain's son-in-law. He came from manufacturing industry and his new executive chairman William Russell was an accountant. Practical businessmen as well as music-lovers (Russell sang in the City of Birmingham Choir), they looked for practical solutions – and despite Weldon's energy, his achievement and his undimmed popularity with audience and musicians, if not with the critics, they saw him as part of the CBSO's problems. Quietly, they approached the Austrian-born conductor Rudolf Schwarz: and having secured his agreement in principle to take over from the 1951–2 season, they summoned Weldon in at the start of December 1950 and suggested (in Russell's words) that 'he might wisely offer his resignation'.

The map contains the following labels:

GEORGE WELDON'S CONDUCTED TOUR-DE-FORCE THROUGH THE MUSICAL WORLD

CALM SEA AND PROSPEROUS VOYAGE

H.M.S. PINAFORE

FINGAL'S CAVE

THE DUCHY OF BALLETOMANIA

LA SOURCE

SLEEPING BEAUTY

SWAN LAKE BEAUTY SPOT

THE SMALL PROVINCE OF WONDERWOTTIS HANDSWORTH (WE DO LIKE TO BE BESIDE THE KEYBOARD SIDE)

PURCELL WASHES WHITER

THE BACH FAMILY TREE

UNIVERSITY (Academic Festival in Process)

QUIET CITY

JUNGLE OF DISSONANT MUSIC, partially cultivated in the early 20th century.

PACIFIC 231

CONTEMPORANIA (LARGELY UNEXPLORED & UNCHARTED, THOUGH GEORGE WELDON HAS PENETRATED FURTHER IN THAN ALMOST ANYONE ELSE)

HUNTING COUNTRY (try to catch a TURIAN)

R. TUONELA

THE UNFINISHED TANN HAUSING ESTATE

R. Blue Danube

HALL OF THE MOUNTAIN KING

THE KINGDOM OF EMOTIA (Luscious country, largely TCHAIKOWSKY)

PERSIAN MARKET

BARE MOUNTAIN (Spend a night here)

THE DEMOCRATIC REPUBLIC OF CLASSICA (Fertile land, very productive of thought)

PASTORAL COUNTRY

CLASSICA CITY Capital of the Musical World (famous for its beauty of form and construction)

EG MONT

Inn The Paradise Garden. (At the street Corner)

GEORGE WELDON'S SPECIAL FIELD. (British Music, especially ELGAR, VAUGHAN WILLIAMS & WALTON)

PORTSMOUTH POINT

FOREST MURMURS

EXHIBITION OF PICTURES

Cathedral of St Cecilia.

OXFORD

FACTORY music makers

CLIFF CASTLE

R. Vltava

AIRPORT Flights by the Bumble Bee & the Dutchman.

GARDENS OF SPAIN (or several here)

PRAGUE

DELECTABLE MOUNTAINS

TINTAGEL

THE ENCHANTED LAKE

REGION OF NOSTALGIA (Land of Mountain and Flood.)

LONDON

NEW WORLD IN THE SOUTH

INDUSTRIOUSLY DEVELOPED AREA (Where one learns to play an orchestral instrument oneself.)

BRIGG FAIR Carnival of Animals

THE GREAT SCHUBERTSEVENIN SEA

Under the editorship of Ruth Gipps, the CBSO's short-lived magazine Play On *provided a witty and often revealing perspective on orchestral life in the year 1949.*

Weldon was not the only one to be shocked. Four hundred members of the CBSO Listeners' Club wrote to him, saying that they felt unable to support another conductor. With some dignity, he told them that their first loyalty should be to music. At his final concert – in aid of the CBSO Benevolent Fund, on 7 October 1951 – the players and staff presented him with a tankard engraved with a man hanging from a noose, and the caption 'The Last Drop'. He finished with the *Enigma Variations* and traffic was delayed in Victoria Square as crowds gathered to see him leave the Town Hall for the last time.

Although Weldon went on to do magnificent work at the Hallé Orchestra, and was in regular demand as a guest conductor and recording artist, he never again directed his own orchestra, and it is hard not to feel that, on some level, the CBSO's new management had made a huge, cruel mistake. Meanwhile, on the last night of the 1951 CBSO Proms, the bass William Parsons surprised Weldon and the audience with his encore: a spoof spiritual to the words 'I'se fired, I'se woefully fired!' Weldon, according to Ruth Gipps, couldn't help laughing. But as she observed, 'Parsons had no idea of tact.'

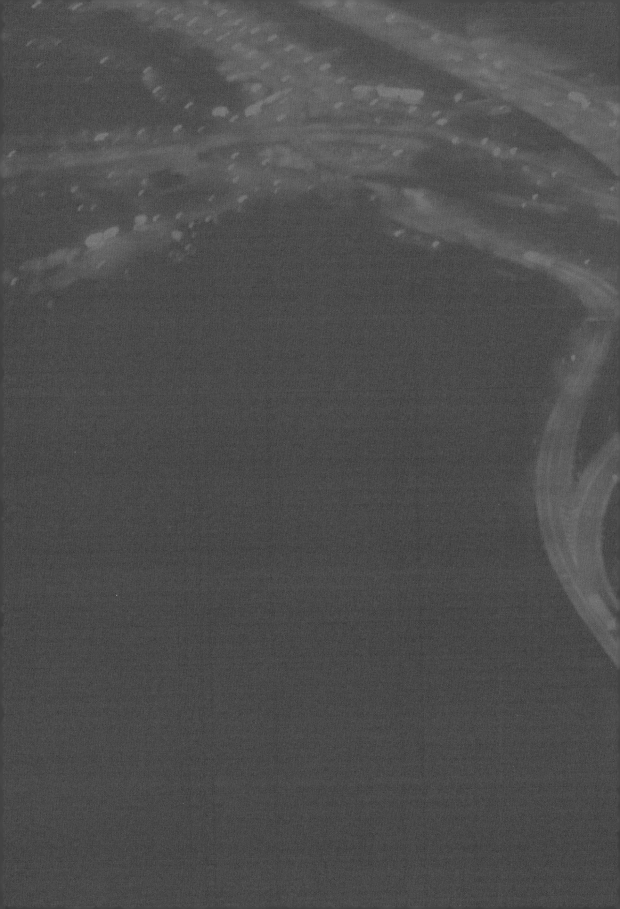

PLAYING FROM THE HEART

Why do you not think Birmingham a good place for meeting people? Besides Mr Mountford & the Rossetti & Burne-Jones & the best Shakespeare library in the world, it contains a race apart, a peculiar people. They look, and are, like no other people in the land. It is impossible to understand England without having stood on that great bridge that runs over the Birmingham [New Street] Station and watched the passers. It is almost necessary for you to get out of your train and view the place and the people. Otherwise you will not understand Life: as I do.

Rupert Brooke, letter to Noel Olivier, 26 March 1910

A Brummie, they say, is someone who knows twenty different ways to get to Erdington, but calls air-sea rescue to get home from Wolverhampton. Birmingham glories in its status as the heart of England: both the physical centre of the country (the literal, geographical centre has long been said to be at Meriden in Warwickshire, roughly midway between Solihull and Coventry), and an economic and cultural engine that pumps people, capital, culture and ideas throughout the UK. It's no coincidence that the city's logo takes the form of a heart, as does the CBSO's.

As Birmingham's orchestra, the CBSO has always, ex officio, been the West Midlands' orchestra too. Naturally, there's been a dose of solid Brummie pragmatism in that relationship. Appleby Matthews realised from the outset that whatever the CBO's aspirations for presenting

symphonic repertoire in the Town Hall, a city orchestra in the fullest sense had to cater for other audiences – for those who liked short tuneful pieces and parlour songs, and for music-lovers who couldn't – or after a hard day's work, wouldn't – hop on a tram to the Town Hall. It might help the bottom line too.

On 8 January 1922, at the 2,000-seat Saltley Coliseum cinema, the CBO gave its first 'Suburban Concert'. Matthews was on bullish form when he explained the concept to the *Birmingham Gazette* – taking particular aim at the upmarket audiences who, he believed, had failed to support the orchestra. 'This new venture marks the definite break with the so-called music lovers of Birmingham – the Edgbastonians – who actually have no use for music or any other art unless they have a "star" to guide them,' he declared.

I believe that it is in suburban audiences that the success of the municipal orchestra and good music lies. I believe that through the suburbs lies the way to musical success and independence of subsidy. I am confident of success. At the Saltley Coliseum, for instance, the municipal orchestra will provide Mozart and Schubert and all the masters at prices ranging from 4½d. to 1s 6d. Think of it! Wagner for 4½d. Can any man do more?

Birmingham has at last got a municipal orchestra. At the Grand Theatre it has been neglected. But we are not put off. Instead, with renewed hope, we go to the suburbs, and if that experiment fails and we are unable to find a home, then we shall play

Birmingham New Street station, prior to 1923. In its early years, the orchestra would book a private railway carriage to take players and instruments to out-of-town concerts.

in the streets. Birmingham must and shall have its orchestra.

The experiment started well. 'Saltley is hardly the sort of suburb which at first sight would be classed as musical,' commented the *Gazette*. 'It is called many things, but rarely that.' Nonetheless, the paper reported an audience of 1,800 and an enthusiastic reception, with many of the audience standing throughout. 'Saltley appreciated it, applauded it, and paid for it, and by so doing, offered a lesson to the city.'

So, Saltley had its orchestra; as in due course did the Gravelly Hill Picture House; Kings Norton Palace of Varieties; the Elite Theatre at Bordesley

Green; the Waldorf Theatre, Sparkbrook; Winson Green Picture House; Villa Cross Picture House, and the Majestic Theatre, Bearwood. On several occasions, Matthews split the orchestra in two and despatched it to two different venues on the same night. But he insisted on conducting at least some of each concert himself – ducking out of the final items of a concert at Gravelly Hill and leaving Godfrey Graham to conduct the rest of the programme while he dashed over to Bordesley Green, where Joseph Lewis had been holding the fort.

You do have to wonder just how impressive these concerts were: Matthews took just twenty-two players to Saltley, and subsequently talked of dividing that orchestra in half. Programmes, despite Matthews' claims to be bringing the 'masters' to the suburbs, tended towards the light: *Eine kleine Nachtmusik*, Delibes' *Pizzicato* from *Sylvia*, some Edward German or Jarnefelt's *Praeludium*, with a couple of drawing-room ballads, and overtures by Suppé, Nicolai or Ambroise Thomas to bookend the evening.

For all Matthews' promises of Wagner for fourpence halfpenny, only the *Siegfried Idyll* and 'Träume' from the *Wesendonck-Lieder* ever made it out to Handsworth or Bearwood (understandably, given the size of the orchestra), and the suburban concerts were quietly dropped next season. Perhaps, in an age where every local cinema and tea room had its own orchestra, the CBO's offering just wasn't impressive enough. Many CBO players already had day jobs performing in those cinemas – a point made, with splendid cheek, by the Grange Super Cinema in Small Heath, when it took out an advert in a CBO concert programme:

> Do you not wonder where all these high-class Artistes get to when there is no big affair on in the Town Hall, etc.? For instance, you will have heard members of the Grange Orchestra here tonight, and their names are on the opposite page. Why not come and hear them 'at home'? They are available every evening.

In fact, as the City Orchestra became more of an accepted presence in the region, lucrative engagements weren't hard to find. Leslie Heward, in particular, was eager that 'the orchestra should be recognised as the body for the whole of the Midland area', and that 'Worcester, Hereford, Gloucester and all such centres of musical culture' should regard the CBO as a 'family affair' – and open their purses accordingly. Certainly, choral societies and festivals – whether big Birmingham choirs such as the City of Birmingham Choir, the long-established festivals in Cheltenham, the Potteries and the Three Choirs counties; in regional centres such as Nottingham, Derby and Leicester, or smaller local concerts in the Black Country – would be an essential part of the orchestra's diary into the 1970s.

Not all were appreciated by the players as much as by audiences: tales of bad journeys, shabby venues and (an eternal constant) incompetent amateur choral conductors are staples of backstage gossip in every UK orchestra. There was definitely an ad hoc quality to many of the CBO's early adventures beyond Victoria Square – with the noisy, smoky glass-roofed canyon of New Street station generally serving as the starting point. Florence Lycett, the CBO's office secretary from 1924 to 1939, told Beresford King-Smith:

> One of the jobs I was given by Mr Shephard [the CBO's general secretary] on out-of-town concert days was to see the players off at New Street station and to give them their tickets on the platform, which was fine if they all turned up, but I never did find out what I was supposed to do if they didn't.
>
> I had some nail-biting experiences. Even the large instruments normally travelled by train, in the guard's van, and I remember on one occasion that the harpist, Winifred

Hunt, arrived on the platform without her harp, which was to be brought down by the porter – a funny little man, known to the players as Black Jack. The train was already late, Mrs Hunt was working herself into a state – there was no point in her going to a concert without her harp – the station master was getting terribly irritable, looking at his watch and preparing to blow his whistle, and there was I, pleading with him to hold the train for a minute or two longer. Eventually, along comes Black Jack, almost invisible behind the harp, which was swaying precariously from side to side on his sack-truck, and we were saved.

Rather like the outbreak of the First World War, the CBO's out-of-town performances often seem to have been defined by railway timetables. Beresford King-Smith, in *Crescendo!*:

In West Bromwich, the CBO's leader Paul Beard found himself faced with an inept local conductor whose tempi in Dvořák's 'New World' Symphony were so laboured that it seemed likely that

Out-of-town: in November 1976, manager Beresford King-Smith and bassoonist John Schroder board the orchestra bus outside the Town Hall: destination, a chilly Worcester Cathedral.

the players would miss their train back to Birmingham. Whispering, 'Follow me, boys,' Beard led off the finale at a cracking pace, leaving the unfortunate conductor waving his arms in rotary backward circles and muttering audibly, in a broad Black Country accent, 'Yow'm going too fast! Yow'm going too fast!'

The cellist Gwen Berry, in diary entries that reek of coal smoke and sterilised milk, gives a vivid picture of out-of-town work in the austerity-stricken late 1940s:

> 10 January 1948: Coventry. Raining again. The town still looks a terrible mess but reconstruction has started.
> 11 January: Sunday concert with H.G. [Harold Gray] conducting the Schubert 'Great'. It went very well. He has improved enormously as a conductor . . .
> 15 January: Hanley. A frightful town but an enthusiastic audience.
> 31 March: Derby. Foul concert. Brass too loud. Basses too close. Horrible hall.
> 6 April: Rehearsals at Dear Dirty Digbeth.
> 20 January 1949: Bath – by train, which was much nicer. Two concerts, both packed house. Schoolchildren in the afternoon . . . At night G.W. [George Weldon] conducting and Denis Matthews in the 'Emperor'. Our digs were a very doubtful proposition at first but turned out better when put to the test. The room Margaret and I shared smelt mouldy, but we had a gas fire so after supper put it on, knitted and chatted . . . Mr

Weldon, Norris [Stanley] and D. Matthews went to Sheriff's, a temperance hotel . . .
> 28 January: Derby – getting very tired of all this trundling to and fro.
> 31 January: Day off, and not before it was needed.

Even once the players were on board their reserved carriage, coupled to the back of a Birmingham-bound train, they weren't necessarily safely home. Ruth Gipps recalled an occasion in 1948 when the train was so long that, as it came to a halt at New Street station, the musicians' carriage was nowhere near the platform: in fact, it was still inside the tunnel at the station throat. The communicating door through to the rest of the train had been locked.

> After calls for attention had passed unnoticed for twenty minutes, the players found their own way to attract notice. To the amazement of railway officials, fanfares on a trumpet and strange unearthly mutters (applied by the double bassoon) emerged from the mouth of the tunnel.

With no purpose-built rehearsal facilities prior to 1998, the day-to-day routine in Birmingham could be uninspiring too. Gwen Berry's 'Dear Dirty Digbeth' – Digbeth Institute – was still in use, a lot dirtier and considerably less dear, in the late 1960s. 'We used to go in there on a Monday morning and it smelled of sweaty wrestlers' jockstraps because they used to do boxing and that at the weekend,' remembers violinist Paul Smith. 'It stank. Beer and sweat and – oh, it was

The CBSO Proms initially featured promenade tickets and potted palms. George Weldon conducts this Prom in July 1947 – note the audience members standing and sitting on the floor.

disgusting. It was a dark, dismal hole. I did my audition in there, actually.'

The CBSO's regular out-of-town concerts around the UK are now planned as thoroughly as any other part of the orchestral schedule, with venue conditions, travel time and meal breaks all carefully regulated. Some once-traditional venues – Wolverhampton, Sutton Coldfield, Kidderminster, Nuneaton and Bedworth – have become less frequent in the CBSO's schedule, as local councils have confronted a new austerity, and amateur choral societies have lost their spending power. In some smaller communities, CBSO chamber ensembles have filled the absence.

Other centres of regional culture – such as Warwick Arts Centre in Coventry; the Cheltenham Festival; Nottingham Royal Concert Hall; De Montfort Hall, Leicester; Victoria Hall, Hanley; and St David's Hall, Cardiff – have developed and sustained impressive programmes. A concert by the CBSO in any venue around the region is prepared with the same commitment, and to the same artistic standards, as a programme at

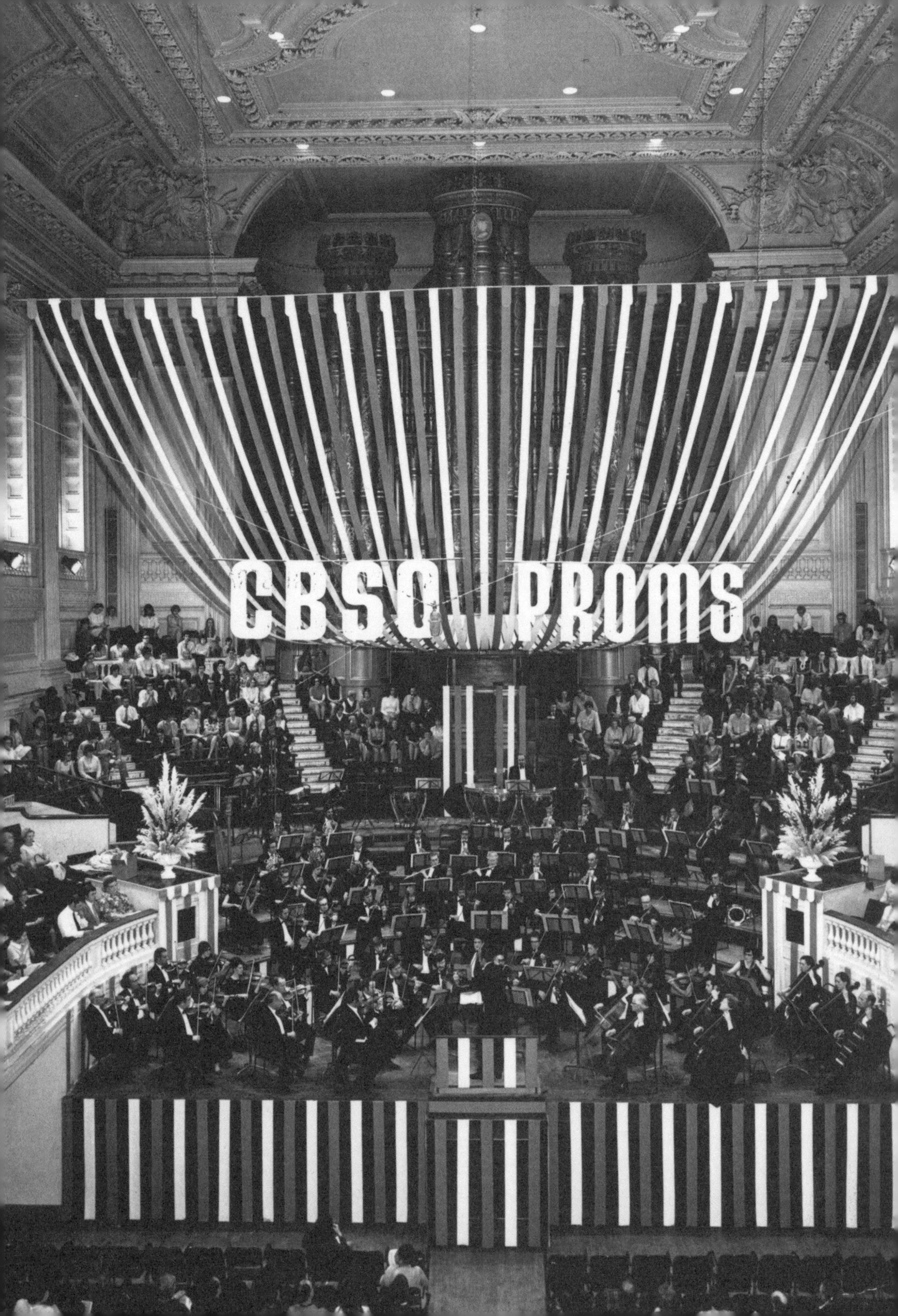
CBSO PROMS

OPPOSITE *The Summer 1972 CBSO Proms featured startling new décor by Beresford King-Smith: 'an interesting visual experiment' which, he recalls, 'proved too expensive to repeat'. Maurice Handford conducted the first night.* ABOVE *The last night of the 1973 CBSO Proms. The CBSO has always prided itself on offering the people of Birmingham an entertaining night out.*

'One of the advantages of being
so rooted in the life of its city is
that the orchestra, by and large,
has been able to read and respond
to changing audience trends'

Symphony Hall. Since the CBO became the CBSO, only four concerts have ever been cancelled due to weather: in March 2018 at Symphony Hall, in December 1990 at Warwick Arts Centre, and in February 1969 at Kings Hall, Derby, all due to heavy snow; and on 25 January 1960 at Kidderminster – when the River Stour rose five feet in sixteen hours and the orchestra arrived to find emergency workers sculling around the Town Hall in rowing boats.

Pops and Popularity

George Weldon was never short of eye-catching ideas, and after noticing the wartime public's enthusiastic response to his short series of summer concerts in 1944, it was probably his idea to name the 1945 season the CBO 'Promenade Concerts'. The success of Sir Henry Wood's Proms in London had been a source of national pride during the war years, and Weldon cheerfully appropriated the winning format: popular programmes, cheap tickets and the seating removed from the Town Hall's stalls to create standing room. The first was on 30 July 1945, and it kicked off in suitably celebratory mood with Walton's *Crown Imperial*. Within a week a correspondent to the *Birmingham Post* was writing about the 'amazing crowds' that the experiment had drawn. The *Post's* own critic noticed how accurately Weldon had nailed the formula:

> The Town Hall floor looked pretty much like that of the Queen's Hall. The absence of a fish pond did not make any great difference – not to the goldfish world,

where orchestral music is said not to be absolutely essential to existence; and there were touches on the platform that helped to suggest the authentic atmosphere, such as the border of decorative vegetation and the carnation in Weldon's buttonhole. If the conductor had grown a beard and dyed it black for the occasion, the illusion might have been more complete.

At least one omission was presently made good: a cooling, palm-fringed fountain was installed for the 1949 Proms, and would for many years serve as a summer holiday home for a family of seven plump goldfish. By now, a successful Proms formula had become established: three close-packed summer weeks of popular classics, themed evenings (Viennese nights, Tchaikovsky nights, Gilbert and Sullivan nights) and last-night pranks. In 1947, during the *1812 Overture*, the bassoonist Vaughan Allin fired a volley (presumably of blanks) from the double-barrelled shotgun that he carried to work each day. In 1972 Fenella Fielding and Michael Flanders narrated Walton's *Façade*, and in 1982 the orchestra's office staff, disguised as cleaners, trooped onstage to operate the vacuum cleaners and electric floor-polisher required for Malcolm Arnold's *A Grand, Grand Overture*.

The 'Last Night' would become Harold Gray's special domain, and he ended each year with Henry Wood's *Fantasia on British Sea Songs* – a tradition continued when Simon Rattle conducted the 'Last Night' in 1982. Rudolf Schwarz tried to refresh the formula by commissioning and conducting a *Fantasia on*

Harold Gray cops an earful during rehearsals for Haydn's Toy Symphony – a favourite on the last night of the CBSO Proms. Percussionist Annie Oakley (left) instructs a scratch band of CBSO board members, supporters and staff.

Songs of the British Isles from Gordon Jacob in 1952 – 'a much better thing musically', thought the *Gazette*, while noting that although the audience hummed quietly along with 'The Ash Grove', by and large they were 'never quite sure what to do with it'. It didn't catch on.

The CBSO Proms would run every summer from 1945 until the mid 1980s, when, without any particular fuss, they were quietly rebranded as summer concerts. The final 'Last Night', complete with traditional flag-waving, took place in 1990, the CBSO's last summer in the Town Hall. 'I anticipated a huge backlash but there wasn't one,' says the then chief executive Edward

Smith. 'It wasn't a big deal. We were just at a point in Simon's tenure where he and I felt there were more interesting things to do – so let's do them. And the city seemed happy with that.' With audiences now thirsty for whatever the CBSO chose to do in the summer months, even without flags or goldfish, the CBSO Proms had effectively accomplished their mission.

And one of the advantages of being so rooted in the life of its city is that the orchestra, by and large, has been able to read and respond to changing audience trends. It wasn't that the audience for light-hearted, accessible music-making at affordable prices had vanished;

lifestyles had simply changed. Throughout the 1990s the CBSO played to a mass audience at a free open-air 'Firework Concert' held each summer in Cannon Hill Park, and promoted by the city (in best City Orchestra tradition) as a civic amenity. In the late 1990s, when the city launched ArtsFest – a weekend-long, city-centre arts festival in early September – the CBSO naturally featured as a headline act. On the first weekend, in 1998, Sakari Oramo pulled out a safety pin and demonstrated to a packed (and non-paying) Symphony Hall audience that they could literally hear a pin drop.

In subsequent years, the ArtsFest performances took place on an open-air stage in Centenary Square – always a risky strategy as the first autumn gales started to arrive – while staff manned a 'Try It' stall, challenging passers-by to get a tune out of a decrepit tuba found lurking, Fafner-like, at the back of the CBSO Centre percussion store. But the real spirit of the CBSO Proms re-emerged first of all at weekday matinees. Classical audiences, went the thinking, have always included a large proportion of retired people – so why not provide concerts at an hour that suits their lifestyle, and can be combined with visits to galleries and shopping? Appleby Matthews would have recognised the rationale. Launched in the late 1990s, they were an immediate and enduring success: Stephen Maddock professes himself baffled that more orchestras don't emulate them.

The turn of the millennium saw the launch of a regular series of Friday-night concerts with an unmistakably popular flavour. As Brindleyplace approached completion, Broad Street and its environs had become Birmingham's own

West End: ground zero for a big night out. The CBSO threw itself wholeheartedly into the entertainment market – well, after a couple of false starts (Oramo's decision to include Sibelius' *Luonnotar* in an evening of orchestral lollipops entitled 'Nordic but Nice' might have been a case of the series trying to run before it could walk).

The formula soon found its feet, and it has evolved over two decades: where once evenings of Lerner and Loewe or Rodgers and Hammerstein guaranteed a lively crowd (and the CBSO briefly surfed the craze for celebrity ballroom dancing, before the BBC re-asserted its *droit de seigneur* over all things *Strictly*), more recent seasons have featured symphonic tributes to ABBA, Queen and David Bowie. With orchestra members dressing up in catsuits, flares and porn-star moustaches for an evening of 'Symphonic Disco', or sharing the stage with Darth Vader for a *Star Wars* night, it's clear that the spirit of the CBSO Proms is pretty much inextinguishable.

Birmingham wants to hear this music – and it's the city orchestra's job to provide it. Whether or not the Friday-night crowd decides to give Beethoven and Mahler a try is immaterial. In a city as diverse as Birmingham, tastes are wide-ranging. There's an enthusiastic audience for Elgar; there's also an enthusiastic audience for John Williams and James Bond – and there's certainly an audience for the music of the Bollywood film industry. That the CBSO should play Bollywood scores in the early 2000s was self-evident: how exactly to go about doing it was another matter. No major Western orchestra had attempted anything remotely similar.

The orchestra booked A. R. Rahman, the

multi-million-selling 'Mozart of Madras' to introduce (and, it was hoped, conduct) two evenings of his own music in 2004. That Rahman had no previous experience with a Western symphony orchestra soon became embarrassingly clear. 'This might sound weird,' he warned the capacity audience at the start of the first concert, and one item broke down entirely onstage, an experience unprecedented for the CBSO in modern times. 'I have written notes about what I have to fix, more lessons in conducting, one can never stop learning,' a chastened Rahman told the *Times of India* afterwards.

But the concerts, on 5 and 6 March 2004, nonetheless attracted enthusiastic attention around the world. 'Rahman concert is a superhit in the UK,' declared one ex-pat Indian blog, and both concerts sold out, with audiences who were overwhelmingly new both to Symphony Hall or their home city's orchestra. CBSO audiences are famously reticent about giving ovations but on both of Rahman's nights with the CBSO the audience almost stormed the stage. 'If music is divine, Rahman is God!' cried one audience member, when questions from the floor were invited.

The learning curve wasn't so much steep as near-vertical, and the lessons have been thoroughly applied to CBSO Bollywood projects since. There have been tribute concerts to Mohammed Rafi, R. D. Burman and Nusrat Fateh Ali Khan, as well as another Rahman night (this time without the man himself). The CBSO's former librarian Timothy Pottier, with experience in both cultures, has created effective orchestrations and worked with conductors

A. R. Rahman, 'the Mozart of Madras', conducted music from his Bollywood film scores in March 2004. 'Rahman is God!' shouted one audience member.

(in particular, Michael Seal) at finding a shared way to bring very different musical traditions together. Preparing these programmes is labour-intensive but rewarding.

'It was a new audience for us, and we learned a few things,' says Michael Seal.

> If we wanted the concert to start at 7.30 p.m., we advertised it as starting at 7.15 p.m. But once the public was in they absolutely loved it. You'd start a number and they'd recognise it and all start applauding. With some of these songs, the only version most people have ever heard is a crackly old soundtrack recording. We'd start some of

these famous numbers, with a live orchestra playing with total commitment, and they'd be out of their chairs.

Apparently in India there was a union rule at the time, that there had to be 200 musicians in the room before the red recording light went on, and most of them were violinists. That's why vintage Bollywood recordings have such a huge string sound. So with the CBSO, it was about the initial contact of bow on string. You couldn't play it like Vaughan Williams; it needed to be more like John Williams on Pro-Plus. And we were also lucky to have Alan Thomas on first trumpet. As a student he'd played in an Indian wedding band and knew exactly how all the trumpet solos went.

The trickiest was working with Rahat Fateh Ali Khan. He's used to starting and finishing a song as he feels like it – Qawwali songs have inbuilt rules of structure, and Tim had transcribed the orchestrations from classic recordings by Nusrat. But sitting to my right were the dholak and tabla-players, and they were like having a big arm around you. When the orchestra started to wobble or the ensemble started to get shaky they'd put in this sort of fill, and somehow we'd all land on beat one again. Absolutely wonderful musicians – we spent most of the time talking about cricket.

The role of cricket in orchestral life has perhaps been under-reported, at least since the days of Neville Cardus. We'll come back to it shortly, but it's worth saying first that projects as innovative and artistically demanding as the CBSO's Bollywood concerts work only when the individual players believe in creating a future for their orchestra, and are committed to making

Birmingham has a huge and enthusiastic audience for Indian film music, and the CBSO has had little trouble finding world class collaborators. LEFT Michael Seal conducts singers Sanchita Pal and Shin Parwana in music by R. D. Burman, May 2012. ABOVE 2018's Best of Bollywood featured choreography by Piali Ray and four different Birmingham-based dance groups.

it succeed. Even a single incident such as the Royal Philharmonic Orchestra's notorious 1969 culture clash with Deep Purple ('You're playing like a bunch of c***s,' declared the conductor Malcolm Arnold, disgusted at the RPO's lack of professionalism) would have undermined these collaborations. But no professional musician working in Birmingham needs to be told how worthwhile it is to play this music.

And the players themselves have been consistently interested in deepening their relationship with their community: you're more likely to witness smiles rather than groans from the musicians when they're asked to play a rush-hour show on the new concourse at Birmingham New Street station (one of the few times they're obliged

to use New Street these days), or to turn out at Birmingham International Airport at dawn to play a fanfare for the first flight on a new route from China. It was on the players' initiative that the CBSO launched its chamber music series 'Centre Stage' after the opening of CBSO Centre in 1998: the aim was to invite the Symphony Hall audience into their new home, and to perform music on a more intimate scale, chosen by the players themselves.

It's about that human connection; though, of course, it's also a means of enriching a musical career based in Birmingham (pet projects have included tango nights, period-instrument ensembles and programmes of Steve Reich and Philip Glass). Every player in the CBSO is entitled to a slot in the series; the choice of

In July 2018, the CBSO and conductor Dirk Brossé play to a 5,000-strong crowd in Sutton Park. OPPOSITE *Playing from the heart: in September 2017, the CBSO performs for commuters on the concourse of Birmingham New Street Station.*

music is entirely their own. After twenty-two years, and nearly 500 lunchtime concerts – even for exiguous fees – there's still no shortage of players wishing to participate.

The sense of player-ownership is vital, but so it has always been with the many different endeavours that have created a sense of 'family' among these ninety-odd Birmingham-based musicians, whether the Benevolent Fund (a friendly society set up in 1944 to support employees and ex-employees through times of medical or financial hardship, and still run by an elected committee of players and staff) or something as informal as the 1960s social

evenings in Moseley (then still affordable to low-paid artists) described by percussionist Maggie Cotton in *Wrong Sex, Wrong Instrument*:

Fairy lights were hung in the old trees and a band was pulled together from CBSO players and friends from the BBC Midland Light Orchestra. Hunks of strong cheese were plonked on the kitchen table, with whole loaves and butter still in wraps. Nothing sophisticated here . . . The cellist owner had painted the empty front room in unrelieved black from floor to ceiling, and this was where loud music, amorous designs and smooch dancing took place. No one asked embarrassing questions, as we all knew the score when it came to entering the Gloom Room.

Or, indeed, the CBSO's sports teams. The CBSO's five-a-side football team plays in shorts that are the bright malachite green of the orchestra's 1980s logo, and with players of the flair of the CBSO's Argentinian principal cello Eduardo Vassallo, it's scored some remarkable victories on tour. The cricket team, unsurprisingly, is more of a home affair. Michael Seal never misses a game.

We've played English National Opera twice – won one, lost one. We've played the Liverpool Phil, and there was a charity indoor tournament at Lords, organised by Mick Doran, a percussionist at ENO. We got to the semi-finals, and the BBC Concert Orchestra was there. I was bowling and this guy was batting. I didn't recognise him as a musician and he hit me back over my head for four or six into the back wall. So I thought, I'm not having that. I moved [trumpeter] Jon Quirk slightly nearer to him and bowled him a bouncer which he fended off straight into Jon's hands. Out! Next day my agent rang, and we were chatting about various things and he said, 'One final thing. If you're going to bowl bouncers at people, and you want to work with orchestras, make sure they are not the chief executive of the BBC Concert Orchestra!'

6

The Viennese Tradition

When Rudolf Schwarz took the stage to conduct Weber's *Freischütz* overture at Birmingham Town Hall on 11 October 1951, the very fact that he was there at all was a sort of miracle. Schwarz was a Viennese musician to his soul, trained in the tradition of Brahms, Bruckner and Mahler. But as far as the Nazis were concerned he was simply a Jew. Imprisoned in Auschwitz, he was set to brutal physical labour, and after ten weeks was selected for extermination. He was saved from the gas chamber (as he told Simon Rattle, decades later) by the intervention of the conductor Wilhelm Furtwängler. Instead, the guards hoisted him up and smashed his shoulder bones. For the rest of his career he was unable to raise his arms above his shoulders. Players who worked under him all mention his restricted but eloquent beat, but CBSO percussionist Maggie Cotton remembers something else. When his shirtsleeves slipped up in rehearsal, you could see the serial number tattooed on his arm.

In that sort of context, the fact that this was the first time that the CBSO had played under a non-British principal conductor hardly seems worth mentioning. Regional music in the UK had a long history of flourishing under foreign-born conductors. In the nineteenth century, the Westphalian Charles Hallé had founded the Manchester orchestra that still carries his name; the Liverpool Philharmonic had welcomed Hallé and Max Bruch as chief conductors. The Birmingham Triennial Festival had thrived for six decades under the Italian-born Michael Costa and the Austrian Hans Richter.

But in the aftermath of the Second World War, the climate for non-British musicians was chilly. With superb exiled and displaced European artists seeking to make new lives in the English-speaking world, there was a perception among some British musicians (and particularly, one suspects, the more mediocre players) that their jobs were under threat. The Musicians' Union, newly empowered by Attlee's Labour government, rushed to see off 'alien musicians'. In September 1947, operagoers attending the first night of a Covent Garden residency by the Vienna State Opera found the venue picketed by around a hundred MU members with sandwich boards and placards. 'Stop Importing Orchestras – We Have the Best' read one banner. 'We have an assurance from Covent Garden that we shall be consulted next time any foreigners are brought over,' said the MU organiser Alex Mitchell. 'Now we want the same assurance from the Home Office and the Ministry of Labour.'

Rudolf Schwarz came to Britain that year, to direct the beleaguered and conductorless Bournemouth Municipal Orchestra. He'd guest-conducted Beethoven's 'Eroica' with the orchestra – the first time they'd attempted it since the war. The symphony, writes Geoffrey Miller in his history of the Bournemouth orchestra, 'magically hung together':

> The conductor had no desk and no score; he directed the concert from memory and gave leads with gentle, almost indecisive movements of his hands. The orchestra sounded as no one had heard it for a long time. Speculation on the appointment

ceased. One man was clearly in possession of the field.

Bournemouth's civic elders had other thoughts, and they were backed more widely. The Minister of Labour, George Isaacs, was challenged on the floor of the Commons: would he, in view of 'the desirability of encouraging native talent', ask Bournemouth to reconsider? 'Can we have an assurance that the Minister of Labour and his colleagues do not favour the application of a closed shop against Mendelssohn, Bach and Beethoven?' retorted the independent MP William Brown. Isaacs would not be drawn, and the satirist Beachcomber, in the *Daily Express*, lampooned musical xenophobia in a spoof letter to the editor. 'Rather than see a foreigner in charge of Bournemouth's music, I would have the Municipal Orchestra composed of substantial tradesmen without a note of music in them, with a citizen of standing to conduct – perhaps the Mayor himself.' 'This,' he added, 'would not be the best orchestra, musically speaking, but it would be British to the core.'

Rudolf Schwarz conducts the CBSO, around 1956. Unable to raise his arms above his shoulders after being tortured in Auschwitz, Schwarz relied upon an undemonstrative beat and his innate musicianship.

But once Stephen Lloyd and William Russell – newly elected as the CBSO's chairman and CBSO executive chair – started to take a serious interest in Schwarz, they needed little persuasion. 'Schwarz is a most delightful man, very alert and keen, possessing both ideas and ideals,' reported Russell to Lloyd after a trip to Bournemouth in November 1950.

> Schwarz feels rather restricted at Bournemouth, but is obviously so grateful to his employers for having enabled him (as he put it) 'to start life all over again' that he feels bound to give them ample time to find a successor . . . He really welcomed my visit, feeling that it offered such a chance as he was seeking.

Unstated – Beresford King-Smith suggests – was the hope that they'd be able to engage a conductor of real pedigree for rather less money than Weldon had commanded. It didn't quite work out that way, financially, but Schwarz's artistic credentials were beyond dispute. Some sources state that as a teenager in Vienna, he'd studied briefly with Richard Strauss. What is certain is that one of his teachers, Richard Robert, had studied under Bruckner; and that another – the composer Hans Gál – was intimate with Brahms's circle. And of course, having played in the Vienna Philharmonic – as Schwarz had done while still in his teens – comes as close as anything on earth can do to guaranteeing the respect of orchestral musicians.

'The job was given without a bat of an eyelid to a foreigner,' grumbled Ruth Gipps later, but she was out of step with the city; Birmingham awaited Schwarz with genuine curiosity. He had guest-conducted the CBSO for the first time in January 1950, when he had snapped his baton into three pieces during Mendelssohn's 'Italian' Symphony. Boult, solicitous as ever, wrote him a note promising him that he would like Birmingham – 'the nicest people, the best water' – and two days before Schwarz's first concert as chief conductor, the Birmingham Daily Gazette published an interview under the headline 'The Conductor from Belsen' – 'tall, greying, and younger-looking than his photographs show': '"I am happy," he said, cigarette in hand. "It is a fine orchestra. I am looking forward to my work. Policy? I want to give our audience a complete symphonic repertoire in one season."'

Lloyd and Russell will have been relieved to hear that, and the first concert augured well. 'His three days of solid rehearsal as resident conductor have produced what seems almost a new orchestra,' wrote the critic of the Gazette. 'The programme, novel and different, attracted a large and more mature audience than has been usual recently,' he continued (this was an era when critics regarded grey heads in the audience as a good thing), concluding that 'Birmingham's concert public are in for an intriguing and vastly interesting season.'

One audience member clearly agreed far too enthusiastically: on Tuesday 13 November 1951 Mrs Lois Cumming of Edgbaston – a latter-day Georgina Weldon – announced in the foyer of the Town Hall that Schwarz was 'madly in love' with her: 'I know he adores me. I shall kill Mrs Schwarz.' Schwarz had never met her. She was refused admittance, arrested and bound over to keep the peace.

But Schwarz's first concert was certainly distinctive – beginning with the *Freischütz* overture, and including Schumann's Fourth Symphony (for only the second time since Heward's death), the Mussorgsky–Ravel *Pictures at an Exhibition* (again, only its second complete performance in Birmingham) and a novelty, Gordon Jacob's two-year-old Suite No. 3 – 'deliciously witty', said the *Gazette*. The inclusion of new British works had been a Schwarz trademark in Bournemouth: he was keen to explore the music of his adopted country.

It was a foretaste of what was to come. Schwarz's first season included music by Reger and Moeran, Roussel's Third Symphony, Ibert's *Divertissement*, Hindemith's *Symphonic Metamorphoses*, Mahler's *Lieder eines fahrenden Gesellen* (the first full-scale Mahler in Birmingham since 1930) and Malcolm Arnold's *Beckus the Dandipratt*. Even his 1952 summer Proms included two premieres and nine other works by living British composers. Clearly, Schwarz felt empowered, planning programmes that required meticulous rehearsal. 'I found that Birmingham was *alive*,' he remembered years later. 'A city with people who work, and are not just lounging around with bucket and spade on the sea front.'

It's easy to tempt fate. Schwarz's advocacy and artistry were impressive, and for the orchestra the chance to work for the first time in a sustained fashion with a conductor grounded in the great Austro-German tradition was simultaneously nourishing and a challenge. Stan Smith, who joined the violin section in 1955

from the defunct Yorkshire Symphony Orchestra, remembers that Schwarz:

> was an entirely different fish to George Weldon. He was an incredibly sensitive musician. He was very musical; it was all very controlled. Even accompaniment figures – he made them all melody. The older blokes didn't like him very much, but the youngsters really liked him.

That was reflected in recruitment to the orchestra. The trombone virtuoso Denis Wick was one of many new hires. In 1955 he would premiere Gordon Jacob's Trombone Concerto with Schwarz and the CBSO, though the one surviving document from him in the CBSO archive is a handwritten note to Schwarz apologising for being late on stage in Cheltenham: 'I am, in fact, almost a teetotaller.'

There were instances of disharmony: when the second violinist, cartoonist and wag Albert 'Rusty' Russell posted a caricature of the trumpeter Arthur Matthews on the orchestra noticeboard, he was startled to receive a letter from Matthews' solicitor threatening a libel suit. (Matthews was particularly affronted to be depicted under a sign reading 'Crumpet Dealer'.) 'I need hardly add that I have no intention of apologising to Mr Matthews,' Russell informed the management.

Nor was musical innovation sufficient to halt the financial slide. The orchestra had been £6,000 in deficit in 1950 and by April 1952 the hole was closer to £18,000. Executive chairman William Russell suggested a desperate scheme: to

'April 1952 was the single greatest crisis in the CBSO's history: the real moment of "life or death"'

merge the CBSO with the Bournemouth orchestra. A single seventy-five-piece orchestra would spend the winter season in Birmingham, and the summer on the south coast.

Bournemouth's councillors – one of whom later described their municipal orchestra as 'a costly toy' – rejected the plan outright. 'Birmingham was concerned with the perpetuation of music; Bournemouth wanted an orchestra for its publicity value and as a tourist attraction,' writes the BSO's historian Geoffrey Miller. '[Bournemouth] was jealous of its proprietorship and preferred to run its own orchestra on a reduced scale rather than share it.' In retrospect it looks like a lucky escape, but the immediate effect was nearly catastrophic for the CBSO. Seeing no other option, Lloyd announced the disbandment of the permanent orchestra and its return to a six-months-a-year freelance band, with a bluntness worthy of Appleby Matthews:

> The Management Committee regrets that it can no longer maintain the orchestra

throughout the year. If Birmingham people share that regret, the remedy is in their own hands. They should fill the Town Hall.

Beresford King-Smith – who handled more than one near-disaster in his own CBSO career – believes that April 1952 was the single greatest crisis in the CBSO's history: the real moment of 'life or death'. Only a timely change of the political wind saved the ship. The leader of the newly elected Labour City Council, Alderman Albert Bradbeer, was 'shocked' at the idea of sharing the city orchestra with a south coast resort, 'where audiences would want a quite different and lighter kind of music to that demanded in Birmingham'. By July, Bradbeer had authorised a loan of £20,000 to be repaid over ten years (incredibly, it was, too), to maintain a permanent orchestra in Birmingham. With political minds now focused, Lloyd lobbied for a longer-term solution, and by the end of the year the annual grant was doubled to £21,000.

Throughout the CBSO's history, existential crises have been followed by artistic innovation. Schwarz's quiet authority and commitment to new music was starting to be noticed. In May 1955 Schwarz and the orchestra boarded three KLM airliners at Elmdon airport for the orchestra's first ever overseas tour – to Holland. In the autumn of that year, with the prospect of a future for the orchestra now secure, the general manager Blyth Major – who'd made the leap from the first violin section into conducting, and then into orchestral management – put out advertisements in CBSO programmes inviting young musicians 'aged

RUDOLF SCHWARZ CBE (1905–94)

Rudolf Schwarz was born into the Vienna of Mahler and Schoenberg. As a teenager he studied with the composer Hans Gál, played viola in the Vienna State Opera, and at the age of twenty-two was appointed first conductor at the opera house in Karlsrühe, Germany. Six years later, as a Jew, he was dismissed by the new Nazi government.

Courageously, Schwarz took the only conducting job open to him – director of the Kulturbund Deutscher Juden, a state-sanctioned Jewish musical organisation. In 1941 he was deported to Auschwitz, where he was reprieved at the last minute from the gas chamber, but was savagely beaten. Transferred to Sachsenhausen, he escaped death again, and he was at Belsen, weighing less than 7 stone and suffering from typhoid, when British troops arrived in April 1945. Schwarz recovered in Sweden, where he met his wife Greta, and in 1947 he accepted a post at the Bournemouth Municipal Orchestra.

Schwarz took British citizenship and went on to be a civilising and profoundly musical formative influence at the CBSO, the BBC Symphony Orchestra and the Northern Sinfonia. He defused problems with Viennese courtesy. When a Bournemouth player told him his beat was unclear, he apologised. 'I know. If there is one thing I cannot do, it is conduct. However, in ten years' time, perhaps.' 'Rudi' was awarded the CBE in 1973 and guest-conducted the CBSO into the 1980s – where the young Simon Rattle regarded him as both mentor and inspiration: 'one of the most compassionate and thoughtful musicians of our time'.

between thirteen and twenty-five' to audition for a new Midland Youth Orchestra.

Meanwhile, a newly international dimension was starting to become evident in Schwarz's choices of guest artists and repertoire. Eduard van Beinum and Pierre Monteux conducted at the Town Hall, Nikolai Malko introduced Shostakovich's Tenth Symphony and, after a nineteen-year absence, Sir Thomas Beecham returned to Birmingham in October 1954 and announced from the podium that the CBSO 'had played like heroes' in Mozart's 'Prague' Symphony. 'I therefore commend them to your attention and applause for the rest of the season.'

On a subsequent visit Beecham dropped out at the last minute, leaving the unsinkable Harold Gray to learn Liszt's 'Faust' Symphony from scratch overnight – he studied the score until 4 a.m. and conducted it later that day. Throughout the 1950s, Gray was getting through industrial quantities of repertoire, and maintaining the all-important schools concerts almost single-handedly, but he was also starting to explore his enthusiasm for Carl Nielsen (then an oddity in the UK) with performances of the Second and Fifth Symphonies.

Eric Coates and Vaughan Williams conducted their own music (Coates' new *Dam Busters* march

topped a 'plebiscite' of CBSO audience members), but there was room for young talent too: Charles Mackerras, Colin Davis and the rising Soviet star Gennady Rozhdestvensky (who brought with him a young protégé, Vladimir Ashkenazy). Guitarist Andrés Segovia, cellist Paul Tortelier, the pianists Semprini, Gina Bachauer and Géza Anda, and the harmonica virtuoso Larry Adler all made Birmingham debuts. Only her final illness prevented Kathleen Ferrier from performing Mahler's *Das Lied von der Erde* with Schwarz in March 1953, and Schwarz repaid another debt to his Viennese past with the first public performance, in March 1955, of his teacher Hans Gál's Third Symphony: the *Birmingham Daily Post* found its slow movement 'faintly reminiscent of the idyllic Mahler'.

Meanwhile, together with a fellow member of the management committee, Professor Anthony Lewis of Birmingham University, Lloyd was working to turn Schwarz's devotion to new music into something more concrete. Negotiations with the John Feeney Charitable Trust started a series of major orchestral commissions from living composers that continues to the present day. Schwarz and Lloyd hoped to reel in an even bigger fish, too. Benjamin Britten had admired Schwarz ever since he'd championed the *Sinfonia da Requiem* in Bournemouth, and in September 1954 Peter Pears had joined Schwarz and the CBSO to give the world premiere of the Symphonic Suite from Britten's new Coronation opera *Gloriana*.

OPPOSITE *23 September 1954. Peter Pears looks on as Benjamin Britten and Rudolf Schwarz leave the stage after the world premiere of Britten's Gloriana suite.*

Britten was enthusiastic about a commission for Schwarz and the CBSO, and promised something for the 1957–8 season. 'There is nothing I would like to do more than write you and the CBSO a special work . . . I will do my best to produce a work worthy of you and the orchestra,' he wrote to Schwarz ('Dear Rudi') on 30 June 1955. But in a note to Lloyd that September he pleaded pressure of prior commissions, while insisting that 'I *wish* to write a work especially for Mr Schwartz [sic] and the Orchestra.'

While Britten hovered, Tippett's Piano Concerto was repeatedly delayed after the first choice of soloist, Julius Katchen, declared it unplayable. Instead, on 31 January 1956, the Town Hall witnessed the Birmingham debut of a thirteen-year-old boy, 'Master Daniel Barenboim', in Beethoven's Fourth Concerto. 'The boy Daniel bore himself bravely, and with astonishing assurance, in the lion's den of the CBSO,' wrote John Waterhouse of the *Birmingham Post*. 'Let us hope that this radiant young musician will not be exploited, as the young Wolfgang Amadeus was.'

The story now takes a familiar turn. Perceptive ears, coupled to deep pockets, noticed what was being achieved in Birmingham. Schwarz felt loyal to the CBSO, and had become a close personal friend of Stephen Lloyd. But an offer from the BBC Symphony Orchestra was hard to refuse, and Schwarz accompanied his official resignation from the CBSO with a personal note to Lloyd in his Viennese-inflected English. 'I feel I must accept the offer,' he wrote on 13 September 1956. 'It is with the utmost regret that I have to ask you, by giving one year's notice, for being released from my contract by 14th September 1957.'

The CBSO issued a statement coupling 'greatest regret' with 'warm congratulations', and added that 'it will be some satisfaction to the orchestra and its supporters that for the second time in the short history of broadcasting the post of chief conductor of the BBC Symphony Orchestra will be filled from Birmingham'. It wouldn't be the last. At a civic dinner hosted by the Lord Mayor in Schwarz's honour, guests enjoyed Poulet Sauté Archiduc and Cérises à la Dubarry, and Schwarz's final concert as chief, on 26 July 1957, was the last night of the CBSO Proms, shared with Harold Gray. Fittingly, he conducted Gordon Jacob's *Fantasia on Songs of the British Isles* and Max Schönherr's *Austrian Peasant Dances*. Britten's enthusiasm for the CBSO cooled the moment Schwarz left. Blaming an 'enormous schedule', he wrote in November 1957 to Stephen Lloyd, 'I am afraid there is now not a chance of me doing a piece for the Birmingham Orchestra in the near future.'

A Composer's Ear

The Polish composer Andrzej Panufnik remains the single greatest creative artist to have headed the CBSO. He is also, with Adrian Boult, the only one to have left his own account of the experience, in his autobiography *Composing Myself*:

> Realising that I could no longer leave my financial survival to fate . . . I put my name forward for the post of Music Director and Conductor of the City of Birmingham

Symphony Orchestra. After an enjoyable and very well-received trial concert I was offered the job. It was a daunting prospect: fifty concerts a year, a huge number of rehearsals, much travelling around the countryside for out-of-town performances, heavy administrative duties including the engagement of soloists and orchestral players, and social appearances as well. To take on this catalogue of responsibilities I would again have to say goodbye to my manuscript paper. A London orchestra would have been less demanding . . .

Although Panufnik had escaped from communist Poland only in 1954, his Irish-born wife Scarlett had already absorbed her share of metropolitan prejudices, and refused to follow him to what she termed 'a dull provincial Midland city'. (Panufnik's contract – like that of all previous CBSO chief conductors – stipulated that 'the conductor shall reside locally'.) And while Panufnik's application for British citizenship depended upon him acquiring the regular means of support that the CBSO job provided, he understood well that his true vocation was as a composer. When Lloyd approached him with a three-year contract, he negotiated it down to two.

In *Composing Myself*, Panufnik presents his years with the CBSO as 'Scenes from Provincial Life': a sort of culture-clash tragicomedy. 'My approach to the classics, strongly influenced by my great Viennese master Felix Weingartner . . . must have seemed "foreign" in a negative sense to most players in the CBSO,' he writes. Yet the orchestra had just spent six years under Rudolf Schwarz, and many of its players had actually performed under Weingartner in the 1930s. Panufnik tells how one senior member of the management committee, puzzled by his accent, asked him where he was born.

> 'Warsaw,' I replied.
> 'Walsall, Walsall, well, that's not far away –' he muttered, looking even more confused. Probably for him a suburb nine miles outside of Birmingham was indeed

far enough away for foreign accents to be normal.

The incomprehension was to some extent mutual, heightened by Cold War tensions and the dramatic story of Panufnik's defection from behind the Iron Curtain. At Blyth Major's suggestion, Lloyd had moved swiftly to secure Panufnik and within eight weeks of Schwarz's resignation note – and even before Panufnik had conducted his trial concert with the orchestra in December 1956 – had arranged for him to be

Andrzej Panufnik returned as guest conductor on numerous occasions. Here, in December 1980, he rehearses his Violin Concerto with soloist Ralph Holmes.

SIR ANDRZEJ PANUFNIK (1914–91)

For Andrzej Panufnik, music was 'a lifelong search'. Born in Warsaw when Poland was still part of the Russian empire, he studied conducting in Vienna and composition in Paris before returning home in 1939. He survived the Nazi occupation, but lost almost all of his music in the flames of the 1944 Warsaw Uprising. Along with his fellow composer Witold Lutosławski, he subsisted by playing piano duets in cafés – and risked arrest by giving secret concerts of banned Polish music on the Warsaw underground.

After the war, the Stalinist regime banned his *Sinfonia Rustica* as 'alien to the Socialist era'. With the aid of his Irish-born first wife Scarlett, Panufnik evaded his Party minders and escaped to Britain while on an official trip to Zurich in July 1954. Denounced as a 'traitor' in Poland, his post with the CBSO was a first step to building a new career in the free world. He went on to take British citizenship in 1961, and to compose ten symphonies.

Panufnik's artistic and moral values remained uncompromised: 'I attempt to achieve a true balance between feeling and intellect, heart and brain, impulse and design.' He continued to speak out fearlessly against human rights abuses in communist Poland, and was greeted by crowds carrying roses when in 1990, after the fall of communism, he finally returned to Warsaw. He lived to see his daughter Roxanna establish herself as a composer, and to be knighted by the Queen for his services to music.

discreetly vetted by Edmund Compton, a personal contact in Whitehall. 'What I have to add off the record is that he would not be in this position if he were viewed with disfavour,' Compton reported. 'I say "Off the Record"; because on principle the authorities don't screen persons for jobs that are not security jobs. And conducting an orchestra is not a security risk.'

In fact, over his two seasons in Birmingham, Panufnik could be said to have been more British than the British. Fascinated by the forgotten composers of eighteenth-century England, he'd often begin programmes with some chamber-scale rarity: a concerto grosso or symphony by John Stanley, Thomas Arne, William Boyce or (a particular favourite) Charles Avison. They would often be coupled with a modern work, and followed by standard Austro-German symphonic repertoire – the 'Three Bs' (Bach, Beethoven and Brahms) were the backbone of Panufnik's second season in Birmingham. Panufnik particularly loved Elgar's neglected tribute to his own homeland, the 'sombre and noble *Polonia*, a work most evocatively echoing the heroic and tragic elements of Polish history'. He conducted it five times in the 1957–8 season, and later wrote a work of his own with the same title, sincerely moved to find this most English – indeed, most Midlands – of composers reaching out in sympathy to a suffering Poland.

Not wanting to be accused of self-promotion, Panufnik refrained from programming his own music, instead premiering symphonies (both Feeney commissions) by Lennox Berkeley and Edmund Rubbra, while Harold Gray and the CBSO's newly appointed second associate

conductor, Meredith Davies, introduced substantial new works by Frank Martin, Darius Milhaud, William Mathias and Alan Rawsthorne. The following season, the committee announced a change of policy. Panufnik, they explained in the 1958–9 season prospectus:

> is also conducting four works from his own pen, these latter at the express wish, and in fact instructions of the Management Committee as he himself was most diffident about their inclusion. It was felt that his *Sinfonia elegiaca* which recently received its first performance in America conducted by Stokowski and acclaimed by the American public, should be a 'must' in Birmingham where we have the composer himself to direct the performance.

'The Birmingham audience was generally appreciative, especially the younger listeners,' remembered Panufnik. Stan Smith recalls that the younger musicians felt the same way. 'Some of the older players just didn't much like foreigners, but I liked him all right – he was much clearer to follow than Rudolf, and he had the nuts and bolts of it. There's a lot to be said for that.' The CBSO clearly hoped and expected that he would extend his contract. Panufnik, however, felt the imperative to compose – though you do wonder if he'd have felt it quite so imperatively had he not become embroiled, in his first season, in a personality clash with the leader, Norris Stanley.

Stanley had been one of Heward's later appointments, though even some of Stanley's

Sir Adrian Boult always looked out for his old orchestra. After Panufnik's departure in 1959 he returned to Birmingham as interim conductor: 'a sort of elderly umbrella to keep some of the rain and snow off'.

contemporaries (notably Gwen Berry) expressed surprise that Weldon had retained him as leader, and Stan Smith was not alone in finding his playing uninspiring: 'He'd been a café player. Everything was there, but it was sort of workmanlike, if you know what I mean?' Nonetheless, Stanley had worked happily with Schwarz: an important point, since Panufnik accuses him of anti-Semitism. Panufnik had told Lloyd that he'd taken the role 'with the all-important proviso that I should be able to make sufficient changes in order to raise the standard

and quality of the orchestra to one of really first class level'. Now, in an internal report, he made it clear that he saw Stanley's 'metallic "café-style" tone' and 'unwillingness to collaborate with the other principals' as a serious obstacle.

Disputes between conductors and leaders only ever end one way. Stanley was eased out in February 1958 with the usual bromides about focusing on a solo career, but not before some ugly moments – when Panufnik commissioned a new arrangement of the National Anthem from Anthony Lewis, Stanley hissed 'Go back to

Siberia!' at the conductor, at a volume clearly audible to the audience. Grievances of this sort can fester for decades in a community as tight knit as an orchestra. Twelve years later, in 1970, Beresford King-Smith clearly felt that the wound was still too raw to reopen in his fiftieth anniversary history of the CBSO. But the new leader, Wilfred Lehmann, started in Panufnik's second season. He proved an outstanding appointment.

Older players such as Berry continued to find Panufnik's forensic rehearsal technique and somewhat formal manner disconcerting. The oboist Tony Miller told Beresford King-Smith that he 'never felt Panufnik was very happy conducting'. 'I realised that they thought me pernickety,' said Panufnik. But the orchestra and audience had acquired a genuine respect for him by the time he told the *Birmingham Mail* that 'it is impossible to conduct a permanent orchestra and compose at the same time'. After his final concert, in July 1959, he was touched to be presented by the players with a symbolic sheet of blank manuscript paper – 'with their sincere good wishes for my continuing success as a composer'.

The management committee was in a hole, and the musicians sensed the uncertainty. The committee had been lining up Meredith Davies to succeed Panufnik a couple of years further down the line, but Davies did not feel ready and was appointed deputy musical director instead. Lloyd turned for a stop-gap solution for the 1959–60 season to an old friend of the orchestra and, as a bemused Panufnik put it, 'announced to the press that the post of conductor had been taken over for one year by Sir Adrian Boult, aged seventy, from Mr Andrzej Panufnik, aged forty-five, who had retired!'

'When the news eventually broke, the dispirited atmosphere in the orchestra lightened considerably,' remembers Maggie Cotton. During Boult's short second stint as chief conductor, George Weldon returned as a guest, Harold Gray conducted Kodály's *Budavári Te Deum* at Worcester in the presence of the composer and Meredith Davies shared an all-Britten programme with the composer himself: Davies conducted the *Spring Symphony* and Britten the *Serenade for Tenor, Horn and Strings*.

Boult conducted the premiere of Robert Simpson's Violin Concerto, and entered the 1960s by revisiting Mahler's Fourth Symphony, three decades after he'd first introduced it to Birmingham. Joan Sutherland was the soprano, and although John Waterhouse of the *Birmingham Post* found himself 'allergic' to Mahler, he conceded that 'there can be no doubt at all that Mahler has a very strong appeal to our present younger generation of intelligent music-lovers'.

He attributed this to the same spirit of rebellion observable in 'Mr John Osborne's Jimmy Porter' – the combative hero of *Look Back in Anger*. The times, they were a-changing. Three years previously in 1956, Sir Adrian had written to Lloyd, 'I have never met a group of musicians with a more happily co-operative spirit than the CBSO.' They were typically generous words, though of course by this time Boult occupied a special place in British musical life. Panufnik, you suspect, might have seen things rather differently.

BIRMINGHAM INTERNATIONAL

T he group of musicians and staff who gathered on the tarmac at Elmdon airport on the afternoon of 19 May 1955 for the CBSO's first international tour were seasoned travellers in one respect. The orchestra had travelled almost continually within the UK, without – in its entire thirty-five-year history – making it further south than Bournemouth or further north than Edinburgh. Any Midlander will tell you that the cultural and linguistic gulf between Birmingham and Wolverhampton is as vast as any in Europe; but no amount (and there was any amount) of dates in Derby, Leicester, Cheltenham or Sheffield provided any serious preparation for what lay ahead: seven concerts in the space of a week in Dutch cities including Alkmaar, Hilversum, Utrecht and Arnhem.

It had happened almost by accident – in as far as the CBSO's chairman Stephen Lloyd let anything happen by accident. Lloyd, as he later told Beresford King-Smith, had been visiting a Dutch subsidiary of his company GKN, and happened to mention to a British Embassy official that the CBSO had never toured overseas.

'Oh,' he said, 'I'm just making plans for a British week in the Netherlands, to be held next year. I think it would be most appropriate if we could get a British orchestra to take part in it.' So the very next day I went over to The Hague and met him and a Dutch lady concert agent, and we fixed up the outline of the tour, then and there! Blyth Major sorted out all the details, of course, later on.

It's doubtful whether Blyth Major thought they were 'details'. To transport seventy-eight musicians and their instruments, plus a sizeable civic party including the Lord Mayor, Major contacted the Dutch airline KLM and chartered three Douglas C-54 Skymasters – 'the biggest planes ever to land at Elmdon', reported the *Birmingham Daily Gazette*. This was a major civic occasion; naturally a photographer was despatched to cover the departure. 'The few spectators at Birmingham's Elmdon airport cheered,' they reported. 'Well, you couldn't just stand and do nothing when a complete orchestra was taking off before your very eyes.' They noticed that each of the three aircraft carried the slogan 'The Flying Dutchman'.

All the 50 crates of instruments had to go through the Customs. 'Nothing hidden in this one,' said a Customs officer as he picked up a triangle. In the second plane was first violinist Harry van der Lyn, looking forward to seeing his own country, which he left during the German invasion. When Rudolf Schwarz, in a bow tie, walked across to the plane, you felt you ought to applaud. But he had a rival. The control officer, waving his arms to guide the pilot, put up a fine performance.

Schwarz and his Swedish-born wife Greta knew what to expect on the Continent in 1955. They weren't quite so sure about the musicians. 'Not only was it the orchestra's first overseas tour, but for many of the players it was their first trip abroad at all,' Schwarz told King-Smith.

Flowers all the way: Rudolf Schwarz and the CBSO pose at Schiphol Airport, Amsterdam, at the end of their first ever international tour in May 1955.

It went to the heads of some of them too, and gave us a few problems; I remember seeing CBSO players sitting outside pavement cafés drinking gin – at 10 o'clock in the morning! I remember too, that I was puzzled to find that although [piano soloist] Denis Matthews and his wife were always given the best room in each hotel, Greta and I were invariably given a poky little room at the back. After a while we realised that they had looked at my name on the register and had assumed I was a hated German.

Players lodged with local families in the smaller towns and while local critics preferred the CBSO's Beethoven (Matthews played the Fourth Piano Concerto) and Dvořák (the Seventh Symphony) to their modern British specialities by Walton, Gordon Jacob and Vaughan Williams, the reception was overwhelmingly warm. 'It was flowers, flowers, flowers all the way during the City of Birmingham Symphony Orchestra's tour of Holland,' reported the *Birmingham Post*.

They saw flowers everywhere. It was the way the Dutch said 'Thank you' for liberation by Allied troops 10 years ago . . . At Arnhem, flowers of remembrance, blue and yellow flowers, in the orchestra's colours, were placed on the Bridgehead

Memorial by Mr Blyth Major, the orchestra's secretary, on behalf of all Birmingham's music-lovers. On Saturday, the orchestra arrived home at Elmdon airport – with garlands of flowers presented by admirers.

A picture shows Rudolf Schwarz wrangling a colossal bunch of lilies down the steps of the plane. The CBSO's first international tour had been an artistic success. More than that, it had been a triumph of cultural diplomacy – a flag-waver for both the United Kingdom and the City of Birmingham, whose potency was not lost on the City Council. The following April, the Mayor of Birmingham threw a civic banquet for the *Burgemeesters* of Alkmaar, Utrecht and Hilversum. Since that time, one of the principal purposes of the CBSO's overseas touring schedule has been to serve as a roving cultural ambassador for a diverse and outward-looking trading city.

Despite the vast and often exhausting logistical effort involved, overseas touring has many other benefits for an orchestra. It is rarely a huge money-spinner (logistical costs can devour concert fees with frightening thoroughness), but it is a morale-booster, a bonding exercise, a means of building and signalling prestige, and it can also be – as we'll see – a period of unique, unencumbered artistic concentration in front of unprejudiced and appreciative audiences. Since the early 1980s overseas tours have been such a frequent part of the CBSO's calendar that they have become part of the orchestra's identity.

But for two decades after that first trip, they were rare and often alarming adventures.

A thirteen-date tour to West Germany and Switzerland in March 1963 (during which opportunistic local promoters billed the orchestra as 'Birmingham Philharmonic, dirigent: Sir Hugo Rignold') drew gratifying reviews ('Beethoven himself would have been astonished at the playing, so competent and sure,' wrote a Basel newspaper) but culminated in the German tour agent 'losing' the instrument van (and all the instruments within it) in a successful attempt to blackmail the CBSO into reducing its fee. May 1968 took the CBSO to East Germany, Poland and Czechoslovakia; in May 1972 they played in Bucharest, Belgrade, Budapest, Bratislava and Košice.

It's hard to explain to anyone born after 1980 exactly what it meant to visit the Communist Bloc before the fall of the Berlin Wall: to enter impoverished, totalitarian police states where Westerners were escorted by official 'minders', hotels and restaurants could not necessarily guarantee the availability of either electricity or food, local currency was effectively worthless and any difficulty with officialdom, however minor, could rapidly escalate into the stuff of John Le Carré novels. 'In those pre-telex, pre-fax days, setting up a tour of this sort required great skill and patience,' comments Beresford King-Smith, with considerable understatement. Problems in 1968 started at Checkpoint Charlie, the heavily fortified entry point through the Berlin Wall into East Germany. 'Well, we couldn't go through because one of the passports was missing,' remembers violinist Stan Smith. 'And it turned out it was mine!' He remembered, at this point, that he'd left it at his parents' house in Northampton.

After a draining exchange with border officials, the orchestra proceeded on tour. In Warsaw, Smith was bewildered by beetroot soup, and uncertain about the correct way of dealing with individuals who approached him in the street, desperate to exchange local money for Western currency. The poverty came as a jolt to many players. 'We had a courier with us,' recalls Smith.

He was a smashing guy, a Pole, and of course we appreciated everything he had done, and wanted to give him a tip. But the only things we had got were these bucketfuls of local change. Like 5p and 1p coins. And we put this all in a hat, and we emptied this all into his hands. And he was . . . you know, embarrassed. And, thinking about it, I thought, 'Why couldn't we have just tried to get some notes or something?'

The next stop was Brno, in Czechoslovakia. It was 13 May 1968: under the liberalising regime of Alexander Dubček, censorship had been abolished only seven weeks previously and a tide of democratic sentiment was starting to rise throughout the country. The CBSO was heading south from Poland straight into the so-called 'Prague Spring'. 'I was in charge of the coaches and we had no problem,' recalls Beresford King-Smith.

But as we approached the border at Cieszyn, in the forest there were tanks, and troop-carriers. Manoeuvres, we were told, manoeuvres. It wasn't manoeuvres,

Behind the iron curtain: Louis Frémaux and the orchestra prepare to board a Czechoslovak State Airlines Ilyushin IL-18 at the start of the May 1972 Eastern Bloc tour.

Timisoara, Romania, May 1972. Young concertgoers discover that Maurice Handford, John Lill and the 'Orchestra Simfonică din Birmingham, Anglia' are in town – playing music by Beethoven, Tchaikovsky, Strauss and 'Tippet'.

of course. They were waiting to go in and crush Dubček.

We got as far as the border and Hugo Rignold and his daughter Jennifer, who'd gone separately in a car, and [general manager] Arthur Baker, who was driving them, were all supposed to be there before us. And they weren't. It turned out they had all the correct visas on their passports, but someone at that border crossing hadn't been told. Because of these 'manoeuvres', they were very sensitive. They thought it was the Western press trying to find out what was going on.

Baker and the Rignolds were arrested, searched, and interrogated for two hours in a soundproof room. 'It was a most alarming experience. The police weren't rough and didn't push us around but they were not exactly polite about it,' Baker told the *Birmingham Post* once the necessary phone calls had been made and the affair straightened out. 'The questions they asked suggested they suspected us of spying.' Back in Birmingham, the press described the whole episode as a 'spy drama' – but also mentioned that the CBSO had been encored at every venue. The Brno Philharmonic presented each member of the orchestra with a commemorative doll.

Organised by the impresario Victor Hochhauser, the 1972 Eastern Bloc tour took full advantage of cheap Eastern Bloc prices, with some unhappy consequences. 'We flew out on an Ilyushin IL-18,' remembers violinist Sheila Clarke. 'I think most of them had already dropped out of the sky by then.' Communist-era Bucharest, she recalls, 'was very primitive. It certainly wasn't Westernised in any way. The shops really didn't have very much to offer, very grey, drab buildings and the whole feeling was one of poverty.' In Ceauşescu's socialist paradise all communication – even music – was mediated by the Party. 'In the concert hall in Bucharest, the audience didn't even hear the music live, but through speakers in the seats – so they got it second hand.' The magnificent Reduta Hall in Bratislava was visibly crumbling; in Košice the CBSO was cheered by a packed house while Yevgeny Mravinsky's Leningrad Philharmonic, the previous night, had been boycotted by patriotic Slovaks and played to empty seats.

'Orchestral tours on which nothing goes wrong exist only in a concert manager's imagination,' writes King-Smith, ruefully, in *Crescendo!*, and it was at the Yugoslav–Romanian border crossing, en route to catch the night train from Arad to Budapest, that history nearly repeated itself. In order to avoid the Vietnam draft, percussionist James Strebing had left his native USA to study in the UK, and his US passport had since expired. Unable to renew it without risking arrest as a draft-dodger, he'd obtained a temporary travel document from the UK Foreign Office. 'What they didn't explain to me at the time was that I would need a visa to go absolutely anywhere,' he remembers.

The coaches arrived at the border and obviously, my passport was slightly different coloured. So, I got hoicked out, and then lots of chatting ensued. The orchestra stayed around for a while, drank everything in the bar and then they thought, 'Well, we'd better send them on.' So they left me with Beresford and [oboist] Richard Weigall, because Richard could speak good German. Eventually, somebody rang me up on the telephone who could speak English. And I explained the situation and they said, oh, OK, and then I bought a round of food for everyone with US dollars – and everybody seemed very happy with that.

It was just very bureaucratic. Nobody knew quite what was going on. And I suppose there were always people standing around with machine-guns, but they really just wanted to get us out of there so we didn't embarrass them. So they sent us off. They just grabbed a couple of people who were driving through and said, 'Take these people to a hotel somewhere.' Taking a fistful of dollars in that part of the world proved very handy.

But long tours can be draining, especially in a socialist economy. Violinist Paul Smith recalls how in Romania:

> We were paid about nine million lei, and the next day we were going to another country so we couldn't actually spend it. I just went to a music shop and bought all the Mozart string quartets for about threepence. In the end we mostly just gave spare currency to people in the station on the way.

Sheila Clarke remembers that in Hungary:

> We were staying thirty miles out of Budapest. Post-concert, one coach would go to the accommodation and another one would stay behind so that we could get dinner if we wanted it. So we were able to experience a traditional Hungarian meal with fiddle-players coming around, which was brilliant. But then we got to our accommodation and they'd overbooked and there wasn't enough accommodation for us.
>
> Well, we had a meal all together, a final fling after the last concert of the tour, and one of our players got up and said what a lousy tour this had been. With the management and Victor Hochhauser and everybody else all sitting right there in the room. After that, Arthur Baker said he

would never take us on tour again. And he never did.

Today Wolverhampton, Tomorrow the World

In the autumn of 1998, chief executive Edward Smith did an audit. Between 1980 and 1998, Simon Rattle and the CBSO had given 209 overseas concerts, in twenty-five countries on four continents. In the 1997–8 season alone they had played in ten different countries, culminating in performances of Beethoven's Ninth and Szymanowski's *King Roger* at the Salzburg Festival. In the CBSO's entire sixty-year history prior to 1980, the orchestra had undertaken only five international tours. The scale of the change is obvious. As the 'Rattle effect' sent its ripples out far beyond Birmingham, the CBSO established a pattern of touring that continues to the present – an annual mixture of long multi-date tours ('I call them dartboard tours cos you're just dashing around,' says Paul Smith), flying visits to international venues, and summer trips to major festivals.

The reason why isn't hard to grasp. Overseas promoters recognised the significance of Rattle's work with the CBSO at an early stage, and as Rattle was succeeded in turn by Sakari Oramo, Andris Nelsons and Mirga Gražinytė-Tyla, the CBSO has maintained an international reputation as the orchestra with which the most significant conductors of their generation do their freshest and most original work. It has become a cliché, but where Birmingham leads, Berlin, Boston, Leipzig and London are likely to follow. During Sakari Oramo's ten years in

Simon Rattle and the CBSO rehearse for their debut at the Berlin Philharmonie on 24 September 1984. The applause was so overwhelming that Rattle had to keep bowing even after the orchestra had left the stage.

Birmingham, the orchestra undertook more than twenty international tours; a total surpassed under Andris Nelsons and looking set to increase further under Gražinytė-Tyla. The CBSO has played in amphitheatres and cathedrals, arenas and palaces, on a floating platform in Abu Dhabi harbour, and beneath the tailfin of an A340 at the Airbus factory in Bremen.

The CBSO performed in Vienna (the Konzerthaus) for the first time in 1982; by 1984 the orchestra had made its debut at the Berlin Philharmonie and, in 1994, in the golden hall

of Vienna's Musikverein. Spain, Italy, Greece, Taiwan and Finland have all joined the CBSO's touring itinerary since then. Japan was a frequent destination between 1994 and 2016. Major USA tours came in 1988, 1992 and 1998; South America in 1997, the United Arab Emirates in 2014 and China (a long-held ambition of Birmingham City Council) in 2016. The Schleswig-Holstein and Salzburg Festivals first invited the CBSO in 1992, and the Lucerne Festival in 1996. 'For a regional British orchestra, this is an astonishing accolade,' wrote one London-based critic from Lucerne in 2012, seemingly unaware that the CBSO had been a regular visitor for nearly two decades. As CBSO violinist David Gregory puts it, 'To be honest, even to this day I think we're more appreciated abroad than we are at home.'

The transforming effect on the orchestra's morale was, and continues to be, significant. 'In a way it really showed us what our worth was. Or at least it gave us an enhanced idea. Especially going to Japan, where we had hardly less than adulation, really,' says Gregory. It took a while for regular touring to become a way of life, however, and there were certainly hiccups along the way. As the orchestra jetted off to a tour of France, Switzerland and Germany in 1984, airline staff complained that musicians had been drinking on the tarmac prior to boarding the plane – and that the aircraft crew detected 'a strong smell of marijuana'. Rosemary Harby, PA to the general manager Ed Smith, took the incoming flak: 'I got a phone call from Brian Summers, who was the boss at Birmingham airport, and he said, "I'm really sorry, Rosemary, but the airline have said they will not bring the orchestra back if there's a repeat of what happened when they went out."'

Orchestras aren't entirely immune to the 'what goes on tour' mentality; some of the orchestra's juiciest touring anecdotes remain, sadly, unprintable. (Many seem to originate in the viola section.) Sheila Clarke, though, as a veteran of that particular tour, dismisses any suggestion of reefer madness from off-the-leash musos.

It was one of our girls – Georgina, a first fiddle – who was trying to give up smoking, and she was smoking herbal cigarettes. That's all it was, but when we got back to Birmingham airport, the police and the dogs were out in force. We all had to sit down while the dogs were sent around our hand luggage; then we had to stand up and they had the dogs sniff around again, and I think the only thing they found was some ham sandwiches, still in their bag.

Frieda Jonas, the chairman's wife, was escorted from the plane for further questioning after a sniffer-dog took exception to her knitting. 'We weren't on drugs at all,' says Clarke. But a few al fresco tins of duty-free Special Brew? 'Oh, quite possibly, yes.'

'Certainly we used to enjoy ourselves in a way that perhaps we don't any more,' says David Gregory. 'But I think that's probably because the job itself has become much more enjoyable.' By the 1990s the CBSO was one of the world's most sought-after touring ensembles, and had raised its organisational game to match. Frank Salomon, Simon Rattle's devoted American manager, handled the US tours, and called them 'a very special experience for all of us'.

'They have become a role model for what a symphony orchestra can become for a community and for the world of music,' he told *Music Stand*, and he was there in Los Angeles when the CBSO completed their May 1998 USA tour with two sold-out performances.

What fantastic audiences they were! The intensity of how they listened, and then the explosion of cheers as they stood to acknowledge the very special musical worlds that Simon and the orchestra created each night, were fantastic rewards for all of us for whom passionate music-making is our lifeblood.

'The CBSO is a very special group of people,' said Rattle to Nicholas Kenyon in his 2001 book *Simon Rattle: From Birmingham to Berlin*. 'One of the things that was most fun for me was seeing the orchestra look after each other on the tour, because I think everybody was dreading a month away. It's very tough and it's very disorientating. Everybody is on the line.' While a tour is still always work – and extremely hard work – musicians and staff have all found their own ways of surviving the experience. The sheer excitement of encountering a different culture can be refreshing in itself. Open-air rehearsals in the Al Jahili Fort in the United Arab Emirates were scheduled around the daily calls to prayer. Players head for beer gardens in Germany, gypsy restaurants in Bucharest, cat cafés in Tokyo; many CBSO musicians pride themselves on having regular post-concert haunts in Vienna, Amsterdam or Munich. Touring in Japan prompts universal enthusiasm.

'There are queues round the block for tickets,' says David Gregory. Sheila Clarke agrees:

After the concert, we'd come out of the stage door and all the tall, fair-haired men in the orchestra were absolutely mobbed by these young schoolgirls. They said they hadn't seen anybody like that and they thought they were all

wonderful. Everything in Japan just works like clockwork, they're incredibly helpful, nothing is ever too much trouble, and the halls are fantastic.

The CBSO's following in Japan has grown only deeper since Rattle's first performances there in 1994; one couple of particularly devoted fans still regularly posts gifts of rice crackers and sweets to CBSO Centre.

In fact, offstage adventures can occasionally leave a deeper impression than performances – sometimes against expectations. Violinist Bryony Morrison remembers one hellish summer day at the Rheingau Festival in Germany in August 2012, when travel arrangements were in meltdown.

It was one of those days when I was very glad I wasn't in management. But we all made it finally to the venue via, I think, nine different routes. They'd managed to rebook everyone, and we got there. We had our brief rehearsal, and there was a real atmosphere of 'We're here, we can do this.' And then we were backstage, eating our sandwiches, just about to line up, when suddenly someone came back and said, 'Andris is in an ambulance.' So it was another reshuffle, and the show went on with Simon Halsey conducting, and speaking to the audience in German. It was definitely a 'yes, let's do it' occasion.

Or there's the overseas exploits of the CBSO's football team: a play-off at the 1998 Salzburg

Festival against the Vienna Philharmonic and the Hallé (the Hallé emerged victorious), and the five-aside match against local lads on Rio de Janeiro's Gloria beach, on the day in September 1997 that news broke of the death of the Princess of Wales. 'One of them had a massive machete in his belt – he'd been out diving for abalone in the bay,' remembers Michael Seal. 'He said, "Do you want to play football – England against Brazil?" Well, we thrashed them 5–1 because we kept our shoes on. And they were just so lovely – they said, "We're really sorry about your Princess. And thank you for the game of football."'

Then there was the time a CBSO side challenged the noticeably fitter and younger forces of the Mahler Chamber Orchestra at Aix-en-Provence in 2000. Unknown to the MCO, the CBSO's principal cello Eduardo Vassallo had called in a friend who lived nearby – an ex-professional footballer. 'It was 9–1 to the CBSO,' says Seal, still unable to prevent himself laughing.

> And they only scored one because [timpanist] Pete Hill was in goal and he jumped out of the way of the ball. The next night when we went into work, Simon told the orchestra that apparently he'd had dinner the previous night with Daniel Harding. And all he kept saying was, 'How did they beat us? They were all so old!'

The musical results, however, are unarguable, and the supreme moments on tour can leave a career-long impression. Seal remembers one night in Berlin in September 1991:

We played Mahler Nine, and as it went on I remembered sitting there thinking, 'Don't screw up. This has been almost perfection. Nobody is screwing up, this is amazing. This is just awesome.' There wasn't even a click or a bang, or anything. And when they finished, we all left the stage and Rattle was going on alone with the score. But I remember standing backstage and there was silence. Normally there's banter, and on this occasion there was total silence. People just putting their instruments away. I don't think it ever happened again in twenty-two years. Everyone knew it was a good one. A really good one.

'I think touring is very good for orchestras,' says David Gregory.

> And there is a simple reason why. And that is, that all you have to think about, apart from eating and sleeping, is playing. That's all your worries are. All the other worries are shelved until you get back home. Plus, it's probably going to be the same music or at least a restricted number of pieces that come round and round, and so with a good music director the standard of the orchestra does improve rapidly, with a concert every day. The tours have got better and better.

That it's Birmingham's orchestra that is taking music-making of this quality to the world remains a source of intense pride, both at home and away. At the end of 2013, forty-four of Japan's

*December 2014: a warm night in the Persian Gulf as Michael Seal
conducts the CBSO on a floating stage in Abu Dhabi harbour.*

leading music critics were asked by the magazine *Ongaku no Tomo* to vote on the best orchestral performance by a touring orchestra that year. They had plenty of options: concerts in Tokyo that year had included performances by Bernard Haitink and the London Symphony Orchestra, the Vienna Philharmonic, and the Berlin Philharmonic under a certain Sir Simon Rattle.

Japanese audiences are knowledgeable, and perhaps less easily swayed by conventional wisdom than Anglophone critics. They trust their own ears. Describing the winning performance,

the critic Junko Yoshida of *Asahi Shimbun*, wrote, 'One rarely attends a concert where the musicians and audience are so firmly united in the same delight, and smiling at each other to this extent.' The concert in question was a programme of Wagner, Sibelius and Dvořák, given at Opera City Tokyo on 18 November 2013 by Andris Nelsons and the City of Birmingham Symphony Orchestra.

7

Concrete City

For things to stay the same, they have to change. Walk into a rehearsal of Hugo Rignold's CBSO in the early 1960s, and the first thing to hit you would have been a fug of cigarette smoke. The percussionist Maggie Cotton joined the CBSO during Boult's interregnum, and in *Wrong Sex, Wrong Instrument*, she describes how in her earliest rehearsals, 'a pall of smoke wreathed its way over the players':

> I watched with fascination as horns tucked half-finished cigarettes into a crook in their instruments, or precariously balanced glowing dog-ends on the music stands. My colleague [timpanist] Ernie Parsons could smoke a cigarette halfway through without dropping any at all . . . My abiding memory of conductor Hugo Rignold is of his chain-smoking through rehearsals, cigarette between yellowed fingers, squinting against smoke while studying the score.

The right to smoke didn't quite extend to the concert platform, where throughout the 1950s attempts had been made to smarten up the orchestra's appearance – to the amusement of John Waterhouse of the *Post*. Tuesday audiences, he noted in 1955:

> now receive additional value from the pleasing prospect of the entire CBSO dressed in white ties and tails (not top hats, at least not within the Town Hall). Dear me, what next? Blue Hungarian outfits for

'Viennese' concerts? Jolly false noses for the Saturday 'pops'? Tiny cupid-wings for 'Music You Love'?

Black ties and dinner-jackets had been the norm under Weldon.

Less obvious to the outside observer (and seemingly lost on Panufnik) might have been the make-up of the orchestra: at least 10 per cent of the permanent orchestra had always been women, but Cotton notes that 'we had players from Australia, Holland, Germany, South Africa, Eastern Europe and all corners of the British Isles. In fact it was quite unusual to hear a Birmingham accent' – apart, that is, from Harold Gray's. The CBO's founding generation was retiring: the violinist Herbert Povey, cellists Harry Stanier and Gwen Berry, and the timpanist Ernest Parsons were among the last survivors of Appleby Matthews' first season.

Parsons finally retired in May 1965. According to Maggie Cotton and Stan Smith, the one-time firebrand had become increasingly erratic and cantankerous, but after his final concert, audience members filed onto the stage for over fifteen minutes to wish him all the best. Harry Stanier was the very last: stepping down in the summer of 1967 at the age of sixty-nine after forty-seven years of service interrupted only by the war. In January 1960 the popular second violinist Albert 'Rusty' Russell collapsed onstage and died at the Town Hall after sprinting up from New Street station in a pea-soup smog: he was laid out in the orchestra ladies' dressing room. 'Poor Albert so still,' wrote Gwen Berry in her diary.

January 1966: Sir Arthur Bliss (left) has a word with Hugo Rignold during the recording of his Meditations on a Theme by John Blow. *Maggie Cotton thought he resembled 'a cross between Peter Rabbit and Queen Victoria'.*

Beresford King-Smith joined the office staff of the CBSO in January 1964, and he too entered a world seemingly unchanged from the ad hoc days of the pre-war City Orchestra. 'The offices were at 60 Newhall Street; the Bradford and Bingley Building Society was just below, and in the basement was Birmingham's oldest-established gents' barbers: a very Victorian set-up,' he remembers.

We were on the third and fourth floors, with a staff of about a dozen . . . there was the general manager, concert manager and an accountant, each with a secretary. There was an orchestra manager who basically accompanied the players on the coaches but prior to that I did all the fixing [booking additional players]. We didn't have our own van until the late 1960s: prior to that I

HUGO RIGNOLD (1905–76)

Hugo Rignold was famous before he'd ever conducted a symphony orchestra. Born into a musical family in Kingston-upon-Thames, he played the Tchaikovsky Violin Concerto under Sir Henry Wood before he was twenty. But another kind of music sparked his enthusiasm, and by the mid 1920s he was a star player in Jack Hylton's famous jazz orchestra. By the late 1930s, Rignold was leading his own band, and was recognised as one of the world's finest jazz violinists. 'There have been only two violinists who have hitherto meant anything to jazz,' wrote *Gramophone* in 1936. 'Venuti, of course, and more recently the French musician Stéphane Grappelli. To my mind Hugo Rignold is a greater artist than any of them.'

War service took him to the Middle East, where conducting gigs with military bands led to concerts with the future Israel Philharmonic Orchestra. As Rignold's biographer Christopher Howell puts it, he became a classical conductor 'if not actually on the road to Damascus, then not all that far from it'. Demobbed, he worked at the Royal Opera House, Covent Garden, and in 1948 took charge of the Liverpool Philharmonic Orchestra, where he found musicians hostile to his planned personnel changes, and audiences prejudiced against his jazz background. Birmingham proved more open to 'Riggy's' qualities. Meanwhile, from 1957 to 1960 he was music director of the Royal Ballet. Ill health limited his later career – although his work with the Cape Town Symphony Orchestra in the early 1970s left a lasting and positive legacy.

simply booked Brown's Removals and they also stored instruments for us.

In King-Smith's first week, the orchestra played six concerts in seven days: a typical schedule at the time, including trips to Cheltenham and Sheffield. Harold Gray took pity on the new boy and treated him to lunch at the Hope and Anchor on Edmund Street – known to the orchestra since 1920 as 'Eli Fletcher's', and still with straw on the floor. It would be demolished the following year as Birmingham's great post-war modernist redevelopment gathered momentum.

'I have never been very certain as to the value of tangible links with the past. They are often more sentimental than valuable,' said the city's radical chief planner, Herbert Manzoni. Work on Birmingham's Inner Ring Road (the so-called 'concrete collar') had begun in 1957 and would continue its onslaught on the city's historic fabric until the 1970s. The old Bull Ring Market, the Victorian Central Library and the CBSO's old venue, the Grand Theatre, all fell. By 1967 the new Bull Ring, the Rotunda and the GPO tower had all risen, and the huge Gravelly Hill motorway interchange was already under construction. 'Spaghetti Junction' would come to represent the futuristic concrete city of 1970s Birmingham as comprehensively as red bricks and machine shops had defined the Victorian 'city of a thousand trades'.

CBSO players had initially feared a similar demolition job at the hands of their new chief conductor. Hugo Rignold had attempted to fire twenty-two players in his previous role at the Liverpool Philharmonic Orchestra – though

he'd also built an impressive reputation as an interpreter and orchestra-trainer. He was a skilled violinist in his own right, and CBSO players came to see 'Riggy' as the antidote to the instability of the previous three years. 'It needed someone who was thoroughly professional, and that's exactly what Hugo was,' said Harold Gray. 'What a nice soul,' confided Gwen Berry to her diary. 'If only we'd had him instead of Panufnik, how different things might have been.'

Any overview of Rignold's era in Birmingham unavoidably suggests musical modernisation – a laying down of the structure of a recognisably modern orchestral schedule. The CBSO undertook its second and third major international tours – in 1963 to Switzerland and West Germany; in 1968 to East Germany, Poland and Czechoslovakia. Wilfred Lehmann was succeeded as leader by Meyer Stolow, then John Georgiadis, and in 1965 by the South African-born Felix Kok, a veteran of Boyd Neel's famous string orchestra who had played under Karajan and Furtwängler in the Philharmonia. He would go on to be the CBSO's longest-serving leader. When the general manager Ernest 'Eddie' Edwards suffered a brain haemorrhage on New Street station in July 1962 and died shortly afterwards, Arthur Baker, formerly of the Bournemouth and Liverpool orchestras, took his place – as it would prove, another appointment with far-reaching consequences.

The orchestra had its first TV engagement, and in January 1966, Rignold took the CBSO into the recording studio for the first time since 1948 to record Bliss's Feeney Trust commission *Meditation on a Theme by John Blow*. It is still an impressive recording: clear, atmospheric, taut, and demonstrating to the full the firm, chiselled string sonorities that Rignold, as a violinist, was able to command. Less happily, the CBSO experienced its first (and so far only) strike, when Rignold, as part of his rebuilding of the string section, required the first violinist Wilfred Pook to move into the second violins.

'Pook's Pique' was how the Evening Standard reported it. Rignold handled the reseating tactlessly: Pook, as Musicians' Union steward, took it as a personal slight, and on Saturday 12 December 1965 the players walked out, wrecking a BBC recording in Solihull. It was all resolved by Monday, and Pook and the CBSO submitted to independent arbitration. 'Wilfred was not a good player, by anybody's standards,' recalls King-Smith. In fact, several of his orchestral colleagues had privately asked for him to be reseated. 'Some of the others were very fed up with him,' remembers Stan Smith. But any orchestra is a community of artists. Individual rights, and individual status, carry genuine significance.

Rignold, however, expected high standards at every level. During a rehearsal of Schoenberg's Verklärte Nacht at Lichfield Cathedral, Meyer Stolow repeatedly misplayed a solo. When Rignold pulled him up, remembers Stan Smith, Stolow retorted, 'Well, am I the only one who makes mistakes?' 'He should not have said that to Rignold,' says Smith. 'Rignold turned to him and said, "But you're the leader!" His face was red!' Their subsequent offstage quarrel could be heard echoing throughout the cathedral. For the newly joined violinist Sheila Clarke, Rignold was 'a nightmare':

If he wanted to find out what was going on, say, in the first fiddles, he would start at the back desk and have them play on their own and then he would have the next desk forward playing it on their own and so on until he got to the front. By which time, they were just a quaking mess.

The audience, however, experienced improvement and enrichment. In the 1964–5 season the orchestra was expanded to eighty-eight players, and the regular routine at the height of the season shows an organisation serving every aspect of the Midlands' musical life: a pattern, recalls King-Smith in Crescendo!,

based on a winter season of twenty Thursday concerts of music covering the entire orchestral repertoire with many eminent visiting artists and conductors, ten Sunday concerts mainly including the established symphonic repertoire, six pairs of 'Music You Love' industrial concerts and sixteen Proms in a three-week season in July. Promotions in other centres included six concerts in Cheltenham, four in Kidderminster, three in Dudley, and two each in Coventry, Nottingham, and the Royal Festival Hall [London]; the orchestra was regularly engaged by local authorities in places as far afield as Leeds and Bristol and by choral societies throughout the Midlands. Seasons with the Welsh National Opera and appearances at the Cheltenham and Three Choirs Festivals ensured a busy life even during the summer months.

Amid all this activity, the orchestra's repertoire begins to take on a more recognisably modern appearance too: and not only because of the thirty-one premieres under Rignold's tenure, ranging from Panufnik's Piano Concerto (a Feeney Trust commission, arranged by Lloyd as a parting gift to Panufnik) to Thea Musgrave's Concerto for Orchestra and the Fifth, Sixth and Seventh Symphonies by Schoenberg's great Viennese disciple Egon Wellesz. The orchestra played Ravel's *Daphnis et Chloé* complete – Maggie Cotton 'revelled in it' – and the 1967–8 season introduced a mini-series of 'Twentieth-Century Masterpieces', including Stravinsky's *The Rite of Spring* (Panufnik had been told it was too expensive to hire the extra players) and Berg's Violin Concerto.

Antal Doráti conducted Mahler's Sixth and Jascha Horenstein Mahler's First (Rignold had already introduced the Ninth to Birmingham, along with excerpts from Berg's *Wozzeck*). Harold Gray explored Peter Maxwell Davies and Nadia Boulanger conducted the music of her sister Lili. She had previously visited Birmingham in May 1966, as a juror in the CBSO's first (and so far only) International Woodwind Competition. William Glock, Adrian Boult and Leon Goossens sat with her, and the CBSO commissioned Malcolm Arnold to write a solo test piece for each instrument. The manuscript of the resulting five *Fantasies* is still at CBSO Centre. They're delightfully inventive pieces, although Arnold's biographers Anthony Meredith and Paul Harris insist that 'these are not works on which he will have spent much time'.

The first prize went jointly to the oboist Maurice Bourgue and a young Irish flautist: James Galway. A couple of months later, to celebrate the twenty-first anniversary of the CBSO Proms, a rose was named 'Hugo Rignold' and everyone in the audience received a bud. Naturally enough the programme included the suite from Richard Strauss's *Der Rosenkavalier*.

One occasion, however, would do more than any other to put the CBSO on the international musical map, and although it occurred under Rignold's tenure, it wasn't under his baton. The world premiere of Britten's *War Requiem* in the new Coventry Cathedral on 30 May 1962 remains a crowning moment in the CBSO's history – unquestionably the most significant premiere the orchestra has ever given. It wasn't that Britten had experienced a sudden fit of conscience over his broken promises of the previous decade. In fact, he was distinctly sniffy when he learned that his huge, unprecedentedly complex new choral work, commissioned by the Coventry Cathedral Arts Festival to mark the consecration of Sir Basil Spence's new modernist cathedral, was to be premiered by what he considered a 'pretty second-rate' orchestra.

A locally recruited amateur Festival Chorus did little to reassure him, and although the soloists were world class – Peter Pears, Dietrich Fischer-Dieskau and Heather Harper (chosen after the Soviet authorities banned Galina Vishnevskaya from participating) – and the London-based Melos Ensemble had been hired to serve as the separate chamber orchestra, Britten declined to conduct the full orchestra and chorus in the premiere. Instead Meredith Davies, who had been working with him at Aldeburgh, and was training the Coventry choirs, shouldered the

responsibility. By way of a compromise, Britten served as assistant conductor, directing the Melos Ensemble in the sections sung by Pears and Fischer-Dieskau.

'We'd rehearsed bits of the piece in Birmingham, but by the time we got to Coventry there were still bits that he either hadn't composed or hadn't had copied,' remembers Stan Smith. The orchestra read through the *Offertorium* for the first time only in the chaos of the incomplete cathedral. Understandably, rehearsals were fraught. The cathedral acoustic was, and is, intractable: 'It seemed to take up the sound and scramble it,' said Davies. Furthermore, the building was still barely finished. 'There was noise – lots of noise – of workmen and cleaners. Carpenters were beavering away,' says Maggie Cotton. 'During rehearsals everyone got used to seeing the composer flitting in and out between the musicians, tweaking mistakes in the complex parts, or slightly adjusting dynamics.' 'He could get a bit tetchy,' says Smith. 'He was working with the little orchestra, and he'd suddenly shout out, "Would you be quiet, please? We're trying to work!"'

And yet the performance made an impact whose echoes can be felt to the present day. 'I recall very clearly the stunned silence at the end,' said Meredith Davies (the programme book had asked the audience not to applaud). 'I looked at Ben and he looked at me and it seemed as if we were going to go on just looking at each other for

OPPOSITE *Coventry Cathedral, 29 May 1962: Benjamin Britten (right) confers with Meredith Davies during the general rehearsal for the world premiere of the War Requiem.*

ever and ever if I didn't put one foot in front of the other and just go off, which eventually I did.' Britten was initially dazed, but later appreciative of what he termed 'a rather wild performance'.

Posterity has judged for itself. Rignold gave notice in 1967 after sensing that the management committee was starting to feel another seven-year itch. They offered him a one-year, rather than a three-year, contract extension and he understandably enough 'took the huff', according to committee member Denis Martineau – but he agreed to see out the 1968–9 season. In the event, illness prevented that. But as 'Riggy' moved on and the CBSO approached its fiftieth anniversary, the orchestra had now, beyond any question, carved its name on musical history.

The New Wave

Louis Frémaux arrived in Birmingham in a flurry of excitement, and left nine years later in even more dramatic style. The 1969–70 season was the orchestra's fiftieth and it was planned as a celebration. The musical comedian and former RLPO flautist Fritz Spiegl (among many other accomplishments, the composer of the BBC Radio 4 UK *Theme*) opened the festivities with a concerto on his celebrated 'Loophonium' – a wind instrument constructed from a lavatory bowl. (Also known as the 'Harpic-cord', it's now in Liverpool's Walker Art Gallery.) A few days later Elisabeth Schwarzkopf sang Verdi and Puccini and comedian Dudley Moore played Mozart's Piano Concerto No. 21 with the orchestra, live on Birmingham's own independent TV station, ATV.

In the middle of all this, on 25 September 1969, Louis Frémaux gave his first concert: a sunburst of energy and light. The programme featured Ravel's second *Daphnis* suite; guitarist John Williams played concertos by Castelnuovo-Tedesco and Vivaldi, and Frémaux exuberantly proclaimed his allegiance to both sides of the Channel, with Britten's *The Young Person's Guide to the Orchestra* and the UK premiere of Henri Dutilleux's *Métaboles*. Kenneth Dommett, of the *Birmingham Post*, was suitably impressed: 'His control of the orchestra and the generous splashes of colour he employed were of a kind Birmingham has been in need of for some time.'

You can see that colour, and that energy, in Frémaux's photographs – the alert, birdlike features and his none-more-*chic* flower-power-era taste for polo necks and flyaway collars. Frémaux was forty-eight years old, but Birmingham had never handed control to a Frenchman before and everything about him seemed charismatic and invigorating, from his personal history, which included a wartime stint in the French Resistance and combat service in the Foreign Legion, to his podium manner. 'He stood very upright, with a straight back, very light on his feet – almost dancing – never crouching, but just leaning towards players or sections when needed,' says cellist David Russell. 'His beat was very clear and precise, and he used his hands and baton to convey this clarity and musicality.'

More to the point, he had an established reputation as a recording artist, and now that Rignold had got the CBSO back on disc, the orchestra's chairman Denis Martineau was determined to keep it there. Frémaux had made some thirty recordings with his previous orchestra in Monte Carlo, and Martineau was captivated by his flair. 'I knew we had to get the best man we possibly could, regardless of expense,' he told Beresford King-Smith, who recounted the conversation in *Crescendo!*:

> I felt that in Louis we had found a man who would build up the orchestra, he would build up our audience, especially with young people; he would attract recording companies; he would get us regular overseas trips and within two years he would be bringing in far more than any increase in salary was costing us.

Martineau wasn't wrong about the recordings. Between 1970 and 1978 Frémaux effectively laid the foundations of the CBSO's modern discography, making some sixteen LP recordings. They served as calling cards for the new precision and verve that Frémaux was drawing from the orchestra. 'Under Frémaux they combine a purity of intonation which metropolitan orchestras might envy with a fluid and spontaneous style of phrasing,' commented the critic Edward Greenfield of the *Guardian*, as early as 1972. The Birmingham audience didn't need to be told: average attendance at Town Hall concerts rose from 67 per cent in the 1968–9 season to 83 per cent in 1970–71, and from January 1973 a new supporters' magazine, *Music Stand*, reflected a growing confidence.

The received wisdom is that Louis Frémaux initiated a step change in the quality of the orchestra's playing. His standards were exacting:

he held pre-season sectional rehearsals, demanding the same commitment from his players as he had decided to give himself. At the end of his first three years in Birmingham he resigned his remaining post in France, at Lyons, in order to devote himself wholly to his British orchestra. 'I am not very interested in the travelling life of a guest conductor,' he told the critic Alan Blyth.

I like to work strongly with one orchestra at a time, and to be concerned with all aspects of developing it. Last season, I conducted nearly seventy concerts with the CBSO, although my contract is only for thirty. This season I'm undertaking almost as

many. You're not really involved with your orchestra if you don't do enough concerts with them.

There was a two-night (literally) flying tour to Holland in April 1970, and in May 1972 an ambitious tour of the Eastern Bloc that included Belgrade, Bucharest, Budapest, Bratislava and Košice. Still, there were limits even to Frémaux's capacity for work, and in 1970, with the diary filling up, Maurice Handford – a former member of the Hallé Orchestra, where he was known as 'the whispering horn-player' for his *pianissimo* playing – was appointed as staff conductor alongside the sixty-seven-year-old Harold Gray. His professionalism was exactly what was

Forward: in the 1970s, new landmarks like the Bull Ring Centre and the Rotunda came to symbolise the remaking of Birmingham as an ultra-modern motor city.

required to get the orchestra through out-of-town programmes on minimal rehearsal. 'He was very, very efficient,' remembers violinist Paul Smith. 'We did Elgar's *Falstaff* on a single three-hour rehearsal. Elgar's *Falstaff*! If he'd been a different character, Maurice could have really made the big time – he'd got a fantastic stick technique.'

But Frémaux's most spectacular initiative was the establishment, in the autumn of 1973, of the CBSO's own chorus. It was a product of the CBSO's and Frémaux's growing reputation as a recording team, and the need for a chorus over which they had complete artistic control. Major choral recording projects such as the Fauré and Berlioz *Requiems* now became practical. Success, in the right circumstances, breeds success, and in 1970 the City Council had started talking again about the new concert hall that it had promised to Adrian Boult back in the late 1920s. A site was identified – that of the decrepit Bingley Hall on Broad Street, an exhibition hall built in the Victorian era to host cattle and pigeon shows. The City of Birmingham Orchestral Endowment Fund commissioned Birmingham's leading modernist John Madin – the architect behind Birmingham's new Central Library and NatWest Tower – to design a hall.

The result, as it appears in Madin's striking preliminary designs, was one of the city's great architectural 'might have beens' – architecturally far superior to Symphony Hall, from the outside at least, though the acoustics (as London's near-contemporary Barbican would demonstrate at astronomical expense) would probably have been wretched. More immediately useful was the fact that by the 1975–6 season the prestige of the CBSO was such that the city's business community was finally starting to see the orchestra as a commercial asset. Imperial Metal Industries (IMI), the jewellers H. Samuel and local radio station BRMB signed up as the CBSO's first private sponsors.

It was one more proof that, in its sixth decade, the 'CB' of CBSO remained central to the orchestra's identity. Beresford King-Smith remembers how, on Thursday 21 November 1974, while Frémaux and the CBSO were halfway through Dvořák's Eighth Symphony in the newly double-glazed Town Hall, when 'a dull thud could be heard, followed a few minutes later by another which made the windows rattle, and then the sound of police sirens'. IRA bombs had exploded in two city-centre pubs, the Mulberry Bush, at the base of the Rotunda, and the Tavern in the Town on New Street.

The terror attack – at that time, the worst recorded in Great Britain – killed twenty-one people and injured 181 more. Eight days later, Frémaux, the CBSO and their new chorus were due to perform Fauré's *Requiem*. The future conductor Jonathan Nott was one of two boy sopranos in the performance, and Mike Cox, a chorus member, told King-Smith that in the circumstances it felt uniquely moving. On 12 January 1976 Frémaux and the orchestra gave a gala concert in aid of the Mayor's Fund for the bomb victims.

By now, Frémaux's identification with his orchestra and adopted city seemed complete – he'd even acquired a taste for fried breakfasts and Sunday roasts. 'When you start in England people are careful, but once they have accepted you, they are very true to you. If you are willing to give your whole heart and mind to this

LOUIS FRÉMAUX (1921–2017)

Only one CBSO principal conductor served in both the French Resistance and the French Foreign Legion; only one was decorated twice for gallantry, and only one was praised for his interpretations by Francis Poulenc and William Walton. Louis Frémaux studied at the conservatoire in Valenciennes and his musical career was interrupted three times by war. Avoiding deportation and forced labour during the Nazi occupation of France, he joined the Resistance; then fought in Algeria with the Foreign Legion before returning to the Paris Conservatoire as a conductor. He was recalled to the Legion to fight in Indochina before Prince Rainier of Monaco intervened to have him discharged from the military. By then he'd been awarded the Croix de Guerre on two separate occasions.

Rainier engaged Frémaux to head the orchestra of the Opéra de Monte-Carlo, where he made a series of acclaimed recordings. In 1969, he was awarded the Légion d'Honneur, and although Frémaux's recorded legacy focuses on French music, his interests embraced contemporary British music and the French baroque. His top choice on *Desert Island Discs* was Britten's *Les Illuminations* and he described the experience of performing it with Peter Pears as 'something I will never forget'. After leaving the CBSO in 1978 he directed the Sydney Symphony Orchestra before retiring in 2005 to the Loire valley with his second wife, the former CBSO cellist Cecily Hake. Although he conducted the National Youth Orchestra in Symphony Hall in 1995, he rebuffed all attempts at reconciliation from the CBSO.

country, everyone will respond to you in the same way – at least, that is what I have found in Birmingham,' he told Blyth. He had become particularly friendly with the CBSO's general manager Arthur Baker, even asking Baker to serve as his agent.

It's possible that Baker and the leader Felix Kok shielded Frémaux from the first signs of dissatisfaction in the orchestra. Baker, like any orchestra manager, aimed to keep the diary full and income regular. That was made easier by the City Council's decision in 1969 to cancel its regular programme of orchestral schools visits. The empty days needed to be filled, and Baker built a good relationship with the impresario Victor Hochhauser, who promoted inexpensive, mass-market concerts of popular classics at the Royal Albert Hall. (His one-time protégé Raymond Gubbay would later follow the same model.) The CBSO played nineteen such concerts in the 1969–70 season alone. What started as a welcome opportunity – regular London dates – became a treadmill.

Busy schedules also made for limited rehearsal – and that in turn led to repetitive programmes and a sense that the orchestra was on a near-permanent UK tour. Player morale started to wilt, even with Frémaux's signature works. 'We got sick and tired of doing *Daphnis, Young Person's Guide, Enigma Variations, The Planets*, over and over and over again,' remembers violinist and players' committee chair Paul Smith. And with good reason: Frémaux and the CBSO would perform Saint-Saëns' 'Organ' Symphony twenty-three times in public between 1972 and 1978.

It's quite fun once in a while but we did it absolutely everywhere, you know? And we only ever did one concert in Birmingham, on the Thursday. The rest of the time we were on the road. We were all over the place: Perth, Huddersfield, Halifax, Edinburgh, Bristol. We used to go to Cheltenham nine times a year.

Split dates, with the orchestra divided in two and dispatched to Sutton Coldfield and Kidderminster, could feel like a particular chore.

Shrewd managers – and perceptive conductors – sense dissatisfaction in an orchestra and move to allay it. Frémaux's personal devotion to Birmingham was beyond question, but he doesn't appear to have realised that Baker was becoming unpopular. Baker's top-down style of management – which had served the orchestra since Matthews' day, with variable results – felt increasingly at odds with the Birmingham of 1970s labour activism, of strikes at the Longbridge car plant and the 1972 mass picket at Saltley coke depot, where police had clashed with members of the National Union of Mineworkers just three miles from the Town Hall. Frémaux, recalls Paul Smith, 'had a little coterie . . . there was Felix, and Arthur Baker and whenever we went on tour there was that little four or five of them. We used to call them the royal party.'

Frémaux's decision to make Baker his personal agent provoked particular suspicion, although Frémaux sincerely believed that the arrangement was 'in the interest of the CBSO' and that Baker 'was never my agent in any real sense'. (Indeed, Frémaux's occasional overseas

Had it been built, John Madin's futuristic new concert hall would have occupied the same canalside location as Symphony Hall. This artist's impression imagines the view from Broad Street.

engagements continued to be handled by his French agent.) Office staff who worked closely with Baker, including King-Smith and the long-serving PA Rosemary Harby, testify to Baker's absolute integrity, but he could be an abrasive colleague, referring to the players, in their presence, as 'musical bricklayers'. 'He wasn't *sympathique*, as Louis would have said,' says Paul Smith. The suspicion grew that Baker was rejecting artistically rewarding work for the orchestra whenever Frémaux wasn't personally attached to it. Smith and his fellow members of the players' committee raised their concerns with the new chairman, George Jonas, and over two years compiled a scrapbook of evidence supporting their suspicions.

Eventually Frémaux started to sense the tension. A dispute between Frémaux and the players' committee over the seating of a

freelance viola-player during rehearsals for Tippett's *Ritual Dances* in February 1978 was one manifestation of a growing friction. 'Every time I went to the rostrum to start a rehearsal there was a member of the players' committee asking to make an announcement,' remembered Frémaux in a personal account, deposited in the CBSO archive and dated November 1989. 'In this atmosphere I could no longer capture the concentration of my orchestra to play well and I was sometimes anxious, disturbed and shaken by a sudden loss of ensemble during a concert.'

The next major project was an important one for the CBSO: a series of performances of the Britten *War Requiem* in early March ahead of a planned EMI recording in June. Illnesses in the orchestra led to another dispute over replacement personnel, and the players' committee made its move. On Thursday 9 March

1978 they called a players' meeting and passed a motion of no confidence in Baker. The following day, in a routine management meeting at the Town Hall, the players told Jonas of the vote and handed over their scrapbook.

Rosemary Harby escorted Baker to that meeting.

> Arthur and I were asked to leave the room. On our return the vote of no confidence was read. He was mortified. He kept saying to me, 'Why have they done this? What have I done wrong?' The man was full of shock and disbelief. We walked back to the office in Newhall Street and that's all he kept saying: 'Why have they done this?'

Baker rang Frémaux the same evening with the news – 'in broken voice', recalled Frémaux. The players had effectively ousted their general manager (he formally resigned on 16 March), but they had severely underestimated Frémaux's personal loyalty to Baker. He seems to have viewed it as a matter of honour. On Sunday 12 March, Frémaux wrote to Jonas demanding to be released from his contract; Jonas responded the following week by warning Frémaux that he would never again work with a UK orchestra. That seems to have been decisive. 'My feelings were sadness and anguish; to see such a mess and so weak a management committee let the situation deteriorate to this point,' writes Frémaux.

> Felix Kok had to stay and work 90 per cent of the job, Arthur Baker had to resign, I was expected to stay. Was he [Jonas] completely in the power of the orchestra? The meeting ended very bitterly and he suggested I should find a good lawyer.

There followed, according to Frémaux:

> letters, press reports, comments, statements, lies, omissions, deformations, insinuations, intimidations, all of that to save the pride of whoever was committed to the CBSO except one punished, Felix, one victim, Arthur Baker, and one scapegoat, myself.

The players' coup against Baker was escalating beyond their control: the CBSO had now lost both a general manager and a chief conductor in the course of a weekend. Outrage (Paul Smith recalls his advice to Jonas as 'sue the bugger!') gave way to concern. 'We wrote a letter, which I took round personally to Louis' flat in Moseley, explaining the fact that none of this was personal to Louis,' says Smith. 'We were more than happy for him to stay on. But he wasn't having any of it and we never saw him again.' Frémaux's estrangement from the orchestra became permanent. After Baker died suddenly of a heart attack at the age of sixty-two in 1988, Frémaux was in no doubt about where the blame lay: 'His unfair dismissal wounded him cruelly, never letting him recover, and was the reason for his premature death.'

OPPOSITE *A Frenchman, Louis Frémaux fought in the anti-Nazi resistance during World War Two and later saw action with the Foreign Legion. But the CBSO players' committee proved to be the final straw.*

ERICH SCHMID (1907–2000)

The conductor and composer Erich Schmid was born in Balsthal, Switzerland, and made a name for himself before the Second World War as one of the most progressive figures in Swiss music – first as an avant-garde composer (he studied with Schoenberg in Berlin in 1930 and 1931, and won the admiration of Theodor Adorno before having his music banned by the Nazis for 'cultural Bolshevism'), and later as the chief conductor of the Zurich Tönhalle Orchestra from 1949 to 1957.

In Birmingham, the sense of tradition that he brought to his May 1978 Beethoven cycle thrilled audience and orchestra alike. 'He had convictions, but didn't shout them at you,' remembers violinist David Gregory. 'He was there just for the music.' In September 1979, in recognition of his special bond with the orchestra, Schmid was appointed as the CBSO's first principal guest conductor, a post he held until April 1982. It was a close and satisfying relationship: Schmid stayed in touch with his Birmingham colleagues for the rest of his life.

Subsequent CBSO principal guest conductors have included Neeme Järvi and (in the late 1990s) his son Paavo, Okko Kamu, Sir Mark Elder, Edward Gardner, and most recently (from 2018) Kazuki Yamada. They have generally been chosen to represent a tradition or an area of repertoire that has complemented the principal conductor's musical interests. So for much of Sakari Oramo's tenure there was no principal guest – Oramo's own musical interests being so wide-ranging that there didn't seem much point in having one.

Frémaux's shock departure had numerous consequences. Immediately, there was an embarrassing media storm, including reports – some utterly fanciful, some suspiciously accurate – in *Private Eye*. Administratively, the cumbersome archaic structure of committee of management and council of management was quickly reformed. The CBSO had not become a player-run orchestra, as some claimed, but from now on two elected members of the orchestra would form part of the organisation's governing body, with full voting rights. Meanwhile, Baker, with impressive loyalty, stayed on for a brief period to help clean up the splatter from his own assassination – booking the veteran Swiss conductor Erich Schmid to take over Frémaux's planned Beethoven Festival that May.

Schmid proved to be an inspiration: Paul Smith recalls that he 'did a wonderful job' of restoring the orchestra's focus on music-making. The Ninth Symphony was cathartic for players and audience alike – according to the *Birmingham Mail*, 'The audience stood, cheered and applauded through the most emotional demonstration I have ever seen in this hall.' Forty years on, violinist Sheila Clarke is still unable to recall that performance without emotion:

> We'd all been dreading the Beethoven cycle with Frémaux because his Beethoven was absolutely awful – nothing to do with German classical style. And then this amazing musician had come in, out of retirement, and saved the day. He was just wonderful. Sheer music came from him.

The whole mess made the CBSO think hard about what it had become and where it wanted to go. Orchestras have long, if selective, memories. The events of March 1978 (sometimes luridly distorted) became first gossip, and then orchestral folklore. Thirty years later, some veteran players still refused to forgive Frémaux. A quieter group favoured a reconciliation. It was all pointless: for the rest of his life Frémaux rejected all olive branches, though a handful of personal friends from within the orchestra stayed in touch.

Looking back, while it is impossible not to regret the manner of Frémaux's departure, it is difficult to regret its consequences – just as it is wrong to overlook the fact that Frémaux had rejuvenated the orchestra, created the Chorus, and left a recorded legacy that still sparkles with energy and charisma. Baker's place was filled in autumn 1978 by Edward Smith – a young manager from the Royal Liverpool Philharmonic Orchestra, with new ideas and a genuine readiness to collaborate with, rather than simply command, his musicians. 'Total breath of fresh air', was Paul Smith's assessment.

Ed Smith had some interesting new contacts too, among them a young conductor whom he'd discovered playing percussion in the Merseyside Youth Orchestra, and who conducted the CBSO in the Town Hall for the first time on 14 December 1978. That conductor's first impression of the orchestra is still the definitive tribute to Louis Frémaux's achievement in Birmingham. The CBSO, in 1978, was 'possibly the best French orchestra in the world' – in the opinion of the twenty-four-year-old Simon Rattle.

THE CBSO AT THE OPERA

Birmingham is one of the largest cities in Europe without a permanent opera house, and it's often fallen to the city orchestra to make up the deficiency. Initially, it was just a matter of taking lucrative bookings: in Bristol, in 1926, the CBO played in the pit for *Così fan tutte*, *Dido and Aeneas* and Ethel Smyth's *Entente Cordiale*.

A 'Grand Opera Week' in the Prince of Wales Theatre in May 1932 saw the orchestra get through *Madama Butterfly*, *Faust*, *Cavalleria rusticana* and *Pagliacci*, and *Tosca* (conducted by John Barbirolli) in the space of five days. In the 1950s the CBSO was regularly hired as a touring orchestra by Welsh National Opera. *La traviata*, *Rigoletto*, *Nabucco* and *Die Fledermaus* all featured; *Carmen* and *Boris Godunov* entered the repertoire in the 1960s.

Simon Rattle began a tradition of regular concert performances of opera, conducting Mozart, Gershwin, and Szymanowski's *King Roger*, and taking Janáček's *Jenůfa* and *Makropoulos Case* on tour to France. Sakari Oramo conducted *Tosca*, *Peter Grimes* and (delightfully) *Iolanthe*; Andris Nelsons built a Birmingham Wagner tradition with performances of *Lohengrin*, *Der fliegende Holländer*, *Tristan und Isolde* and *Parsifal*, as well as Strauss's *Der Rosenkavalier*, while Mirga Gražinytė-Tyla has already tackled *Idomeneo* and Debussy's *Pelléas et Mélisande*.

But perhaps the CBSO's most significant operatic collaborations have been on productions by Graham Vick's Birmingham Opera Company. Vick's radical, site-specific re-imaginings of *La traviata* (2007), *Khovanshchina* (2014), Tippett's *The Ice Break* (2015) and Shostakovich's *Lady Macbeth of Mtsensk* (2019) all drew international acclaim.

Chrystal E. Williams sings the title role in Birmingham Opera Company's Lady Macbeth of Mtsensk, *staged in the derelict Tower Ballroom, Edgbaston in March 2019. Alpesh Chauhan conducted.*

VOICES OF THE CITY

E dward Elgar was aware that he didn't need to go into much detail. As he addressed the assembled dignitaries at the University of Birmingham on 29 November 1905, he knew that everyone present would have taken, as a matter of established fact, Birmingham's status as a centre of choral singing – and the unique position that amateur choral music held in the musical life of the nation:

> Our chorus singers have long been our great insular wonder and pride: and so much has been said on the choral work of this country that it will be immaterial for me to go into detail. In the last few years we have had choruses trained – perhaps over-trained in some instances – to a perfection of finish and attack never before attempted.

His listeners only had to look around them for evidence. Many of the crowd would themselves have been participants in (and certainly audience members at) the Triennial Festival's great choral performances. In the years between Triennial Festivals the Birmingham Festival Choral Society (founded in 1843) maintained a local core of highly trained amateur singers, giving concerts in its own right and ready to be supplemented by singers from around the country when Festival years came around.

By the late nineteenth century at least a half-dozen further choral societies were also active in the city. Birmingham's first orchestras were assembled from scratch to serve the needs of the choral community. But with the dissolution of the Triennial Festival after the First World War, and the founding of the CBO, there seems to have been genuine anxiety over the continuance of choral music in Birmingham. The Festival Choral Society continued to prepare for a festival that was never to return. It gives concerts to this day, laying claim to the inheritance of the Triennial Festivals as one of Birmingham's longest-surviving secular musical institutions.

In 1921, the founders of the new City of Birmingham Choir chose instead to follow the city's motto and look forward. Its founding objectives – as its historian W. G. A. Russell put it in 1946 – were 'to specialise in the performance of unaccompanied choral works, and to collaborate with the then new City of Birmingham Orchestra'. 'The association with the City Orchestra has been well maintained,' Russell added – as well it might be, with Granville Bantock as the choir's founding president, and a list of musical directors that would grow to include Appleby Matthews, Meredith Davies and the eminent chorus trainers David Willcocks and Christopher Robinson. With the orchestra in regular demand across the Midlands as an accompanist for choral societies, the close but informal relationship with the City of Birmingham Choir effectively provided all the choral support that the CBSO required for its first half-century. So Louis Frémaux's decision, in 1973, to found a brand new symphonic chorus, managed by and devoted entirely to the CBSO, initially looked like a snub.

'I think it was essentially about artistic control,' says Philip Rawle, the CBSO Chorus's archivist, and a founder member of the Chorus.

Simon Halsey (then 24) and Simon Rattle (28) brief the CBSO Chorus in the Great Hall of Birmingham University prior to recording Britten's War Requiem, February 1983.

To thrive, any amateur choir has to satisfy its members, and under Christopher Robinson, the City of Birmingham Choir's artistic ambitions extended far beyond providing a line of women to 'ooh' and 'aah' for five minutes at the end of *The Planets*, or sitting through the three wordless movements of Beethoven's Ninth. Frémaux had his own choral agenda, and he asserted his artistic control from the very first auditions, in September 1973.

Frémaux had appointed as chorus master the baritone Gordon Clinton, principal of the Birmingham School of Music. They both knew

what they wanted. 'Standards will be high – they must be,' said Frémaux to the *Birmingham Post*. The upper age limit was set at forty-five. 'We looked for good voices that would blend to a texture we had in our imagination,' Clinton explained in *Music Stand*. 'The voices must then belong to people who had personality, projection and musical appreciation.' But with Clinton and Frémaux personally supervising all 250 initial auditions, the impression they made on aspiring singers was formidable. 'Nerve shattering!' was how one tenor, Terry Bailey, later remembered it:

There was a panel for the audition including Frémaux and Clinton. Scales/arpeggios and sight-singing a chorale – in German! Ruth Gerald the accompanist played very sensitively and most reassuringly, especially as we were asked to prepare an aria. Thank goodness for the *Messiah*!

The 120 successful applicants met for the first time at Birmingham School of Music on 3 October 1973. 'We knew, as a chorus, that he'd chosen us individually; there was always that edge of excitement,' remembers alto Elaine Russell. 'Louis arrived and thanked us all "for the gift of your beautiful voices",' recalls another founder member, alto Joan Boothroyd. 'We were all handed a copy of a Bach chorale [Clinton had chosen the final chorale of Bach's *St John Passion*] and we opened our mouths. Out came an incredibly beautiful choral sound. It was an amazing moment.'

'It was very fresh and new. It was Louis' baby, he'd pushed for it, and he wanted it to be the best it could – he wanted a clear, young sound,' says Elaine Russell. The full extent of Frémaux's ambition for his new choir wasn't long in revealing itself. The CBSO Chorus sang for the first time in public on 31 January 1974, in a performance of Berlioz's *La damnation de Faust*; the following night they repeated it in the Royal Festival Hall in London. The programme opened with Britten's muted arrangement of the National Anthem. 'All Birmingham's musical world was waiting to hear what sound we made,' remembered Boothroyd. There was a spontaneous burst of applause at the end of the Anthem.

The triumph seems to have come as a shock to some members – around thirty singers resigned before the next project, a Gilbert and Sullivan night with Harold Gray in April. John Falding, of the *Birmingham Post*, blamed the 'anticlimactic' choice of repertoire for that second concert, and the CBSO's general manager Arthur Baker conceded that it might have been a mistake ('though not a very serious one'). 'There can now be no doubt that the members want to be worked hard, and need to be treated as the professionals they can sound like,' concluded Falding.

He made a vital point. Relatively few of the City Choir's members had crossed over to the new CBSO Chorus, and in fact, with its low age limit, the CBSO Chorus had recruited an ensemble without any of the retirees who form the backbone of amateur music-making. The CBSO Chorus had demanded a serious and intensive commitment from members who already had busy lives – all in the service of the orchestra's artistic agenda. In return, it had promised ambitious, exciting music-making at the highest professional level.

The bargain works both ways, and that unspoken contract would become the basis of the CBSO Chorus's ethos. The upper age limit has long since been lifted (although strict re-auditioning rules apply to all members). But although the Chorus's members have included teachers, lawyers, doctors, writers, vicars, architects, dancers and at least one former US beauty pageant queen, the word 'amateur' has been abolished. The CBSO Chorus's members are treated, and expected to perform (in Simon Halsey's phrase), as 'unpaid professionals'. The results could be heard as early as April 1975, and the Chorus's first major recording: Berlioz's *Grande Messe des morts*, taped in one of the few spaces in Birmingham then realistically capable of containing such a colossal work, the Great Hall of Birmingham University.

Elaine Russell recalls the *Grande Messe* sessions as 'awe-inspiring', and for Louis Frémaux it was a manifesto of his ambitions for Birmingham, embodied in the pairing of orchestra and chorus: nothing less than a re-assertion of Birmingham's place in the musical world. 'We were not afraid at that time to perform and offer to record one of the most spectacular pieces of the repertoire,' he said, in 1989. 'It symbolises the scale of our ambition in spite of the small possibilities of our provincial place.' In June 1975, an ailing Benjamin Britten leapt from his seat at the Aldeburgh Festival with a yell of 'Bravo!', as Frémaux, the orchestra and chorus whirled to the end of Ravel's *Daphnis et Chloé*. Two weeks later a Chorus cricket team beat the orchestra's XI by nineteen runs at the BBC's Pebble Mill sports ground.

By then, artistic wickets were tumbling with increasing regularity to the new Chorus. Frémaux's recording of Fauré's *Requiem* (December 1977), said *Gramophone*, 'emphasises the devout quietness of the piece'. Meanwhile, the Chorus was slipping into another crucial part of its ongoing role, in CBSO performances of Holst's *The Planets*, Debussy's *Nocturnes*, Beethoven's Ninth Symphony and Mahler's Second and Third Symphonies (both encountered for the first time under Frémaux in 1975). In time, the Chorus would learn to sing most of them from memory.

These orchestral staples – each containing just too little choral music to be worth the time of a conventional choral society – remain part of the CBSO Chorus's *raison d'être*, and a major part of its difference from other amateur choirs. 'Put it this way,' says founder member Philip Rawle. 'We've almost never had to sing the *Messiah*.' The Chorus's first Christmas carol concert with the orchestra, on 18 December 1975, launched another annual tradition: guest presenters have included Johnny Morris, Humphrey Lyttelton, Juliet Stevenson, Alan Titchmarsh and Simon Callow.

Gordon Clinton had been sixty-two when he launched the new choir. In September 1979, after five years of concerts and in declining health, he retired, handing his creation over to Richard Greening, a composer and former organist of Lichfield Cathedral. Greening died of a heart attack after his second rehearsal with the choir, aged only fifty-one. Clinton immediately stepped back up until Nicholas Cleobury took over in July 1980 – in time for the Chorus's first concert with the twenty-five-year-old Simon Rattle: Szymanowski's *Stabat Mater* and Mahler's 'Resurrection' Symphony, at Leeds Town Hall on 20 September 1980.

Singing to the World

The new artistic direction was evident from the outset. Rattle's two concert performances of Gershwin's *Porgy and Bess* in August 1981 weren't the Chorus's first full-length opera (they'd done *The Mikado* in 1978), but they were certainly the most ambitious – although for a chorus that had recorded Janáček's *Glagolitic Mass* that January, it seemed refreshingly straightforward: at least there was no need of the language coach who'd been hired to bring their Old Church Slavonic up to scratch. Berlioz's *Béatrice et Bénédict* came in the summer of 1982, by which time Cleobury had decided to focus on orchestral conducting. It was simply coincidence, however, that on the night the Chorus was told of his resignation, their weekly rehearsal had been taken for the first time by Simon Halsey, the twenty-three-year-old director of music at the University of Warwick.

'One day in September 1982 I got a call from Beresford King-Smith saying, "Could you come and take one rehearsal?"' Halsey recalls.

> And I went to take one rehearsal, at Carrs Lane Church. I had a lovely time, and I was heartbroken because Nicholas had only just taken the job. I wanted to work with a symphony chorus, and the only one in the Midlands had just gone to a man of twenty-seven. And at the end of the rehearsal, Beresford came and said, 'I'm terribly sorry, ladies and gentlemen, I've got to tell you that Nicholas will be leaving us.' And I thought, 'Yes!' – but I couldn't show it!

> And I can clearly remember on 5 November – this is such a significant thing for me – I was sitting in my office at Warwick, when Ed Smith rang me, and said, 'We are minded to offer you the job of chorus master.' I was so excited that I ran in a circle around the whole campus of the university, trying to get the excitement out of my system. I began on 1 January 1983,

and the first thing we did was to record the Britten *War Requiem* in Birmingham University's Great Hall.

Simon Halsey has continued to direct the CBSO Chorus to this day – a four-decade record of service unmatched by any of the CBSO's principal or staff conductors apart from Harold Gray. His appointment wasn't entirely a foregone conclusion – the baritone Brian Rayner Cook was also under serious consideration. But Rattle had been aware for some time of Halsey's work at Warwick; he'd endorsed his appointment there, and clearly recognised an artist who shared his own ambition and energy. Mutual respect was tempered with honesty, most decisively when Rattle saw that Halsey was starting to nurture orchestral ambitions. Halsey has never forgotten one particular exchange.

> When I was twenty-five, Rattle, twenty-eight years old himself, took me aside and said, 'Look, this is not going be an easy conversation, but why don't you try to be the best chorus master of your generation and forget being an orchestral conductor? Because the world has too many second-rate orchestral conductors, and every generation only has one or two legendary chorus masters.' It was a good conversation. I had a very bad night, and then woke up the next morning feeling like the whole world had been lifted off my shoulders, and I could finally be who I actually was. It was one of the most liberating and extraordinary experiences of my life.

The CBSO Chorus draws 'unpaid professional' singers from the whole spectrum of Birmingham life – members have included doctors, teachers, parliamentary candidates and at least one beauty pageant queen.

Within a year of Halsey's appointment the Chorus had undertaken its first overseas trip – sending a semi-chorus to Dusseldorf in October 1983 to sing *The Dream of Gerontius* under Sir Charles Groves. Under Halsey and Rattle, a large, highly drilled and responsive chorus was central to increasingly ambitious plans: whether the *Gramophone*-award-winning 1986 recording of Mahler's 'Resurrection' Symphony, the UK premiere of John Adams' *Harmonium* in 1987, or a tour of the west coast of the USA, performing Beethoven's Ninth with the San Francisco Symphony. A July 1990 tour of Spain, along with the orchestra, found

the Chorus singing Beethoven's Ninth under a full moon at the Alhambra in Granada. 'That performance was magic from beginning to end,' remembered alto Lesley Nickell in 1995. 'Even the trombone section said so.' Naturally, the Chorus participated in the CBSO's final regular concert in the spiritual home of the Birmingham choral tradition, Birmingham Town Hall, with a performance of Beethoven's *Missa solemnis* on 15 May 1991.

It had already sung in the official opening concert of Symphony Hall on 15 April 1991 – Ravel's *Daphnis et Chloé*, followed by Mahler's 'Resurrection' Symphony on 12 June. Later that year, the eighty-seven-year-old Sir Michael Tippett conducted choir and orchestra in a recording of *A Child of Our Time*: Chorus members relate that his beat was so unclear that the orchestra's leader, Peter Thomas, discreetly directed the performance instead. Meanwhile, for the Chorus, as for the orchestra, the superb new hall offered both an opportunity and a serious challenge. 'We had to get bigger to go into Symphony Hall,' says Halsey.

> In the Town Hall we could put 110 singers on stage from a membership of 120. Basically everyone did every concert, and there were only six concerts a year. And then Simon wanted more and more, and we had to have more and more singers, because we were doing Szymanowski, Janáček and Stravinsky, and all that sort of thing. It hardly looks revolutionary now, but then he'd come to me and say, 'Can we do *The Raft of the Medusa* by Henze?' We had to up our game with language coaching and recruitment. Suddenly we had to have 180 people to put 130 on the stage. The nature of the choir changed.

The transformation wasn't just reflected in repertoire, although the works that the Chorus tackled during Rattle's ten-year *Towards the Millennium* festival – Schoenberg's *Gurrelieder*, Martinů's *The Epic of Gilgamesh*, Szymanowski's *King Roger* – show how far it had travelled. There was a growing appreciation that this was a world-class ensemble in its own right: a fitting partner for an orchestra whose international standing had never been higher. 'The relationship with the

orchestra has definitely changed,' commented founder member Jenny Mason as the Chorus celebrated its twenty-first anniversary in 1995.

> They were at first suspicious and a bit resentful of the 'amateurs' who were muscling in on their concerts and growing reputation. Now I think we've proved ourselves able to keep up with them whatever they've thrown at us, and we're accepted and even welcomed as part of the team.

In 1998 Sakari Oramo inherited a choral ensemble at the peak of its form; supported by newly formed youth choruses and capable of rising to such new challenges as Sibelius' *Kullervo* (April 1999) Britten's *Peter Grimes* (March 2001), and Oramo's growing passion for the English (read Birmingham) choral tradition. A centenary performance of *The Dream of Gerontius* in Symphony Hall on 3 October 2000, with Anne Sofie von Otter as the Angel, felt like a belated act of atonement for that unhappy Birmingham premiere a hundred years earlier, and the moment at which *Gerontius* joined Britten's *War Requiem* and Mahler's Second as one of the CBSC's (as the Chorus was known between 1995 and 2009) house specialities.

Between 2000 and 2006 Oramo, the CBSO and its Chorus would sing their way through centenary performances of all Elgar's Triennial

OVERLEAF *On 30 May 2012 – the fiftieth anniversary of the premiere of Britten's* War Requiem *– Andris Nelsons conducts the CBSO and CBSO Chorus in Coventry Cathedral. The performance was televised internationally.*

SIMON HALSEY CBE

Simon Halsey grew up to the sound of choral music. Educated initially at New College School, Oxford, Simon won choral scholarships first to Winchester College, and then to King's College, Cambridge. His father, the choral conductor Louis Halsey, worked closely with Benjamin Britten. Even before he left school Simon had met Stravinsky and Britten, and witnessed innumerable choral premieres.

His first job was with Scottish Opera, collaborating with the young director Graham Vick on innovative community projects. ('No one in Port Glasgow knew I had this stupid posh accent – I was just English as far as they were concerned,' he remembers.) In 1987, inspired by the same ideals of accessibility, Vick and Halsey founded City of Birmingham Touring Opera (now Birmingham Opera Company). Meanwhile, in 1980 Halsey

had been appointed director of music at the University of Warwick: partly on the recommendation of Simon Rattle, whose sole reservation was that the twenty-two-year-old Halsey might be 'a bit young'. (Rattle was twenty-five.)

In 1983 he took charge of the CBSO Chorus. From 1997 to 2008 he was chief conductor of the Netherlands Radio Choir; from 2001 to 2015 the artistic director of the Rundfunkchor Berlin, and since 2012, ahead of Rattle's appointment as the LSO's music director, he's been chorus director of the London Symphony Chorus. But he continues to live in Warwick and to base his work around the West Midlands – where, as well as directing an ambitious choral programme at the University of Birmingham, he's approaching his fortieth year with the CBSO Chorus.

Festival oratorios, culminating in Elgar's 150th birthday in June 2007, and performances of *Gerontius*, *The Apostles* and *The Kingdom* over one weekend. In September 2002 the CBSO and Chorus had returned to Coventry Cathedral for the fortieth anniversary performance of Britten's *War Requiem*. The Coventry acoustic proved as unmanageable now as it had then; abandoning historical accuracy, this and subsequent performances have compromised by utilising the opposite end of the nave from the original 1962 performance.

'Oramo was clearly a great musician, but he knew he didn't know how to conduct a choir,' remembers Halsey.

> So, rather sweetly, he would come to chorus rehearsals initially and I would co-take rehearsals with him. He very quickly got the hang of it, and now I would put him in the top two or three of chorus conductors in the world. By which, I don't mean a conductor that conducts choruses. I mean a choir trainer: with an instinctive understanding of how to get colours out of voices. It's extraordinary. And he learned this all with the CBSO Chorus.

But this was, by now, a chorus with a major international reputation – in demand far beyond Birmingham, independently of the orchestra. The BBC Philharmonic Orchestra, in Manchester, does not have its own chorus, so starting with a 1999 recording of music by Lili Boulanger, it has cultivated a long-term relationship with the CBSO Chorus. In 2002 Rattle flew the Chorus

'Every choir has to be reborn all the time, and this could be the beginning of another golden period'

out to Austria to record Beethoven's Ninth with the Vienna Philharmonic, and the Chorus joined other massed choirs to sing Mahler's Eighth Symphony at the opening not just of the 2000 Sydney Olympic Games but also the 2002 Commonwealth Games in Manchester. In 2008, and 2010, the Chorus flew to Kuala Lumpur to sing with the Malaysian Philharmonic Orchestra – Vaughan Williams' *A Sea Symphony* and Berlioz's *La damnation de Faust*. The Chorus has sung in Finland, Hong Kong, Israel, Canada and Mexico.

In each case, the logistical commitment boggles the imagination. Since 1993, with the appointment of Justin Lee, the Chorus has had its own dedicated full-time manager and assistant manager. In addition to Halsey, the musical staff has expanded to include an associate chorus director, Julian Wilkins – who is also conductor of the CBSO Youth Chorus – an associate conductor, David Lawrence, and a designated vocal coach, Alison Chamberlain. A members' committee assists the management with everything from serving rehearsal refreshments at CBSO Centre to planning social events. But Chorus members remain unpaid; most have day jobs, and with tours as well as the regular schedule of rehearsals and Birmingham concerts, membership makes serious demands on members' personal time.

In return – well, the original deal holds good. The members' commitment has been rewarded with the opportunity to sing under Andris Nelsons in Wagner's *Lohengrin* (2010) *Tristan und Isolde* (2012), *Der fliegender Hollander* (2013) and *Parsifal* (2015), as well as 2012's fiftieth-anniversary performance of Britten's *War Requiem* – and diving even further back into Birmingham's musical history, to record Mendelssohn's *Lobgesang* with Edward Gardner in Birmingham Town Hall. Not to mention, in 2013, a celebration of the music of Bollywood legend A. R. Rahman.

The CBSO Chorus, in other words, is not, and never has been, a conventional choral society, and if it was created to complement the orchestra, the two ensembles are now unarguably on an equal footing. The Chorus gave its 900th performance on 17 February 2018 – a performance of Orff's *Carmina Burana* under Michael Seal. Two months later it was singing Lili Boulanger under Mirga Gražinytė-Tyla, and a few weeks after that, the women were en route to the BBC Proms, where Andris Nelsons and his visiting Boston Symphony Orchestra had stipulated that if they were to perform Mahler's Third Symphony, no other British choir would do. Gražinytė-Tyla's relationship with the Chorus has so far been wholly distinctive: Haydn's *The Creation,* Mozart's *Idomeneo*, and in November 2018 the UK premiere of Roxanna Panufnik's specially commissioned *Faithful Journey*.

'With Mirga's feet under the table, we're ready for another rebirth. Every choir has to be reborn all the time, and this could be the beginning of another golden period,' says Simon Halsey. Whatever her artistic plans, the CBSO Chorus is there at her disposal; a chorus of international stature, ready to serve the orchestra and the city as Birmingham's choral tradition moves forward into its fourth century.

8

Ten Pieces from a Revolution

1. Boulez: Rituel in memoriam Bruno Maderna

At first glance, Boulez's *Rituel* looks less like a piece for the rebirth of an orchestra than an act of deconstruction. The individual sections are broken up, and reassembled on stage in eight completely new groupings, carefully positioned. A gong chimes once, and what, to an unfamiliar or hostile ear, sounds disorderly, even chaotic, slowly begins to assemble itself into a musical structure of extraordinary refinement and emotional power.

The *Rituel* wasn't exactly the first thing that Town Hall audiences heard under Simon Rattle's artistic leadership: that had been Janáček's *Sinfonietta*, on 18 September 1980 – a suitably optimistic flourish for a new beginning and the CBSO's sixtieth anniversary season. But five days later, on 23 September, coming immediately before only the CBSO's third performance of Mahler's *Resurrection* Symphony, it was a bold first indication of the road that Rattle intended to travel with his new orchestra.

Boulez had given the world premiere with the BBC Symphony Orchestra in 1975; since then the piece had gone completely unperformed in the UK. It wasn't only the CBSO that had never played a note of Boulez. 'Composers like Boulez, Berio, Lutosławski, were basically unplayed by the British orchestras apart from the BBC Symphony,' says Rattle. 'What I would consider the great living European composers – most of the British orchestras simply did not feel that this was their remit.' In his second week on the job, the CBSO's new principal conductor was already thinking in international terms.

In hindsight, the audacity looks breathtaking. In fact, like much of what was to follow over the next two decades, it was the work of clear heads building on sound principles. Rattle had conducted the CBSO for the first time in Oxford in 1976. Ed Smith, who had managed the Merseyside Youth Orchestra when the teenage Rattle's potential first became clear, managed to get Rattle and the CBSO in front of a Birmingham audience (with Nielsen's 'Inextinguishable' Symphony) in December 1978. The events of that spring had effectively revolutionised the CBSO's management culture: the players, it was understood, henceforth had a say in the organisation's artistic direction. Smith respected that. Nonetheless, he was pleasantly surprised when the players organised a vote and requested that the vacant conductor position be offered to Rattle.

'Now, had they said, "No, we think we should wait a bit longer, we should see X, Y or Z, or Okko Kamu's coming in three weeks' time", I don't know what would have happened,' recalls Smith. 'But they felt they were the guiding light for the whole United Kingdom orchestral scene. Once the dust had settled from Frémaux's departure I think they thought, "We've got our man in – Smith – as our general manager, we've flexed our muscles. The Board has listened to us. So now we need a new music director, and Rattle is exceptional.' Rattle, for his part, was thrilled to be courted. 'I've never done this before or since, or even put my name forward to a job, but when Ed Smith – who I'd known since I was in my mid-teens – became manager, I did say to him, "Look, if you ever wanted to work together, I would be with you like a shot."'

The official announcement was to be on 2 July 1979, but it was scooped by the *Birmingham Post* on 22 June: 'New conductor heralds CBSO harmony' was the headline. Rattle was scheduled to start from the 1980–81 season, but he already had a keen sense of an orchestra that was eager to work.

This was an orchestra which knew it was in trouble because of the chaos around Louis' departure. They realised that having endless guest conductors was fascinating, but that they weren't doing the basic dental hygiene of being an orchestra. They were absolutely determined not only to keep themselves afloat, but to get better and better. And as a very young conductor, I was given the chance to create what their playing style would be. I don't know whether an orchestra which was more in their own groove would have put up with a young conductor asking so many things, some of them good and some of them ridiculous. But basically it felt like they were up for anything.

It was very clear from the beginning: they wanted to know, are we going to play this on or off the string? How are we going to hold notes, how are we going to tune chords? Well, I didn't always quite know what I was asking. And some things I was asking for were kind of impossible. We all grew up with this process, together.

Apart from being a powerful declaration of artistic intent, *Rituel* was a starting point for a longer-term process. With the orchestra dismantled into Boulez's eight sub-ensembles, Rattle got to know and work with individual players outside their usual orchestral context. Sectional rehearsals would become a central component of Rattle's artistic process: it was like stripping down and cleaning an engine. Now it was time to put it back together and see how well it could perform. 'What was clear was that they were not settled at all, but were extremely ambitious,' remembers Rattle. 'There was no ceiling placed on what was possible.'

2. Sibelius: Symphony No. 7

Early rumours of Rattle's plans – and pieces like the Boulez – disconcerted some audience members. Ed Smith wrote to the *Birmingham Post* to allay their concerns:

> Please don't imagine that Mozart, Beethoven, Brahms and Tchaikovsky are about to disappear from CBSO programmes . . . What I am afraid we sometimes tend to forget is that the twentieth century is now eighty years old and its composers include Mahler, Sibelius, Elgar, Ravel, Rachmaninoff and Stravinsky.

In fact, Rattle drew support and encouragement from a deep well of Birmingham tradition – from the principal guest conductor Erich Schmid ('the great saviour after Louis left') and from Rudolf Schwarz: 'Really central for me – he could tell me what it was like playing under Strauss or Toscanini. Just extraordinary

stories.' And from the nonagenarian Sir Adrian Boult – who had conducted the CBSO for what would be the last time in September 1977, aged eighty-eight, and now encouraged Rattle, as he had encouraged Heward and Schwarz decades before.

Town Hall audiences grew as word of Rattle's galvanising effect started to spread: average sales were 90 per cent in the 1980–81 season, and 96 per cent by the end of the 1984–5 season. Innovations such as Janáček's *Glagolitic Mass*, Gershwin's *Porgy and Bess*, Weill's *Seven Deadly Sins*, a string of early Britten rarities and Messiaen's *Turangalîla-Symphonie* make for striking-looking programmes even today. (Only H. K. Gruber's *Frankenstein!!* really backfired – perhaps not an ideal choice for a Last Night of the CBSO Proms. 'The audience just sat there bewildered,' remembers Ed Smith.) The 1981 BBC Proms responded by inviting the CBSO twice in one season – unprecedented at the time. Rattle was empowered to take risks by Smith: together with Smith's supremely capable PA Rosemary Harby, they formed an unbreakable, mutually supportive team. Simon Halsey saw them in action shortly after joining in 1983:

> Simon and Ed were an extraordinary, powerful combination. Ed would chair meetings in which he'd be entirely silent, and let everyone make a fool of themselves, speak too much, and so on.

OPPOSITE **Conducted Beautifully, Simon's Orchestra:** *summer 1982, and the Birmingham public gets into the spirit of the annual CBSO Proms. Home-made banners with topical acronyms were a Proms tradition.*

And then Simon would give two passionate sentences about how we should do it – everyone would realise that's exactly how we should do it – and Ed would simply write down the conclusion: to do exactly what he and Simon wanted to do.

Sceptics in the orchestra were being won over too. 'Early on, may heaven forgive me, I thought he was just a whiz-kid,' remembers violinist Stan Smith. 'Just shows you what I know.' Rattle's approach to programming in the early 1980s could put a fresh spin even on familiar repertoire. One October 1985 programme interleaved Sibelius' two symphonies in C major – No. 3 and No. 7 – with all three of Beethoven's *Leonora* overtures. 'Blind faith,' says Ed Smith. 'And what a wonderful programme it was!' Sibelius quickly became a touchstone of the partnership, and a weekend-long cycle at Warwick Arts Centre and London's South Bank in April and August 1983 showed that Rattle's vision for this music ran far deeper.

The Fifth and Seventh Symphonies, in particular, were enduring Rattle favourites, and a recorded cycle, laid down between 1984 and 1986, would become a benchmark. 'A mighty account of the work, one which has enormous breadth and power,' declared *Gramophone* of the Seventh. 'It is the measure of a great performance that it can persuade the listener that this is not only a new and refreshing point of view, it is the only one.' A world far beyond Birmingham – and the UK – was starting to notice what was happening in the Town Hall.

3. Messiaen: Turangalîla-Symphonie

The pianist Peter Donohoe still remembers Rattle and the CBSO's August 1982 BBC Proms performance of Messiaen's *Turangalîla-Symphonie* as one of the greatest musical experiences of his career. Frémaux had introduced Messiaen to Birmingham, but it was Rattle who recklessly attempted to squeeze the gargantuan forces required for *Turangalîla* onto the Town Hall platform on three occasions between 1981 and 1991 – as well as performing it eleven times on tour, in venues ranging from Wells Cathedral (Messiaen himself appeared, unannounced, in the audience) to Hong Kong Cultural Centre.

The 1986 EMI recording – followed almost immediately afterwards by a recording of Mahler's 'Resurrection' Symphony – showed that as Rattle and his Birmingham forces thought bigger and bigger, so too did their recording partners. In 1988, that 'Resurrection' disc was named Record of the Year in the *Gramophone* awards, in terms that made the strongest claims yet published for the partnership:

> None of this could have been achieved, of course, without the CBSO, who here emerge as an orchestra of world class. With such supple and rich string-playing, such expressive woodwind and infallibly accurate and mellow-toned brass, could anyone, coming upon this recording unawares, be blamed for identifying these players as belonging to Vienna, Berlin or Chicago?

4. Haydn: Symphony No. 70

Orchestral development in the 1980s wasn't a one-way process. If it seemed at times as if Rattle and the CBSO were simply on a mission to play ever more challenging twentieth-century works with ever more virtuosity and style, Rattle himself was acutely aware of other trends – particularly the revolution in so-called 'authentic performance' of music from the Classical and Baroque periods. 'We had done a lot of Classical music, but my realisation that it was absolutely imperative to go along the historically informed route really came about through my discovery of *Idomeneo* and through it, Nikolaus Harnoncourt and his writings,' says Rattle. In time, Rameau's *Les Boréades* would enter the CBSO repertoire; there would be concert performances of *Le nozze di Figaro* and *Don Giovanni*.

But Haydn was already a Rattle favourite, and from 1986 onwards, one particular middle-period symphony would serve as a testbed for a radical – effectively untried – idea: to see whether a modern symphony orchestra could assimilate and use the lessons of historically informed performance. Rattle invited specialists such as Nicholas McGegan and Nicholas Kraemer to work in Birmingham; in 1985, Iona Brown was appointed guest director. Until his retirement in 1988, leader Felix Kok was an enthusiastic collaborator in this new line of artistic enquiry and his successor Peter Thomas would prove just as open-minded. Rattle and the orchestra would perform Haydn's Symphony No. 70 some twenty-two times between 1986 and 1990. Rattle again:

This tiny symphony – less than twenty minutes – has so many of the building blocks of that style. That was the first piece with which we really tried to apply those lessons. And what's interesting is how much modern orchestras now know about this style. You only have to say a couple of things and everybody clicks in. It's become very much the mainstream, and I think that the CBSO was part of that.

Other plans required efforts beyond the purely musical. In the summer of 1986 Rattle and Smith presented to the Arts Council a 'Development Plan' – a fully worked-out scheme to enable the CBSO to expand in numbers, to pay its players and staff better, and to move into an artistic league with the great orchestras of Europe and the 'Big Five' of the USA. To impartial observers, it was merely a logical next step from the fact – recognised by critics and audience alike – that this was now the most important orchestra–conductor partnership in Britain, and a model for the future that went far beyond the UK. (After the CBSO's Berlin Philharmonie debut in 1984, a Berlin newspaper printed a photo of Annie Oakley and Maggie Cotton: the sight of two female percussionists in a major orchestra was so novel as to be newsworthy.)

The Arts Council's chairman, William Rees-Mogg, was enthusiastic: 'With London orchestras, where players are paid by the session, the quality goes up and down too much.' Heads of those London orchestras duly spluttered with indignation. Yet many CBSO players were also ambivalent – older players suspected an attempt to erode hard-won contractual rights (in fact, by abolishing the old, derogatory term 'rank and file' for section string players, Ed Smith hoped to enhance their professional standing), and feared a purge. The plan did allow for multiple section leaders, but some long-serving players certainly felt threatened. Michael Buckley – violinist turned general manager – handled the Musicians' Union negotiations, and a vote by the orchestra, held in the Library Theatre in Paradise Circus, squeaked through by 44 votes to 39 (with one abstention) in January 1988. Over 600 candidates applied for the eleven new positions in the orchestra.

The Arts Council had very publicly acknowledged that the CBSO was a special case among UK orchestras, and now funded an expansion unparalleled since George Weldon recruited the permanent orchestra in 1944. But quangocrats come and go. Later Arts Councils would be less supportive, while the CBSO's newly expanded financial commitments remained unchanged. 'They abandoned us,' said Rattle in Nicholas Kenyon's 2001 book *Simon Rattle: From Birmingham to Berlin*. He raged against Rees-Mogg's successors, and their apparent determination to punish the CBSO for its ambition. ('You are the villains of British orchestral life,' said one Arts Council apparatchik to Ed Smith. 'You've let people get above themselves.') 'Shame on the Arts Council for knowing so little, for being such amateurs . . . shame on them.' Today, Rattle stands by what was achieved.

'Orchestras do not stay on a steady state, they either go down or they go up,' he says.

I don't think we had any option other than to have the Development Plan, which was basically a way of increasing both the size of the orchestra, and the depth of ability. It certainly was not a thing of 'unless you do this, I leave'. But I think I was very honest about saying: what is the future? The level we were able to reach in that time simply wouldn't have been possible without the new influx of players and the new type of working conditions, and the possibilities it gave us. It simply was the only way.

5. Nicholas Maw: Odyssey

Composed between 1973 and 1987, Nicholas Maw's *Odyssey* is sometimes claimed to be the longest continual span of purely orchestral music in existence. In the all-bets-off second half of Rattle's first decade in Birmingham, the idea that such a work might not only be performed (and to an appreciative audience, too) but recorded was still just surprising enough to make headlines, and after it finally happened, in October 1990, an overwhelmed Maw declared, 'We are all fortunate to be living through the Rattle era.' Another legend was born: that Rattle's personal clout was now so great that he'd refused to renew his contract with EMI until they agreed to record it. Rattle denies this: 'They were open to the idea – it would absolutely not have been the first thing that they chose, of course – but EMI at this point knew that this was important. I'm delighted we could and I still think it's an astonishing piece.'

The recording is still astonishing, too, with blistering playing from the trumpets under their long-serving principal Alan Whitehead – although it's also a late document of the limitations of Birmingham Town Hall. 'The middle part of the upper gallery was fine. In the side bits, the sound deteriorated. Downstairs was a complete write off. No one would ever want to sit anywhere there,' remembers the critic Richard Whitehouse, a concertgoer in the 1970s and 1980s. 'We just couldn't hear what was going on, especially in loud music,' remembers violinist David Gregory. Rattle is still incredulous:

> When I think how we squeezed people on to the stage, I don't know what the Fire Department were doing. The public response to the orchestra was so huge, that we would just simply cram as many people into the hall as we possibly could. If it was a smaller orchestra, there would be seats on the stage as well. It would absolutely not be allowed now.

By the time of *Odyssey*, something better was already in sight.

6. Mahler: Symphony No. 2 ('Resurrection')

Nothing galvanises local politicians like international attention. Birmingham City Council had been promising a new concert hall at intervals since at least 1918. The civic redevelopment plans that emerged in the mid 1980s initially centred on the International

OPPOSITE *Simon Rattle rehearses the CBSO in Birmingham Town Hall. By the mid 1980s, orchestra, conductor and audience were rapidly outgrowing their historic home.*

Convention Centre, but the city's chief executive Tom Caulcott was sympathetic to the CBSO's cause, and expert at leveraging European funding. And with Rattle and the CBSO emerging as Birmingham's most exciting artistic success story since the Triennial Festivals – this at a time when the sheen had long come off the city's ultra-modern 1960s image, and the national media tended to present Birmingham in terms of *Crossroads* and Spaghetti Junction – the argument that culture could drive urban renewal finally seemed unanswerable.

Town planners have since talked of a 'Birmingham effect'. And whether or not the remodelling of Victoria and Centenary Squares and the commissioning of public art by Antony Gormley and Dhruva Mistry had any direct connection with the CBSO, they were widely perceived as part of a broader civic resurrection, whose flagship was the city orchestra and whose poster boy was its curly-headed, disarmingly youthful conductor. It was he who insisted that the new International Convention Centre's Hall 2 should be designed by the world-leading acousticians Artec, and who was astonished to find receptive ears. 'It could not have been built without the input of Europe,' says Rattle.

March 1988: Simon Rattle's celebrated mane vanishes beneath a hard hat as he inspects building work on the future Symphony Hall.

And the memory of the foundation stone being laid by Sir Keith Joseph and Jacques Delors together – probably the people in their two countries who loathed each other the most – and the fact that both of the major political parties in that city, people who would fight like cats and dogs about anything else, could come together without an eyelash of disagreement on the Convention Centre – well, I was a young guy. I didn't realise how unusual that was.

After seventy-one years, the CBSO gave its last regular concert at Birmingham Town Hall on 15 May 1991. It had been rehearsing in the barely believable new acoustic of Symphony Hall since January; now Rattle, the orchestra and the chorus gave an unofficial first concert on 15 April 1991 – Ravel's *Daphnis et Chloé* and Stravinsky's *The Firebird* – before the official opening by Her Majesty the Queen on 12 June 1991. The main work was Mahler's 'Resurrection' Symphony, the piece that had helped launch Rattle's first season and which, in recorded form, had brought the partnership to international attention. It had never sounded like this, though. 'Symphony Hall puts city on top of the world' was the headline in the *Birmingham Post* – a sentiment that continues to find an echo three decades later.

Even thirty years on, no UK or European city has a more acoustically perfect orchestral venue. It continues to hold the CBSO to a formidably high standard. 'Once we were there it was very clear again that the ceiling had been lifted off the orchestra's possibilities,' says Rattle. David Gregory agrees: 'I think Symphony Hall has possibly done as much as any of our music directors to improve the orchestra.'

7. Patrick Doyle: Henry V

By the 1990s Birmingham had become a glamorous – even seductive – destination. The violinist heroine of Jilly Cooper's novel *Appassionata* (1996) 'was deeply impressed by the orchestra and the awesome acoustic of Symphony Hall. Her hero, Simon Rattle, however, was in Vienna and the guest conductor was a charming, wily old fox called Sir Rodney Macintosh . . .'

> She was relieved when he suggested supper in the apartment in which the orchestra put up its visiting conductors . . . when he returned five minutes later, however, he was brandishing the nearly empty bottle, reeking of English Fern and wearing nothing but a blue-and-white-striped butcher's apron. Rodney's down beat may have been wavery, but nothing could have been more emphatic than his upbeat, which was relentlessly lifting the striped apron like a shop blind.

Cooper had spent time with the CBSO while researching the novel; it has been suggested that the CBSO's education manager Ann Tennant and trombonist Danny Longstaff might have used a pinch of salt when answering such authorial enquiries as 'Could you bonk a *small* woman on a glockenspiel?' The point remains: the CBSO was mainstream, and it was sexy. Rattle and his orchestra were the universally recognised faces of classical music at its most stylish, exciting and accessible. Who else would you choose to present and perform in a seven-part TV documentary series on twentieth-century music? *Leaving Home* aired on Channel 4 in 1996.

And in 1989, when the young Royal Shakespeare Company star Kenneth Branagh claimed the mantle of Laurence Olivier by directing and starring in his own film of Shakespeare's *Henry V*, he wanted the most charismatic names on his soundtrack. That meant Rattle and the CBSO. 'We jumped at it,' remembers Rattle – and the CBSO's first, and so far only, film score (a score for Hugh Hudson's *My Life So Far* was recorded in 1999 but spiked by Harvey Weinstein), was a thrilling experience.

The orchestra was magnificent. I remember Patrick Doyle running in after the first take. I asked, 'Pat, do you have anything to say to us?' 'Yes,' he said. 'It's f***ing wonderful!' And then ran out. But I remember this wonderful thing of all these actors and actresses coming in just to hear how it was, hanging around.

One by one, Kenneth Branagh, Emma Thompson, Judi Dench, John Sessions, Brian Blessed and Derek Jacobi sidled in to eavesdrop on their musical counterparts.

8. Mark-Anthony Turnage: *Three Screaming Popes*

'Far from an angry young man's unremitting onslaught' was the verdict of Anthony Bye in the *Musical Times* after Rattle and the CBSO gave the world premiere of Mark-Anthony Turnage's *Three Screaming Popes* on 5 October 1989. The tone of surprise is significant, even though the review acknowledges the twenty-nine-year-old Turnage's 'defiant gestures and desperate eruptions'. But wasn't that what was expected in Birmingham by then – the shock of the new? In fact, *Three Screaming Popes* was the latest in the distinguished line of Feeney Trust commissions for the CBSO, and neither the first nor the last to become an instant classic.

Rattle and Smith had a particular knack for taking an established Birmingham practice and cultivating it into something bold and big. Rattle's appetite for new music had found a ready response from the younger members of

the orchestra: the players took the initiative in setting up the semi-independent Birmingham Contemporary Music Group in 1987. But from this raucous, supremely confident new Feeney Trust commission followed another idea: that the CBSO should have a living composer as part of the creative team. Turnage was appointed composer-in-association in 1989; Judith Weir followed him in 1995.

Meanwhile, sitting (or so he later said) in a Birmingham rush-hour traffic jam and chatting with Michael Vyner of the London Sinfonietta, Rattle conceived the idea of an arts festival on an unprecedented scale – a retrospective of the twentieth century that would itself occupy the entire final decade of that century. Starting in 1990 with the 1900s, and proceeding by a decade each year, *Towards the Millennium* would last ten years and climax in 2000 with brand new commissions for the new century – music that had not even been written when the festival started. The festival would embrace all the cultural institutions in Birmingham, not just the musical ones, and would be presented jointly in London too, with the Sinfonietta (under Oliver Knussen's artistic guidance) and the CBSO playing in both cities.

Starting in the era of Rachmaninoff and Mahler, the aspiration was that by the year 2000 audiences would flock enthusiastically to programmes comprised entirely of (to take one programme from the '1990s' instalment) Henze,

OPPOSITE *15 April 1991: the first concert in Symphony Hall. Simon Rattle, the CBSO, the Chorus and a capacity audience discovered that it had been well worth the seven-decade wait.*

Ligeti, Tippett and Simon Holt. The programmes were Rattle at his most gleefully eclectic: Martinů's *Epic of Gilgamesh*, Stockhausen's *Gruppen*, Birtwistle's *Earth Dances* (Rattle did some discreet touching-up of the orchestration), Suk's *Asrael Symphony*, Turnage's massive jazz suite *Blood on the Floor*, further performances of *Odyssey*, and Messiaen's *Éclairs sur l'au-delà*.

'The idea contained the seeds of its own destruction,' joked Smith's successor Stephen Maddock; not strictly fair, although the marketing challenges grew progressively tougher. Years later, the CBSO's press officer Rachel Burrows still blanched visibly at the mention of Henze's *The Raft of the Medusa*. But no pre-millennial festival anywhere else in the world matched *Towards the Millennium* for scale and scope – and nothing since has run it even slightly close.

9. Szymanowski: *King Roger*

Symphony Hall presented challenges as well as opportunities. 'The first thing was that it was much more difficult to play in,' says Rattle.

> You could really hear everything, everybody had to find new ways of playing. Immediately the word went around the country that people who played the oboe or the bassoon would have to find other equipment to play there. It was so sensitive: you actually had to make other types of reeds. And it really takes a while to get to know how to play in a great hall.

But once the musicians had learned how to 'play' the new space, the artistic potential was boundless. 'I think it changed our lives really,' remembers David Gregory. 'I was hearing things I had never heard before, in familiar pieces of music.' And while Rattle probably wouldn't have hesitated to stage the modernist blockbusters of *Towards the Millennium* in the Town Hall, the new acoustic gave certain areas of repertoire an opportunity to blossom as never before. One passion that really flowered was Rattle's love for the music of Karol Szymanowski, whose super-saturated post-Romantic textures seemed to flush with new colour in the clarity of Symphony Hall.

'I think Rattle had an unerring way of finding out what the next big thing was going to be – finding a piece of music that should have been heard before and hadn't been,' says Gregory. A series of Szymanowski recordings between 1993 and 2006 documented the experience, and – as he had throughout his tenure – Rattle sought out soloists who could teach the orchestra something about the stylistic world they were discovering. 'I think it was Thomas's sound that he was wanting the orchestra to take on,' says Gregory of the 1995 recording of Szymanowski's violin concertos with Thomas Zehetmair, 'a very fine-spun vibrato, a very clear, bright sound, almost over-the-top: ecstatic. This is the side of Simon that loves all things sensuous and exotic. The clue for me was his concert moccasins in black suede.'

The ecstasy peaks in Szymanowski's opera *King Roger*, recorded live in 1998, Rattle's final summer in Birmingham. The Chorus's closing

SIR SIMON RATTLE OM CBE

Birmingham has repeatedly drawn its musical talent from Liverpool. Simon Rattle's childhood enthusiasm for music was so strong that the Royal Liverpool Philharmonic Orchestra let him join the Merseyside Youth Orchestra as a percussionist a year early. As an eighteen-year-old student at the Royal Academy of Music, he conducted a scratch orchestra in Mahler's 'Resurrection' Symphony. His triumph – just six months later – in the 1974 John Players International Conductors' Competition led to an unhappy stint at the Bournemouth Symphony Orchestra and a happier one at the BBC Scottish Symphony Orchestra, although the RLPO voted against offering him the post of principal conductor.

'Now you're now the second Scouser who's become conductor of this orchestra,' said the ninety-year-old Sir Adrian Boult to the twenty-four-year-old Rattle, when Rattle was offered the Birmingham job in 1979; 'Marvellous place, Birmingham: very good orchestra, wonderful water.' In an age of jet-set maestros, Rattle's wholehearted commitment to the CBSO over eighteen years redefined what a conductor–orchestra partnership could mean. Knighted in 1994, Rattle left the CBSO in 1998 with a game-changing legacy – including the building of Symphony Hall and CBSO Centre – but no clear plans for his own future. But with the announcement in 1999 that he had been appointed principal conductor of the Berlin Philharmonic, he achieved a status in the musical world unsurpassed by any British-born conductor, before or since. He stepped down in 2018, having become music director of the London Symphony Orchestra in 2017.

incantations echoed from on high: orchestra, chorus, conductor, soloists, audience and venue all coming together to achieve something that would have been impossible a decade earlier, and was even then impossible anywhere else in the world.

10. **Thomas Adès: Asyla**

A decade after discovering Turnage, Rattle and the Feeney Trust backed a hunch about another young composer. Thomas Adès was only twenty-six but *Asyla*, the work that Rattle and the CBSO premiered on 1 October 1997, didn't sound it: at least, not if you ignored its freshness, its certainty and the pounding, rave-influenced dance rhythms of its *Ecstasio* third movement. This was a symphonic work for a new millennium: so obviously a masterpiece that Rattle chose to reprise it ten months later, in August 1998, as the opening item in his last concert as music director of the CBSO.

He had announced his departure to the orchestra in February 1996. 'It was a sad day. Whether you could say it was a shock is another thing, because we all knew, after sixteen years, that the time was coming to an end,' recalls Michael Seal. 'Of course, any time the managers turned up at Symphony Hall, something major was going on, and I remember thinking, "Right, something big's coming up."' 'I remember the silence afterwards,' says David Gregory. 'You could cut it with a knife.'

Rattle had no specific plans beyond the CBSO: he simply felt that it was time, for everyone's benefit, to do something new:

In retrospect, maybe I could have said, look, I'll stay to 2000, it's a nice round number – but in the gut, it felt like the right thing to do; that maybe everybody needed something else, and that we should finish while it was still going well. It was simply an instinct. Eighteen years is really a long time, particularly in this modern world. And I think it was the perfect time for Sakari Oramo to take on and develop the orchestra further, in a different way. I don't know whether I could have helped them much more.

Of course, I did have to think enormously about it, but telling the orchestra was one of the hardest things. We'd always been very honest with each other. It was fascinating that almost the minute I told them about it, the relationship changed, and it was actually much easier. The feeling that, 'oh, this person is not in charge of the rest of our lives' can also be helpful.

Rattle had long surpassed Leslie Heward's record as the CBSO's longest-serving principal conductor, and the final season was, by any definition, a high – tours to Europe, South America, Japan and the USA, *King Roger* in Birmingham and Salzburg, and a complete Beethoven cycle in which Rattle paired the Ninth Symphony with Birtwistle's *The Triumph of Time*. 'Come his very last hurrah, they will probably block off the ring road and chain him to the podium,' predicted Anthony Holden in the *Observer*. Instead, Rattle hired the Chung Ying

'In 2020,
Simon Rattle is
still an important
part of the
CBSO's life'

Garden restaurant in Chinatown, and treated the entire orchestra, chorus, board and staff to a 'thank you' dinner. The farewell concerts, on 29 and 30 August 1998, ended – of course – with Mahler's 'Resurrection' Symphony. Channel 4 filmed the concerts (the crew wore T-shirts with the slogan 'Arrivederci Brum'), both performances were sold out, and Smith took the decision to open the general rehearsals to the public. Flowers were thrown and tears flowed both onstage and off.

In 2020 Rattle is still an important part of the CBSO's life. The unfinished business of *Towards the Millennium*, the ongoing Szymanowski recordings and two long-planned projects – a tribute to Duke Ellington with Ellington's former orchestrator Luther Henderson in 1999, and Mahler's Eighth Symphony in 2004 – saw him make regular returns to Birmingham, though after 2002 his new role at the Berlin Philharmonic was necessarily his first priority. There was also the matter of allowing his successor Sakari Oramo space to forge his own relationship with orchestra and audience: Rattle yielded the October 2000 centenary performance of *The Dream of Gerontius* to the new music director.

And as ever, where Birmingham leads, London (eventually) follows. Despite a sometimes jaded press, if Rattle can achieve with the London Symphony Orchestra what he achieved in Birmingham – a rejuvenated orchestra, engaged audiences and a genuinely world-class concert hall (the capital's first) – it'll be another long-term manifestation of the 'Birmingham effect'. Meanwhile, Rattle is not – and never can be – 'just' a guest conductor in Birmingham. Even though players and staff have changed, he's still intrinsically part of the CBSO's (and the city's) musical make-up.

In May 2014, he gave his services for free to conduct the annual CBSO Benevolent Fund concert – Rachmaninoff's Third Piano Concerto, with Peter Donohoe, and Brahms's First Symphony. Bryony Morrison joined the violin section in 2012, fourteen years after Rattle's departure. Old hands had told her what to expect, but she remained sceptical: 'The temptation is to think, "Are you really that great?"' she says. 'Then he started and it was: "Oh wow. Yes." It was like being under a spell – exhausting, but amazing.' The funny thing is, Rattle felt the same: 'We had one rehearsal on the afternoon, and it was one of the best concerts I can remember, absolutely unforgettable. It was astonishing. And above all, such a feeling of, oh God yes – we really do know each other.'

SYMPHONY HALL

When the plans to create a new International Convention Centre took shape in the mid 1980s, civic leaders had been promising Birmingham a new concert hall since at least 1918. The city's chief executive Tom Caulcott and council leader Bernard Zissman were both committed supporters of the CBSO. But to avoid political controversy (and to secure European Commission funding), they employed subterfuge: Hall 2 of the ICC was described on plans as a multi-purpose hall, which just happened to be suitable for concerts.

It was Simon Rattle who, after meeting the acoustician Russell Johnson, insisted that Johnson's firm Artec be given the design contract. Johnson in turn insisted that the new hall be designed from the inside out, with acoustic needs dictating architectural design. The new hall would have adjustable acoustic chambers, an orchestra pit beneath the stage, 2,262 seats and near-perfect soundproofing. Its entire 40,000-tonne weight rests on hundreds of rubber blocks, to cancel any sound or vibration from the mainline railway tunnel directly below.

Acclaimed upon opening as a 'Stradivarius of a hall', the new venue was christened 'Symphony Hall' by CBSO chief executive Ed Smith (he'd originally pondered 'The Meridian' – 'the centre of music in the country, the centre of excellence' – but was anxious that it might be mistaken for the Warwickshire village of Meriden). At least one concertgoer was overwhelmed: convinced that Symphony Hall's spectacular lighting canopy had mystical powers, for many years she arrived early before concerts in order to commune with it in silence.

The gleaming red and chrome décor of Symphony Hall embodied the resurgent confidence of Birmingham during the Rattle revolution, and its acoustic remains unsurpassed.

WORKSHOP OF THE WORLD

In 2006, a manuscript dealer in Cheltenham advertised for sale a collection of documents associated with Sir Edward Elgar. Elgar wasn't the only composer who featured: these were his letters to Isaiah Burnell, the former head of music at Bromsgrove School and a friend of Elgar in his later years. The dealer, understandably, was less interested in the rest of the bundle, which comprised songs, choral music and a couple of orchestral scores by Burnell himself. Among them was an incomplete set of brass parts for a work entitled *Overture: Bromsgrovia* – a piece completely forgotten, assumed lost, and, as it happens, the very first new work to be premiered by the eight-week-old City of Birmingham Orchestra on 1 November 1920.

There's almost no record of this performance, or the reaction to it. In May 1939, the *Birmingham Mail* reported that Burnell's *Concert Overture* had been performed by the CBO and Adrian Boult; whether this was the same piece, misremembered, is impossible to say, though Boult did conduct Burnell's *Elegy* with the CBO in 1928. 'The music has a gentle sadness and falls pleasantly on the ear,' reported the *Birmingham Daily Gazette*, and Elgar, too, was kindly about his friend's 'well-wrought and poetical' music.

It is hardly the grand statement of a premiere with which we might, with retrospect, wish that the CBSO had launched its century-long commitment to new music. But it is exactly the sort of piece you can imagine Appleby Matthews, with his roots in the amateur choral scene and Midlands-wide network of contacts, championing as a favour to an acquaintance, or out of a more general belief that Midlands talent ought to be encouraged. New music, in 1920, was not a rarity, a challenge or a cause that needed special pleading – not that this stopped Matthews. Returning from Germany in 1922, he told the *Gazette*,

> They regard their composers as gods, whereas we are apt to regard ours as eccentric simpletons who would do much better to take a berth in an office. Hence, German composers have international reputations, in spite of the fact that, in so far as modern music is concerned, English composers are of higher rank.

Music was, as Elgar once put it, in the air, and less than a decade had passed since the last major premieres of the Triennial Festival. Matthews' very first season with the CBO had opened with a contemporary work by a Midlands composer – Granville Bantock's overture *Saul* – and the 'First Symphony Concert' would include more of the same. Elgar's inaugural programme contained no music that was more than ten years old. Guest appearances in those early seasons – whether from Midlanders such as Gustav Holst and Ralph Vaughan Williams, or celebrities from further afield, such as Sibelius, Ethel Smyth or Arthur Bliss – were a draw to audiences, not a deterrent.

Still, there seems to have been more to the CBO's early commitment to contemporary music than a mere desire to establish an artistic profile or to capture a bit of reflected glamour. A city orchestra doesn't exist merely to sustain itself, or provide commercial entertainment. It is a civic amenity: it has a duty, like the central

Under George Weldon (seen here rehearsing in 1948) the orchestra championed new music by British composers including Ruth Gipps, Elisabeth Lutyens, Arthur Bliss and the orchestra's bassoonist Vaughan Allin.

library, botanic gardens or museum and art gallery, to give its city access to a cross-section of what is new, good and important, both at home and abroad.

Some conductors have taken that duty to broaden the city's artistic horizons intensely to heart. Simon Rattle tells a story of how in later life Adrian Boult spoke to him with pride of his pioneering Mahler and Bruckner performances in Birmingham in the late 1920s. 'People would come from miles to hear them,' he remembered. Rattle responded that he hadn't realised that

Mahler and Bruckner were favourites of Sir Adrian. 'Not at all!' replied Boult. 'I thought they were terrible rubbish!'

Boult never quite dropped that public-school mask of studied flippancy, but in fact he championed new music throughout his career, including (in Birmingham) works by Bartók, Dohnányi, Medtner, Cyril Scott, Granville Bantock and Holst. His autobiography *My Own Trumpet* contains an eight-page list of his premieres – clearly a source of pride. Until the 1950s, at least, new music continued to be in the air. Leslie

Heward – a composer himself, though he rarely used his Birmingham position to advance his own music – gave UK premieres of works by Ernest Bloch, Glazunov (the Saxophone Concerto) and the Swede Lars-Erik Larsson alongside home-grown produce by Victor Hely-Hutchinson.

Under George Weldon in the late 1940s, in fact, the spirit seems to have been one of 'Dig for Victory'. The orchestra's double-reed section was practically a composers' workshop, with Weldon premiering three works (*Trivia*, *Nocturne* and *Two Pastorals*) by the oboist Mary Chandler, some five orchestral works by the bassoonist Vaughan Allin and, most significantly, the Piano Concerto and the first two symphonies by the orchestra's second oboe Ruth Gipps, who conducted her prelude *The Cat* in October 1948. Amid the epic quantity of repertoire performed by Weldon, there was plenty of scope to explore the orchestra's own creative resources alongside Weldon's more idiosyncratic UK premieres, including works by the Turkish composer Ahmet Adnan Saygun or the American Don Gillis' swinging Symphony No. 5½ (its third movement is entitled *Scherzofrenia*).

Rudolf Schwarz's outlook was even more cosmopolitan – including a belated UK premiere for the imposing *Symphonie concertante* for organ and orchestra by Joseph Jongen and, in 1958, Ernest Bloch's Symphony for Trombone and Orchestra, with the CBSO's former principal trombone Denis Wick as soloist. 'Concertgoers with a thirst for modern British works seem likely to have a friend in Vienna-born Rudolf Schwarz,' reported the *Gazette*, shortly after his appointment.

He has conducted many 'moderns' including several first performances in England. A high percentage of his coming programmes in Birmingham contain recent British works – and in seven of the twelve Thursday concerts they are works not previously performed by the orchestra in Birmingham.

This was the era of the so-called 'Cheltenham symphonies' – not necessarily symphonies, or indeed premiered at the Cheltenham Music Festival, but a catch-all term for traditional forms coupled to a brisk, communicative, broadly late-Romantic or neoclassical musical language. The CBSO, with its geographical proximity to Cheltenham, was well placed to take advantage of this post-war boom. Throughout the 1950s and 1960s the orchestra premiered a string of large-scale works by British and British-resident composers, many in Cheltenham itself (Alan Bush's Symphony No. 1, Arthur Benjamin's Piano Concerto, Egon Wellesz's Symphony No. 6, Peter Racine Fricker's Symphony No. 4) and still more in Birmingham (Hans Gál's Symphony No. 3, Robert Simpson's Violin Concerto, Gordon Jacob's Sinfonietta No. 3, Alun Hoddinott's Piano Concerto No. 2).

Andrzej Panufnik was reticent about promoting his own music, but Hugo Rignold's interests were far-reaching – including, between 1965 and 1968, three of Egon Wellesz's symphonies. The most important premiere of this period, Benjamin Britten's *War Requiem* (still the CBSO's single most significant world premiere), occurred on 30 May 1962. By this time, however, critical fashion was starting to

As music director, Andrzej Panufnik was reluctant to promote his own music, but in time both he and his daughter Roxanna would receive major commissions from the CBSO.

turn against the Cheltenham tendency. At the premiere of Malcolm Arnold's Fifth Symphony in July 1961 (given by the Hallé, not the CBSO), broadsheet critics were observed in the foyer of Cheltenham Town Hall phoning dismissive reviews through before the symphony had even finished.

There's a slight (but understandable) impression, throughout Hugo Rignold's and Louis Frémaux's tenure, of an attempt to give audiences new music without taking the box-office risk implied by the emerging avant-garde – though with works such as Dutilleux's *Métaboles* (September 1969), and John McCabe's beautiful song-cycle *Notturni ed Alba* (a 1970 Three Choirs Festival commission), and such rediscoveries as Martinů's Violin Concerto No. 1 (receiving a belated UK premiere in February 1975), that didn't have to mean any sacrifice in musical quality. It's telling that the CBSO's UK premiere of Leonard Bernstein's extraordinary, psychedelic *Mass* didn't take place in Brum, but safely out of town at the

Royal Albert Hall, London, 19 July 2015: John Woolrich (left), Andris Nelsons and the CBSO's contrabassoonist Margaret Cookhorn (right) acknowledge the applause after performing Woolrich's contrabassoon concerto Falling Down. *This was Nelsons' final appearance as music director: the CBSO has frequently put new music at the centre of landmark concerts.*

Coventry Theatre on 16 May 1976, filling a slot immediately after the *Danny La Rue Show*.

The CBSO had performed extracts from *Mass* at Camden Roundhouse in April 1973, but this was the whole shebang. 'Mass Hysteria,' predicted the *Birmingham Post*. 'It must disturb and perhaps offend those unable to be open-minded in their belief,' and after a flurry of protests in the regional press – including from at least one CBSO supporter, who denounced the orchestra for performing 'this blasphemous and

sacrilegious work' and threatened to withdraw future patronage if it went ahead – the original plan of staging it in Coventry Cathedral was dropped. The performance was arranged by the University of Warwick. The CBSO played in the pit while Cameron – described as 'a professional and musically competent rock group' – performed onstage with the student chorus. Roy Wales conducted, with Bernstein's personal blessing.

'It was not polished,' commented the *Coventry Evening Telegraph*, and the performance was repeated at the Royal Albert Hall the following night. Paul Griffiths, in the *Financial Times*, reported that 'given such poor material, this performance was almost a miracle of transubstantiation. The playing of the CBSO was full, bold and vigorous.' 'All I got was a headache,' said the critic of *The Stage*.

Made in Birmingham

By the time Simon Rattle arrived in 1980 – initiating a transformation in the depth and range of the CBSO's commitment to new music – the organisation already had twenty-five years' experience of commissioning composers in its own right. This was an unexpected (and belated) benefit of an act of nineteenth-century civic philanthropy. John Feeney (1839-1905), born in Sparkbrook, was the son of the Irish journalist who founded the *Birmingham Daily Post*. Over the course of forty years as the *Post*'s proprietor, Feeney accrued a sizeable fortune, and on his death, he left 9 per cent of his entire estate to fund a charitable trust 'for the promotion and

October 1991: Sir Michael Tippett records A Child of Our Time *in Symphony Hall. His Piano Concerto, premiered in 1956, was the CBSO's second Feeney Trust commission.*

cultivation of art in the City of Birmingham, or for the acquisition and maintenance of parks, recreation grounds and open spaces in or near the city'.

Feeney's legacy can be seen all over Birmingham – in the galleries that bear his name in the Museum and Art Gallery, the paintings (including works by Burne-Jones and Joseph Wright of Derby) that his Trust acquired for the city, or on the slopes of the Clent Hills, which Feeney's trustees helped save from development in the 1930s. The Trust had been one of the original guarantors of the CBO back in 1920. But it seems that it took until the mid 1950s – and

During his time as the CBSO's first composer-in-association, Mark-Anthony Turnage wrote a series of now-classic scores.

the formidable civic networking power of the CBSO's chairman Stephen Lloyd – before any of Birmingham's musicians thought of making use of the John Feeney Charitable Trust. The first Feeney commissions were aimed squarely at the top table of British music. On 13 December 1955 Rudolf Schwarz conducted the premiere of Arthur Bliss's *Meditations on a Theme by John Blow* (1955). Michael Tippett's Piano Concerto and Peter Wishart's Concerto for Orchestra followed in 1956, and Edmund Rubbra's Seventh Symphony in 1957.

Symphonies by Lennox Berkeley (his Second), Alan Rawsthorne (ditto) and Robert Simpson (his Third), Andrzej Panufnik's Piano Concerto and Elizabeth Maconchy's *Serenata concertante* all helped set an enduring pattern for Feeney commissions – substantial works by figures of national and international significance. The journey from commission to premiere was not always straightforward. Britten slipped the net, and in June 1956 Lennox Berkeley's publisher pointed out that the proposed fee of £75 for a new symphony 'is entirely inadequate for a composer of such high standing'.

'After he has paid income tax, there would only be some forty odd pounds left as recompense,' they added, not entirely unreasonably. Tippett, meanwhile, offered a work that was already under way – a piano concerto that he'd originally intended for the pianist Clifford Curzon and the 1955 Edinburgh Festival, but which was now seeking a pianist and premiere. 'Tippett is a slowish worker, so if we did not get the piano concerto we might have to wait a little while for a major work from him,' management committee member Anthony Lewis counselled Lloyd. The pianist for whom Tippett had originally conceived the work, Noel Mewton-Wood, had committed suicide in December 1953. Now, in the absence of Curzon, Julius Katchen (according to Tippett) 'declared it unplayable' and withdrew shortly before the advertised premiere in January 1956. Louis Kentner took it on instead, and premiered it from memory on 30 October 1956.

Tippett was disappointed. Schwarz, he wrote later, 'concentrated so much on the individual notes (a Teutonic bad habit) that the sense of the music was lost'. (You wonder whether the Viennese and Jewish Schwarz would have appreciated being called 'Teutonic'.) 'Well, it was a bit confusing,' remembers Stan Smith, who played in the first violin section that night. 'It didn't help that the manuscript parts were so awful.' Music publishers, then as now, are sometimes more punctilious at negotiating fees than providing usable sheet music.

Regardless, it was a high-profile launch for the Feeney commissions. By the time of Thea Musgrave's Concerto for Orchestra – in which, in the spirit of 1968, the first clarinet attempts to launch an insurrection against the full orchestra – Hugo Rignold's highly drilled CBSO had no concerns about presenting the premiere in London, at the Royal Festival Hall. And under Frémaux, the Feeney commissions reflect an increasingly broad musical perspective that embraced Nicola LeFanu's *Columbia Falls*, Richard Rodney Bennett's Violin Concerto, the extraordinary flute concerto for James Galway, *Mandala ki Raga Sangeet*, by the Kolkata-born John

Mayer (1977), and John Tavener's piano concerto *Palintropos*. 'Incomprehensible,' wrote the *Birmingham Post*'s Barrie Grayson after the Tavener premiere, with pianist Stephen Bishop-Kovacevich.

Simon Rattle's arrival changed the direction of the Feeney commissions, just as it changed the entire direction of the CBSO's programming. Most noticeably, he dropped the unspoken understanding that British composers would be the beneficiaries of the scheme. So the Feeney Trust can take the credit for works of the quality of Toru Takemitsu's *Vers, l'arc-en-ciel, Palma* (1984), Tristan Murail's *Time and Again* (1986) and Sofia Gubaidulina's *Zeitgestalten* (1994). From young British composers favoured by Rattle came two landmarks of contemporary British music: Mark-Anthony Turnage's *Three Screaming Popes*, and *Asyla*, the first large-scale orchestral work by the twenty-six-year-old Thomas Adès. 'Totally original, uncompromisingly serious, utterly of our time and a teasing, tingling delight to the ear. This is music that orchestras are going to want to play, and audiences to hear, again and again,' predicted Andrew Clark of the *Financial Times*, with complete accuracy.

The Feeney commissions continue: as of mid 2018, some seventy-five works in total, of which fifty-seven were for the CBSO with a further four (by Tansy Davies, Charlotte Bray, Ben Foskett and Daniel Kidane) for the CBSO Youth Orchestra. But they have never been the entire story. The orchestra's prestige under Rattle led to premieres such as John Adams' *Lollapalooza* (1995) – 'a fortieth birthday present for Simon Rattle, who has been a friend and collaborator for many years' said Adams – Hans Werner Henze's

At the opening of CBSO Centre in November 1998, Judith Weir conducted Free Standing
Flexible Structure – *a fanfare performed from the Centre's acoustic galleries.*

Tenth Symphony (at the 2002 Lucerne Festival) and a raft of new works by Magnus Lindberg, Henze, Simon Holt and Judith Weir commissioned for the year 2000, and the final instalment of the decade-long *Towards the Millennium* festival.

By then, Birmingham's own new music ensemble – Birmingham Contemporary Music Group (BCMG), established in 1987 by two CBSO cellists, Ulrich Heinen and Simon Clugston – was a wholly independent organisation, with its own commissioning agenda and international profile. Together with the Feeney Trust, it would commission Oliver Knussen's final completed work, *O Hototogisu!* in 2017. Rattle also pressed for the CBSO to appoint its first composer-in-association, and Mark-Anthony Turnage began his formal relationship with the CBSO in 1989. 'We wanted to have a composer actually working with us,' said Rattle to Nicholas Kenyon (in *Simon Rattle: From Birmingham to Berlin*). 'We gave Mark Turnage a laboratory to create his very best music, let him go to rehearsals and meet players, so it wasn't just a matter of writing works in isolation.'

The results included some classics – including *Momentum* and *Drowned Out*, and the cello concerto *Kai* (for BCMG) – and one major unsuccessful experiment: the choral work *Leaving*, subsequently withdrawn. 'I think it was a psychological block I had with the English choral tradition,' says Turnage. Turnage's successor, the future Master of the Queen's Music, Judith Weir, followed in 1995, with a radically different philosophy: 'I did feel an ambivalence about working with orchestras,' she told Kenyon, in *Simon Rattle: From Birmingham to Berlin*. 'So I approached the scheme in a slightly unusual way, which was to do a lot of work with small groups from the orchestra, out in the country or in the suburbs.' She also forged a special artistic bond with the CBSO's fledgling Youth Chorus: *Storm* (1998) and *We Are Shadows* (1999) have both entered the repertoire.

Sakari Oramo's enthusiasm for new music was easily the equal of Rattle's, and he was active in choosing Julian Anderson as the CBSO's third (and so far final) composer-in-association. Anderson was determined to use all the resources placed at his disposal. 'The set-up is arguably the best in the country,' he told the *Guardian* shortly before taking up the post in 2001. 'There are so many levels, from the composing point of view alone – the orchestra, the Birmingham Contemporary Music Group, the choruses – and they're all so well integrated.

'I have found the orchestra enormously open, very sympathetic and very interested,' he added – and Anderson's first work for the CBSO, *Imagin'd Corners* (2002), was conceived as a showpiece for the CBSO's horn section in the acoustic of Symphony Hall. *Symphony* (2003), *Book of Hours* for BCMG (2004) and *Four American Choruses* (2004) for the unaccompanied CBSO Chorus all sprang from the relationship, with its final product – the exquisite, Brancusi-inspired *Eden* for orchestra – being premiered at Cheltenham in July 2005.

'When Mark was first appointed in 1989, that was the first such appointment in this country,' says CBSO chief executive Stephen Maddock. 'That was very advanced thinking at that point. By the time we got to 2005, everyone had a composer-in-association.' It was time to explore other ways of presenting and creating new music. Five years into Sakari Oramo's tenure, he fulfilled a personal ambition in April 2003 with a long weekend entitled drolly, if bafflingly, *Floof!*

The name, it turned out, was the title of a work by Esa-Pekka Salonen: the sound made by a robotic poet when trying to say the word 'love'. The festival was almost like a house party – with Oramo inviting his wife, the soprano Anu Komsi and his friend Salonen for four days of deliriously colourful new music spread between CBSO Centre and Symphony Hall, and between the CBSO and BCMG. Oramo took up his violin to perform Salonen's fiendish, unaccompanied *Lachen verlernt*, while Julian Anderson, Philippe Schoeller, Simon Holt and the Sutton Coldfield-born experimentalist Jonathan Harvey, introduced their own music alongside UK premieres from Franco Donatoni, Magnus Lindberg, Hanspeter Kyburz and Mauricio Kagel. 'Jonathan was a great personality and I miss him dearly,' remembers Oramo (Harvey died in 2012). 'His music was something of a revelation for me. Yet the orchestra had never played a note of it.'

The improvisatory spirit had its drawbacks. Not all listeners relish the challenge of new music, and although there was nothing to match the yell of 'Absolute bilge!', later found to have come from a former CBSO board member, that had interrupted the world premiere of Leif

Segerstam's Symphony No.35 ('Flashbacking Backwardsly') in November 2000, *Floof!* was only a qualified commercial success. The effort involved in pulling together such an extravaganza had left relatively little time for marketing, and Geoff Brown of *The Times* remarked that Symphony Hall 'had so many empty seats that they could have held a dentists' convention at the same time'.

As any venue manager will confirm, it is actually quite difficult to gauge the precise emptiness of a hall by eye alone. In drawing audiences of between four and five hundred at short notice for such uncompromising programmes – some of the largest ever seen in Birmingham for new classical music – the CBSO's marketing team had pulled off something of a triumph. As Brown added, these were 'concerts of red-hot artistry, important UK premieres – Donatoni, Kagel – and some of the fizziest, most attractive new music this side of a crate of champagne'. On the Saturday evening, a jubilant Oramo issued an impromptu invitation for the entire audience to stay for a drink afterwards – catching the CBSO management entirely unawares. Some swift words with the Symphony Hall bar staff, and a hefty cheque behind the bar made sure that the party atmosphere continued into the night.

The precise combination of conditions that made *Floof!* possible proved impossible to replicate during Oramo's remaining five years in Birmingham. Among premieres by Peter Sculthorpe, Per Nørgård. Isabel Mundry, Kaija Saariaho, Henri Dutilleux, Elliott Carter and the Birmingham veteran John Joubert, Oramo did,

however, bring the CBSO its first Holst world premiere (his withdrawn 1903 symphonic poem *Indra*) and just missed out on what was, perhaps surprisingly, its first Elgar premiere – in 2005, eighty-five years after Elgar had conducted the orchestra's first symphony concert in 1920.

Elgar's exquisite little orchestration of 'The Holly and Ivy', rediscovered in an antique shop in Bewdley, was given its modern premiere by the CBSO at Worcester Cathedral on 11 August 2005, and subsequently recorded by Oramo on the CBSO's first and only own-label CD. Meanwhile, Oramo's one-man mission to revive the music of John Foulds led to belated world premieres in 2004 of *Lyra Celtica* and *Mirage* – a statement of sincere artistic belief in (as Oramo put it) 'a genius whose music is brilliantly inventive and yet distinctive', and whose *Three Mantras* represent, for Oramo, 'the peak of all British orchestral music written between the two world wars'.

Different conductors have different priorities. Andris Nelsons was more than game for the baffling but oddly listenable *Work No. 955* by the Turner Prize-winning artist Martin Creed, performed in Symphony Hall on 23 September 2008 as part of a collaboration with Birmingham's Ikon Gallery. A similar collaboration with the Ikon Gallery in 2001 – Ceal Floyer's *Nail Biting Performance* – did not go quite so well. The idea was for the artist to stand on the conductor's podium and bite her nails down a microphone in front of the full orchestra. The orchestral management, fearful that the players would break out in uncontrollable giggles, took the decision for them to stay offstage.

But while Nelsons' instinctive musicianship meant that the premieres he did give – including first UK outings for Jörg Widmann's *Antiphon* (2009), Brett Dean's trumpet concerto *Dramatis Personae* (2014) and Hans Abrahamsen's ravishing song-cycle . . . *let me tell you* . . . (2014) – were compelling musical occasions, the economics of commissioning new music have meant that, increasingly, large-scale new works have required collaboration or co-commissioning. Still, who wouldn't have wanted Sir James MacMillan to conduct the world premiere of his own *St Luke Passion* in December 2014, or to have had the energising verve of Diego Matheuz to partner Johannes Moser in Enrico Chapela's electric cello concerto *Magnetar* (March 2013) – one of the Feeney Trust's most unexpected commissions yet?

The commission for Gerald Barry's Organ Concerto (March 2018) was shared between the CBSO, London's Southbank Centre and Irish state television, but Birmingham had the first hearing – and Barry's deadpan musical gags will surely never land with more hallucinatory strangeness than in the pristine acoustic of Symphony Hall. New works by Kaija Saariaho, Raminta Šerkšnytė, Jörg Widmann and Roxanna Panufnik featured in Mirga Gražinytė-Tyla's first seasons, as well as belated UK premieres for Mieczysław Weinberg's Symphony No.21, and Mikalojus Konstantinas Čiurlionis' 1907 symphonic poem *The Sea*.

'The most exciting point for me is the combination or balance of two things: the entreaties, or the immediate emotion, so to speak, and then the rational and intelligent and brain-challenging stuff as well,' Gražinytė-Tyla

told the *Irish Times*. 'That's the sign of a real masterwork.' So just as Appleby Matthews' first season in 1920 was filled with the music of living composers, there was never any doubt that the CBSO would celebrate its centenary, true to Birmingham's civic motto, by looking forward.

Twenty composers have been commissioned, drawing on the CBSO's heritage, its networks, and simply an enduring curiosity about what's new, what's good, and what Birmingham needs to hear. Thomas Adès, Unsuk Chin, Brett Dean, Anna Thorvaldsdóttir, Thomas Larcher, Julian Anderson, Thea Musgrave, Gary Carpenter, Bent Sørensen, Jörg Widmann, Matthew Aucoin, Mark-Anthony Turnage, Kerry Andrew and Raminta Šerkšnytė head the list, at time of writing. A further twenty emerging composers have been invited to write short encores, making some forty premieres in total.

British audiences, said Elgar at the University of Birmingham in 1905, are 'intelligent: they do not want treating sentimentally, we must give them the real thing, we must give them of the best because we want them to have it, not from mere curiosity to see how they accept it'. Elgar, Appleby Matthews and even Sir Adrian Boult might have been surprised to see that in its centenary season, the CBSO and its family of ensembles would give as many premieres as it managed in the entire first twenty-seven years of its existence. But they would have recognised – and applauded – the spirit.

BIRMINGHAM CONTEMPORARY MUSIC GROUP

As classical music entered the second half of the twentieth century, composers increasingly turned away from the full symphony orchestra, specifying small, distinctive chamber-sized ensembles (often with highly unusual combinations of instruments) shaped by the precise demands of the sounds they wanted to create. Starting in 1968, the London Sinfonietta had pioneered the idea of a flexible, virtuoso new-music ensemble in the UK. Two CBSO cellists, Ulrich Heinen and Simon Clugston, felt that Birmingham should have something similar, and with the support of Simon Rattle and the CBSO – who realised that anything that enriched Birmingham's musical ecosystem could only benefit the orchestra – BCMG gave its first concert on 21 June 1987, in Birmingham Conservatoire's (then new, since demolished) Adrian Boult Hall.

BCMG rapidly established itself as an independent sister organisation of the CBSO, promoting its own concerts and building its own pool of regular players, many (but by no means all) drawn from the CBSO. Simon Rattle, Thomas Adès, John Woolrich and Oliver Knussen have all provided artistic leadership, and although in 1998 BCMG moved both its offices and its concert series into CBSO Centre, it pursues a wholly autonomous artistic policy. Particularly influential has been its 'Sound Investment' commissioning programme – effectively, a crowdfunding scheme for new music, decades before the term was invented. Through it, since 1991, BCMG and its supporters have commissioned and premiered over 175 new works from composers including Judith Weir, Osvaldo Golijov, Thea Musgrave, Helen Grime, Gerald Barry and Harrison Birtwistle.

BCMG performs in CBSO Centre, September 2018. Since its opening in 1998 the CBSO's purpose-built rehearsal hall has proved a remarkably versatile concert venue for contemporary music, chamber recitals and jazz. Electric fans, thunder sheets and exotic percussion instruments are not uncommon features of BCMG concerts.

Beyond the Millennium

On Thursday 24 September 1998 at Symphony Hall, perhaps the only person who wasn't measuring Sakari Oramo against his predecessor was Oramo himself. Rattle's final concerts had taken place less than a month earlier and Oramo's choice of programme for his inaugural concert as principal conductor looked, from that perspective, like a straightforward raid into Rattle's heartland. Sibelius' *The Bard* and Mahler's First Symphony framed Henri Dutilleux's violin concerto *L'Arbre des songes*, with Olivier Charlier as soloist.

It didn't sound like it, though, and few British listeners will have had any reason to know that what they were hearing that night was also a quintessential Oramo programme. The carefully chosen, slightly left-field homage to his Finnish heritage (Rattle, for all his love of Sibelius, had never performed *The Bard*); the fascination with contemporary music, from the perspective of a virtuoso violinist (Oramo had begun his career as leader of the Finnish Radio Symphony Orchestra); the unprejudiced willingness to tackle a warhorse such as the Mahler – that these would all become hallmarks of Oramo's decade in Birmingham was not, in fairness, something that anyone could have deduced from the handful of concerts that Oramo had given with the CBSO prior to that date.

'It was in 1995: somebody cancelled, and we were looking for a replacement,' recalls Ed Smith.

An agent sent me a tape of this completely unknown guy conducting Fauré's *Requiem* in that wonderful stone church in Helsinki.

And I put it in the video machine when Simon was with me, at home, and I can't remember if it was me or him that said, 'Yeah, and look, he's smiling. He's loving the sounds that he's being able to generate from this group – yes, let's take a risk on him.'

'And so in May 1995 I had this debut with the CBSO,' says Sakari Oramo. 'It was clearly the best orchestra I had conducted so far. We played *Don Juan* and *Lemminkäinen Legends*. And yes, I felt happy. And then I got a pretty late invitation to do a summer concert in the following year.' By then – the summer of 1996 – Rattle's departure had been announced. 'But, of course, I didn't have a clue that I could be even considered for the position, because I didn't have any experience. Not for a job of that magnitude.'

The assumption in the world beyond Birmingham was that the CBSO would be looking for an established name. (The CBSO's former principal guest conductor Mark Elder was often mentioned.) The years since 1980, however, had given the players an extremely clear idea of what they needed in a conductor – with, at the back of it all, a collective awareness that in 1979 they'd backed a hunch about a youthful unknown. Although he admits to a certain amount of 'manoeuvring', Smith allowed the musicians to reach their own conclusion; a process that has become standard procedure in CBSO conductor searches.

'Robert Heard, the chairman of the players' committee, met me in the reception of our offices at Paradise Place and said, "We really think

He's started and he's Finnish. The appointment of Sakari Oramo to succeed Rattle raised eyebrows, but Oramo's youthful appearance and quiet humour masked a fierce musical intelligence and the instincts of an orchestra-builder.

that Sakari is our man." I thought, bloody hell, that's wonderful,' says Smith. Together with the CBSO's leader Peter Thomas, Smith flew out to Helsinki to offer him the job. 'The orchestra had quite suddenly become united in knowing what it wanted,' explained Thomas in *Music Stand*. 'It was an extraordinary fusion of opinion, both on a cerebral, and more profoundly for a musician, on a gut-feeling level. Sakari Oramo is an artist overflowing with talent and musicianship . . . He is just the right musician to forge a new direction for the orchestra.'

Forward: the city orchestra lived up to the city's motto again. The announcement certainly prompted surprise. I remember players in the Royal Liverpool Philharmonic's bandroom expressing bafflement that Rattle's super-orchestra would stake everything on 'some Japanese conductor'. A small group of commentators predicted, with a little more haste than in retrospect looks seemly, that the CBSO was now about to go backwards. Jokes were made about Oramo's unshowy appearance (a 'bank manager' was one particularly vacuous comparison), and in January 1998, under the headline 'So glum for Brum', the *Guardian* pronounced Oramo a 'letdown'. His performance of Mozart's Symphony No. 39, it pronounced, 'had no redeeming feature whatever'.

Pre-judgements like these – made before Oramo had even taken up his position – leave an uncomfortable feeling that the national media was in slightly too much of a hurry to put a lid on the Birmingham phenomenon. 'Will the orchestra slip back to provincial status?' asked the *Independent*. 'It all looks desperately uncertain.' Three misapprehensions were at work. First came the notion that the quality of the CBSO's playing was a sleight-of-hand, sustained by Rattle's charisma, and destined to evaporate on his departure. Second was an unfamiliarity with Oramo's method of working. And, third, came a fundamental misreading of the CBSO's relationship to its audience, and its city. Birmingham audiences thrilled to Rattle's achievement, but it was the orchestra that they backed. They swung behind Oramo, as they'd swung behind Rattle and Frémaux, organising coach parties to support his concerts, and even baking him birthday cakes.

Yet two decades on, Oramo remembers:

> Birmingham was a cultural shock for me. I'd never seen a city more scarred by various phases of development. Symphony Hall just stood there alone – Brindleyplace didn't exist yet. I didn't fall in love with the city immediately, I have to say. But I wasn't overly nervous before I started – just normally nervous. I didn't take notice of the 'Rattle effect', of the Rattle phenomenon. There were some press articles, but they died down quite quickly.
>
> Then I remember an early outing to Paris, where Rattle conducted one concert and I conducted one, at the Cité de la Musique. It was in late 1999. It was a very, very difficult occasion for me – because of the comparison. I think that's really when it struck me for the first time.

That was a high-profile occasion – a weekend in which the Cité de la Musique flew out BCMG as well as Rattle, Oramo and the full orchestra for a festival entitled simply *Carte blanche à l'orchestre de Birmingham*. It was an early indication that the CBSO's reputation beyond the UK was still on the up. The CBSO would undertake almost as many overseas tours during Oramo's decade as it did during Rattle's entire eighteen-year tenure – a reassuring sign as the 1980s and 1990s CD boom slumped, and public funding continued to dissolve.

Ed Smith stepped down as chief executive at the end of September 1999, after twenty-one years (Turnage composed *Ed's Farewell Fanfare* to mark the occasion). Smith's successor – Stephen Maddock, a former manager at the BBC Proms – found that if the CBSO's artistic problems were illusory, the credit-card bills for Rattle's years of achievement were starting to roll in. 'I'd worked in London for nine years, and in those circles there was a sort of theory of orchestral gravity – that what goes up must come down. One critic said to me, "Oh, well you will want to get rid of that conductor, won't you?"' remembers Maddock.

What I was told when I took the job was that the deficit was £250,000 – that was it. But that was by the end of the previous year, and I found that it was going to be the same again in the current year. So that would be nearly half a million. Don't get me wrong, the organisation was fantastic, but the CBSO was putting truly wonderful work on the stage with a fairly creaky back office, if I'm honest. So the deficit got much bigger very quickly.

Unavoidably, then, a major preoccupation in the new century was to steady the bottom line. The CBSO applied to join the Arts Council's Stabilisation scheme, a belated acknowledgment from the Council that consistent underfunding had left even the best-run UK orchestras in a precarious position. The Arts Council's own consultants, recalls Maddock, were frank in their appraisal of the CBSO's position: 'It's very well run. It's doing the right things. It's connecting with its audience, all of that. It just needs more revenue funding. Of course the Arts Council didn't want to hear that, so we never got additional funding.'

A £5 million stabilisation injection did, however, allow investment in an expanding organisation. The back office that had served Rattle and Smith was essentially an expanded version of the same set-up that had served George Weldon. The organisation had acquired a rudimentary website in 1996 (believed to be the first for any UK orchestra) and email in 1998. Now there was a rebranding – the 2001–2 season saw the introduction of a new multicoloured logo (promptly dubbed 'the splat') – an enlargement

of fundraising capacity, of community and education work, and of financial management.

This was no paper exercise. Symphony orchestras are no more cost effective in the twenty-first century than they were in the 1920s, and the effort involved in raising the money necessary to give ninety musicians a living salary is immeasurably greater than when the only other show in town was the Hippodrome panto and the only other charity was the dogs' home. A city orchestra in modern Birmingham has to justify its claims on the public purse with ever more vigour and conviction. Compared with US or European orchestras – or even the wealthier London bands – the CBSO remains understaffed, and the decision by management staff to unionise in 2003 reflected a feeling that greater recognition of the role played by the back office in keeping the musicians on stage was seriously overdue. A threat of industrial action the following September was resolved amicably.

The CBSO was also, for the first time in its history, running its own building. Orchestra, chorus and staff moved into CBSO Centre, a purpose-built rehearsal hall and office building, in August 1998. Artec had designed the main hall, which doubled as a chamber-sized concert hall. The players launched a chamber music series, Centre Stage, and the Centre also found a use as a venue-for-hire outside orchestral rehearsal hours. The first concert in the Centre, appropriately enough, was a reworking of Mahler by the American jazz musician Uri Caine.

Here too, expansion was required. The initial plan to run the building with just three staff – a hall manager (the author), a technician and an apprentice – proved wildly overambitious. By the time Prince Edward opened CBSO Centre on 23 November 1998, the staff had been working for forty-three days straight. The building's concept, however, was subsequently emulated by the LSO at St Luke's, and the Royal Liverpool Philharmonic and Hallé orchestras in their respective cities, and among its many logistical advantages, CBSO Centre brought staff, chorus and players into the same building on normal working days for the first time in the organisation's history. They could eat lunch together, and the whole building resounded when Oramo and his wife Anu Komsi left Maddock to babysit their two-year-old son Leevi, whose screams of protest could be heard from Broad Street.

Centre Stage, meanwhile, prompted a flowering of small ensembles, as players formed string quartets, piano trios and brass ensembles. Bass trombonist Alwyn Green formed the ten-piece Berkley Salon Ensemble and cellist Eduardo Vassallo – a family friend of Astor Piazzolla – set up his own quintet, El Ultimo Tango. Guest artists ranging from Stephen Hough and Imogen Cooper to Lisa Batiashvili and Janine Jansen were invited to join CBSO players for chamber music, and Oramo himself led Spohr's Nonet.

Up the road at Symphony Hall, Oramo was directing some of the most eclectic programmes in the CBSO's post-war history. Early seasons included Enescu's Third Symphony, Sibelius' Kullervo, Constant Lambert's Summer's Last Will and Testament, Esa-Pekka Salonen's LA Variations, Jean-Féry Rebel's Les Élémens and the UK premiere – eighty-five years after it was composed – of Rued Langgaard's Symphony

No. 4. Oramo's second season paired a cycle of Sibelius symphonies with Prokofiev piano concertos and contemporary Scandinavian works: a recorded Sibelius cycle followed.

Oramo took up his violin to partner principal oboe Jonathan Kelly in Bach's C minor Double Concerto, and a box set of Saint-Saëns piano concertos with Stephen Hough won a string of major record awards. There were misfires: a reconstructed Schubert symphony was dropped in rehearsal with an admission from Oramo that he'd misjudged the work's quality. But still, 'short of selling programmes and serving the interval drinks, there's not much more that Sakari Oramo could be doing for the CBSO,' wrote Christopher Morley in the Birmingham Post.

Perhaps the greatest surprise – and, for Birmingham audiences, the greatest pleasure – was Oramo's growing fascination with British music. Most non-native heads of British orchestras will readily perform a token 'Enigma' or Planets. Oramo chose to champion Vaughan Williams' Sixth Symphony, Bax's Tintagel, Gilbert and Sullivan's Iolanthe, and the music of Frank Bridge – whose suite The Sea opened Oramo's first Prom with the CBSO, in the summer of 1999. A concert performance of Britten's Peter Grimes in March 2001 ('Compelling from the start, and got better as the evening progressed,' wrote the Guardian) was the moment that, for many, made it clear beyond question that the boyish-looking Finn was now master in his own house. The four-day new music festival Floof! in April 2003 was a source of particular pleasure to Oramo. 'It was a kind of carte blanche,' he remembers.

SAKARI ORAMO OBE

Sakari Oramo's mother was a pianist and his father was a musicologist. He trained as a violinist – in Holland, in Vienna, but mainly at the Sibelius Academy in Helsinki. Straight out of college, he became a founder member of Avanti! – a virtuoso Finnish chamber orchestra with a mission 'to shake up normal practice'. In 1989, he became leader of the Finnish Radio Symphony Orchestra, and meanwhile enrolled in the famous conducting class taught by Jorma Panula, whose pupils included Esa-Pekka Salonen and Osmo Vänskä. 'Mainly to find out what it was all about,' he says.

It was a tape of Oramo conducting Fauré's Requiem in Helsinki that brought Oramo's conducting to the attention of Ed Smith and Simon Rattle in Birmingham. Oramo prefers not to remember the exact performance. 'There was a glitch in the organ and it suddenly blasted full power – we had a huge cluster which kind of shook everyone. I haven't done the piece since.'

In Birmingham, amid a hugely diverse repertoire, he found a special connection with British music – mastering a remarkably convincing Brummie accent in the process. Meanwhile his wife, the soprano Anu Komsi and their two young sons Taavi and Leevi became familiar parts of the 'family' at CBSO Centre. After one year as the CBSO's principal guest conductor (2008–9) he held principal conductor posts with the Finnish Radio Symphony Orchestra and Royal Stockholm Philharmonic before, in 2013, following his CBSO predecessors Adrian Boult and Rudolf Schwarz to become chief conductor of the BBC Symphony Orchestra.

MICHAEL SEAL

Michael Seal discovered his vocation as a violinist in the Kent County Youth Orchestra. As an undergraduate at Birmingham Conservatoire in the summer of 1991 he auditioned for the first CBSO String Training Scheme. To his astonishment he was offered work as a paid CBSO extra player, becoming a full-time member of the CBSO's second-violin section from 1992 to 2014, as well as playing in the CBSO's six-piece educational ensemble, the Little Big Time Band.

But the opportunity that launched his conducting career almost never happened. In 1999, a rehearsal session with the orchestra was made available to players who wanted to try conducting. 'Ten people applied for four slots,' he recalls. 'We literally drew straws, and mine was the last one out.' He went on to study with Sakari Oramo's mentor Jorma Panula, became the CBSO's assistant conductor in 2005, and in 2011 was appointed associate conductor – the first since Harold Gray's retirement in 1979.

A fixture of the CBSO's season, with a particular taste for twentieth-century and British music and a special relationship with the CBSO Youth Orchestra, Seal also guest-conducts across Europe and the UK. He's regularly 'rescued' cancellation-stricken concerts – notably in Heidelberg in March 2012, when Andris Nelsons was called away to a family emergency, leaving Seal to accompany tenor Jonas Kaufmann. (Simon Rattle spoke to Kaufmann the night before, and assured him that he was in excellent hands.) A stalwart of the CBSO's cricket team, Michael Seal is currently the orchestra's second-highest-scoring batsman.

Stephen even said, 'You don't have to think about ticket sales, audience, whatever.' And so I did it. There were relatively small audiences, but of course it didn't matter at all. It was a statement, and it was something I really wanted to do and loved doing. It was exhilarating and I think it did a lot of good, also, for my relationship with the orchestra. They saw this was something original, something I had put together without any constraints.

No constraints applied, either, when Oramo made his latest British discovery – the music of the forgotten pre-war composer John Foulds. Over three seasons from 2004 to 2006, orchestra, audience and the record label Warner Classics backed Oramo's belief that Foulds' music deserved to be heard.

I met a German journalist, very passionate about forgotten music, and he woke up my interest in this totally unknown composer. So he gave me the score of *Three Mantras*. I mean, I was trapped by the awesome intensity and energy of that piece. But then, of course, we discovered *Lyra Celtica* and *April-England*, this wonderful, wonderful little fantasy, and that made it possible to make another disc. I had a feeling the orchestra were, a bit . . . well, I mean, they wanted to make it work, very much, but they were a bit bewildered. 'What is this music? How do we perform it?' But I think the results still bear listening.

Birmingham's unsuccessful bid to be 2008 European Capital of Culture had at least one happy musical consequence, too – IgorFest, a four-year project, starting in 2005, to perform every single work by Stravinsky. As anniversary followed anniversary, Oramo found himself drawn not just to Britten's *War Requiem* (the fortieth anniversary performance took place in Coventry Cathedral in September 2002) but to Elgar's great series of Triennial Festival commissions: *The Dream of Gerontius*, *The Apostles* and *The Kingdom*. 'I count Elgar as one of my three favourite composers of all time,' he says.

I'm just fascinated by his invention, by the wealth of detail in everything he wrote, and by the sincerity of his message. I'm not a religious person at all. But I approach them as great works of art with a distinct human message, and a strong sense of invention and beautiful writing.

'He conducts English music superbly,' wrote the *Guardian* after *The Kingdom* in October 2006. 'Everything moved with total assurance . . . the sound was consistently glorious.' In 2008 Oramo was awarded the Elgar Society's Elgar Medal. His in-house recording of *Gerontius* (2007) shows how he stripped away a century's varnish from these works, probing beneath the surface, clarifying textures without any sacrifice of poetry or passion. It also reveals how masterfully he'd refined the CBSO's sound, from the strings upwards. Far from suffering a fall in standards after 1998, the consensus across the orchestra remains that Oramo improved the CBSO's tone quality and ensemble. It had been one reason why the players pressed for his appointment.

'After Rattle it was so refreshing,' says David Gregory. 'Rattle knew the music so well that he felt we should know it too. So we just loved the way Sakari did what a conductor should do, which is to show you where you are. He had clarity, and the inspiration to go with it.' Sheila Clarke agrees: 'Being a fiddle player himself, he was wonderful for string-players. Sakari got the strings playing in a much more fluid way, with a much greater depth to the sound.' Oramo acknowledges that this was one of his aims:

> When I started, I felt that the orchestra was pulling in very different directions, musically. I have enormous appreciation for Simon. He's a great musician. But his style of preparing and rehearsing – it had been so detailed that I felt there was a lack of spontaneity, of initiative in the orchestra. I found it really hard to pull them together at first.
>
> But I found a way, by working with the strings in great depth and length. I remember we did several string pieces in my first days, and I remember particularly Bartók's *Divertimento*, which was an eye-opener. Maybe something could happen here; something good, musically, in the way I wanted it to happen. And so I think the result was a less percussive, more string-based sound. I think that was my achievement, in my time in Birmingham. It didn't happen without wounds and scars. I feel it took more or less all of the ten years

I was there, but I had the orchestra I wanted to have in my last two seasons.

By then, of course, everyone was a decade older. Like the cells in a human body, every member of an orchestra changes over time, yet the identity of the whole remains the same. Rattle's woodwind 'royal family' of Kevin Gowland (flute), Jonathan Kelly (oboe) and Colin Parr (clarinet) had moved on. (Kelly followed Rattle to the Berlin Philharmonic.) Michael Seal had emerged from the second violin section to become assistant conductor; Peter Thomas had been succeeded as leader by Laurence Jackson. Martyn Davies (clarinet), the last playing member of the CBSO to have performed in the premiere of Britten's *War Requiem*, retired in 2004. When, in 2006, Oramo announced that the 2007–8 season would be his last in Birmingham, newer members such as the principal flute Marie-Christine Zupancic, principal horn Elspeth Dutch, first oboe Rainer Gibbons and trumpeter Alan Thomas, had never known any other music director.

'Sakari did a lot of concerts – around four hundred in total, of which a hundred were overseas,' comments Stephen Maddock. 'It takes time and energy and input and involvement to make that happen,' says Oramo.

> And of course my family was in Finland and my kids were still quite young. And whether I was in Birmingham or at home I always felt that I was in the wrong place. That's a dilemma of international conductors of course; you're always in the wrong place, no matter what. I felt it was fair for everybody

that I would leave it there. I was quite clear about it. I didn't have any second thoughts, ever. I think it was a good period, ten years, and a really strong development.

Sakari Oramo conducted his final concert as CBSO music director on 12 June 2008 – Janáček's *Sinfonietta* and Beethoven's Ninth, followed by a party in the International Convention Centre. A decade earlier, the *Birmingham Post* had reported his first concert under the headline 'He's started and he's Finnish'; now his final pre-concert talk was billed as 'Right to the Finnish'. Oramo's quirky sense of humour and unfussy podium style had concealed a fiercely intelligent, often intensely emotional musical personality and an uncompromising orchestra-builder. Perhaps the real monument to his tenure is that in 1998 the conversation about the CBSO had been almost entirely about the immediate past. In 2008, it was about the future.

The Nelsons Touch

About the last place anyone expected CBSO history to be made in 2007 was Birmingham Town Hall. It had been more than sixteen years since the CBSO had played there, and more than a decade since it had been closed to the public for a renovation that many Brummies doubted would ever be completed. But on the evening of Sunday 2 September 2007, the remodelled Town Hall was almost ready for its new public, and the CBSO was booked to play an 'acoustic test' with the only conductor who happened to be at hand – twenty-eight-year-old Latvian Andris Nelsons, making his

first visit to Birmingham to record Tchaikovsky's Violin Concerto with the violinist Baiba Skride.

Nelsons and the orchestra quickly rehearsed a test programme of Strauss's *Don Juan* and Dvořák's 'New World' Symphony, and a small audience of CBSO staff, friends and close supporters was quietly invited. Violinist Paul Smith had retired a few weeks previously, but was called back in to fill a gap. He is still wide-eyed when he describes what happened next.

I was driving into town and I thought, you must be mad, you've just retired. And what are you doing now? You're going to go and rehearse the bloody 'New World' Symphony. I started the rehearsal, and after about ten minutes I thought, this is a new piece. It was absolutely extraordinary. And at the break everybody just said, well, this boy's just got it.

Sheila Clarke remembers:

There were only about a hundred people in the hall, and yet he conducted as if there were two thousand people there. It didn't make any difference to him at all, and it just brought us all alive. The players' committee asked every single player in the orchestra individually whether we should appoint him and everybody said yes. There might have been a couple who weren't quite sure, but no more than two. So we went straight to Stephen Maddock, and said, 'Look, you've got to book this man. We've got to get him. We've got to have him.'

A rule of thumb: if you want to gauge whether an orchestra is enjoying itself as much as you are, look at the players' faces, and examine their body language. The sound, as Nelsons launched into *Don Juan*, was one that no one present will ever forget: the overwhelming physical immediacy of the Town Hall's new acoustic on that sunny September evening, and the way every line within the music's texture seemed to surge and glow. But almost as gripping was the sight of seventy-odd players swaying and nodding like soloists, eyes locked onto this gangly young conductor and smiling as they played. Musicians (and writers) talk a good shout about the transforming power of music, but this genuinely felt like an orchestra, a conductor and an audience falling in love at first sight. 'There was just no controversy at all,' says David Gregory. 'It was the obvious choice. It was magic.'

Well, any sufficiently deft piece of orchestral management is indistinguishable from magic. Stephen Maddock had been discreetly placing unattached conductors in front of the CBSO ever since Oramo had announced his departure. A search committee of players, board members, staff and music staff identified potential candidates. The process then, as with Rattle's successor, was to let the musicians reach their own consensus. (CBSO players complete anonymous appraisal forms for every

OPPOSITE *Andris Nelsons was another CBSO discovery. His easy-going manner could cause headaches for managers, but on the podium he carried everything before him, and his relationship with the orchestra was like a seven-year honeymoon.*

conductor and soloist with whom they work.) Gustavo Dudamel had conducted the orchestra in February 2007; by the first rehearsal break, players were pressing for him to be offered the post, unaware that he already had plans with Ed Smith's new band, the Gothenburg Symphony Orchestra. 'Thank goodness,' comments Sheila Clarke. 'He was so like Rattle that it wouldn't have worked in the end.'

Plans for a director-less season in 2008–9 were already being made when Maddock spoke to Richard Wigley, general manager of the BBC Philharmonic. Wigley was already sizing Nelsons up for his own orchestra, so Maddock moved swiftly to set up an audition in Birmingham. 'We called it an acoustic test for the Town Hall, on the lines of plausible deniability. So if it didn't work, or if the orchestra didn't like him – well, concert, what concert?'

For Nelsons himself, the memory of those days is of something 'unreal, a miracle'.

> I knew that anyone who was coming as a guest could be a potential candidate. Really, though, I've never in my life had career plans, or some idea of where I should be or where I could be. I really was not following that model. But I remember it was a very family feeling, from the very beginning. I wasn't really thinking about where it can or would lead; I just focused on making music, meeting the orchestra and also to play these two pieces in the Town Hall. The decision the orchestra made was a very big surprise and an extremely great honour for me.

The CBSO announced Andris Nelsons as its new music director barely a month after he'd worked with the orchestra for the first time and before he'd conducted a single public concert with them. After the experience of Rattle and Oramo, the musical world was more ready to accept the judgement of the CBSO players, and it helped that Nelsons already had a growing reputation on the Continent. A hastily planned 'get to know you' matinee in November 2007 confirmed that the choice was justified. 'Having appointed, at the eleventh hour, a young Latvian whom the Birmingham public had never seen, there was an understandably excited rush to get him on the podium. Yet Andris Nelsons seemed not to be aware of any pressure,' wrote Rian Evans in the *Guardian*. 'He is, quite simply, a commanding presence, without a trace of ego, intent only on creating music and pulsating energy.'

Nelsons' energy in performance, his seemingly innate mastery of vast musical forms, and his near-supernatural capacity for creating sonic beauty went together with an irrepressible good nature and lack of affectation. He rented a flat in the newly refurbished Rotunda and CBSO staff got used to finding him attempting to microwave canned soup while still in its tin, or carrying energy bars for when he lost track of time and simply forgot to eat.

Meanwhile, in rehearsal, he'd be sculpting a Wagner prelude with the kind of command not heard since Furtwängler. 'He has a phenomenal conducting technique,' says David Gregory. 'He came to the orchestra like it was a grand piano, and he played it like Horowitz.' Nelsons' bond of trust with his musicians made

extraordinary things possible. 'He was one of the few conductors who didn't try and get rid of anybody in the orchestra,' remembers Sheila Clarke. 'He wanted to get the best out of his players, and he never gave you the feeling that he was the most important thing on the platform.' That Nelsons built on Oramo's work to draw from the CBSO some of its finest playing in living memory is an impression shared by older and younger players alike. Bryony Morrison's childhood love of music was sparked by Simon Rattle's 1996 *Orchestra* CD-ROM; she joined the CBSO's second violins in 2012:

> Andris has got the most incredible range of facial expressions, and there's something about his technique as well that's simultaneously very, very precise, and also super-expressive in terms of phrasing. So he has this amazing ability to make the big moments really count, maybe because he paces it so well. One of my favourite Andris moments was when we did *Der Rosenkavalier* with him: the Silver Rose scene. I just remember thinking, 'This is extraordinary. This is like nothing in life.' And yes, it was just one of those moments that really stays with you forever – transformative.

Nelsons wasn't the first CBSO music director to champion opera, but – alongside an orchestral repertoire that favoured late Romantics and twentieth-century masters – the scale and ambition of Nelsons' operatic projects was unprecedented. He opened his first official

ANDRIS NELSONS OBE

If there was a time in Andris Nelsons' life when he wasn't preoccupied with music, he struggles to remember it. At the age of five, at a Latvian State Opera production of Wagner's *Tannhäuser* in his native Riga, he remembers being 'overwhelmed by the music'. He took up the trumpet at the age of twelve; and later sang as a bass-baritone. As a deputising trumpet-player in the Oslo Philharmonic, he caught the ear of his future teacher and mentor Mariss Jansons; by 2003 he was principal conductor of the same Latvian State Opera that had fired his childhood love of music. He began his first *Ring* cycle in 2006, at the age of twenty-seven.

When he came to the CBSO's attention in the summer of 2008, Nelsons was chief conductor of the Nordwestdeutsche Philharmonie in Herford, Germany, but his reputation was growing, with bootlegs of his performances circulating among concert managers across Europe, and engagements at Bayreuth and the New York Metropolitan Opera already in his diary. In Birmingham, he initially rented a flat in the Rotunda: 'It is both in Birmingham, and above it,' he observed. His genial manner and fondness for luxury cologne gave his time at CBSO Centre the air of an extended honeymoon. Players, staff and audience alike all felt that his departure was premature. He has since taken posts in Boston, USA, and (from 2018) as Gewandhaus-kapellmeister in Leipzig – one of the oldest and most distinguished conducting positions in the world.

season in 2008 with *La Bohème*. *Der Rosenkavalier* came in May 2014. As the final trio filled Symphony Hall, Nelsons hung off the podium like a sailor in the rigging, letting the waves of sound crash over him. But Wagner was, and is, at the heart of Nelsons' ambitions; and after *Lohengrin* in 2010, *Tristan und Isolde* followed in 2012, *Der fliegender Holländer* in 2013 and *Parsifal* in 2015. Concerning rumours of a Birmingham *Ring* cycle, Stephen Maddock says only that 'Andris has a tremendous, mischievous sense of humour'.

Nelsons' successes at Bayreuth meant that the Wagner performances that he did give in Birmingham drew international attention – and brought the CBSO together with singers of the celebrity of Jonas Kaufmann, whose rehearsals for Mahler's *Kindertotenlieder* in 2012 were briefly halted when it was discovered that solo and orchestra parts were in different keys. Nelsons' relatively narrow repertoire gave guest conductors scope to explore: John Wilson conducted Vaughan Williams; Ilan Volkov devised idiosyncratic modern programmes, and principal guest conductor Edward Gardner (appointed in 2010) joyously rediscovered all five Mendelssohn symphonies. On two ear-splitting evenings in October 2009, the CBSO and Chorus squeezed on stage alongside the combined orchestral and choral forces of the Mariinsky Theatre, St Petersburg, as Valery Gergiev conducted Prokofiev's *Cantata for the Twentieth Anniversary of the October Revolution*.

And while the aftermath of the 2008 global crash was not an ideal environment for artistic growth, ticket sales were actually buoyant.

Nelsons, like Oramo and Rattle, guaranteed a great night out and audiences who were forced to prioritise leisure spending opted for quality. But half a decade of management effort was squandered on a project by the City Council to merge Symphony Hall and the CBSO – until now, wholly independent organisations. Since the city part-funded both, it looked logical enough, superficially at least. Symphony Hall had been booking second-string London orchestras to perform popular classics in direct competition with the CBSO, in defiance of artistic or financial logic. That ceased, but draining, destabilising arguments dragged on for several years before the scheme was decisively thrown out by the CBSO's board under its new chair, Bridget Blow. (Acting chair Kumar Muthalagappan had eviscerated the project after the death of his much-loved predecessor Ronnie Bowker in 2010.)

'I can absolutely see why the funders wanted to have that question asked and then answered,' says Maddock. 'But the truth was that we're both working on pretty tight margins with pretty skeletal staffing, so simply by putting organisations together, you weren't achieving many savings.' Nelsons, however, like Boult, Heward, Schwarz and Rattle before him, was an asset with a rocketing market value. In May 2013, he accepted the post of music director at the Boston Symphony Orchestra. He intended, he said, to hold both posts simultaneously, and even talked about plans for the CBSO's centenary in 2020. The reality of holding down two positions on different sides of the Atlantic, as well as maintaining a home life in Latvia with his wife and their baby daughter, would make that impossible. That didn't make the inevitable conclusion any less painful.

'It was such a difficult decision, and one of the reasons, too, was that when I took the position at Boston, I hoped that I would continue as far as I could to fulfil the tasks of music director of both orchestras,' says Nelsons.

Of course I could have just reduced my weeks with Birmingham, and then reduced Boston, and continued with two orchestras, just as now I have two orchestras, Boston and Leipzig. But Birmingham has more concerts and a longer season than either of those. I could have continued several years, but I would have been steadily reducing my commitment. It wouldn't be fair towards the orchestra and wouldn't be fair also towards me.

'I said, "We want you to carry on of course, but I can't make the decision for you,"' says Stephen Maddock.

I didn't want to get to a situation where, yes, Andris was going to do it, but all we would end up with was six or eight weeks – and end up spending most of them on tour, so he had no presence in Birmingham. Because we've never done that. Even when our conductors have had another job going, the CBSO has always been number one. In the end, there were no hard feelings about it at all.

Nelsons announced his resignation in October 2013; his official farewell concert was with

Mahler's Third Symphony on 18 June 2015. It was the severing of a relationship which, after seven years, still felt like a honeymoon.

'Emotionally, there was no reason to leave,' says Nelsons.

Maybe people think some frictions had started. It was the opposite. Each year our music making together got closer and closer and deeper and deeper, and there was no reason to think about leaving the orchestra at all. I always thought it's better to leave earlier, rather than to leave too late when everyone says, 'Oh, we are so fed up with him', and I'm glad that never happened. But I miss the orchestra. I felt very looked after. There was a feeling that we were doing it together, and we supported each other as partners – orchestra and conductor. I think that's very rare.

Nelsons' very last concert as CBSO music director would be under the eyes of the world, with Beethoven's Ninth at the BBC Proms on 19 July 2015. Bryony Morrison remembers that too:

I remember doing his last Prom, and yes, it was one of those concerts that you'll always remember. I went home thinking, 'How are we ever going to move on from him?' And then we had two free days, and the next day, we were due to play *Sleeping Beauty* with Mirga Gražinytė-Tyla – who we'd never come across before.

CBSO CENTRE

Very few British orchestras rehearse full time in the venue where they perform, and for seventy-eight years, when not at the Town Hall or Symphony Hall, the CBSO led a peripatetic existence. After considering the former Presbyterian Church on Broad Street (now the Popworld night club), the CBSO acquired a ninety-nine-year lease on Rowe Bros' former lead-plumbing factory on Berkley Street. As part of its ground rent, the CBSO was required to give the King Edward VI Schools Foundation a copy of every new recording it releases.

Deputy chief executive Richard York led the conversion project, and everything but the 1921-vintage factory façade was demolished, to be replaced with offices, studios and a 300-seat rehearsal and concert hall, modelled on the Swan Theatre in Stratford-upon-Avon. CBSO Centre was officially opened by Prince Edward on 23 November 1998, to the sound of a new fanfare by Judith Weir. A time capsule beneath the main hall contains a copy of Simon Rattle's first contract, an Argos catalogue and a bottle of whisky.

It's now the base for most CBSO rehearsals, as well as the Centre Stage chamber music series and the administration of BCMG and the chamber choir Ex Cathedra, as well as the CBSO. It is regularly hired out to other users – a useful source of income, which has seen the CBSO hosting the *Jazzlines* contemporary jazz series, BBC One's *Question Time*, script conferences for *The Archers* and a private rehearsal for the late Luciano Pavarotti. Unable to fit through the front door, the great tenor entered via the emergency exit.

CBSO Centre's Holliday Street façade shows just how much of the structure was purpose-built. The arched roof spans the main rehearsal hall; the wooden lattices proved to be a popular nesting site for local magpies.

10

The City's Orchestra

'I will be blunt,' says Mirga Gražinytė-Tyla, remembering her very first rehearsal with the CBSO in July 2015.

We started with Tchaikovsky's *Sleeping Beauty*. It was the very last concert of the season, and I think the musicians were very tired. I remember at some moments thinking, 'Whoa!' – and not in a good way. I expected more in the first rehearsal. But there was this other thing, and it was very strong – they were making music as if they were a youth orchestra. This communication – a sense of 'Ah! Let's do this together!' And on the second day I thought, 'Wow, this is where we start.' It was impressive how much they'd changed, the speed with which everybody worked. And in the concert, they gave more. They'd given a lot in rehearsal, but they gave more.

It could so easily have been routine. In the twenty-one months since Andris Nelsons had announced his departure, Stephen Maddock and the conductor search committee had been taking every opportunity to place unknown or promising conductors in front of the orchestra, even if that meant a season or two of interregnum. Orchestral life has changed since Boult's 1959–60 stint as 'umbrella'; with international air travel making it possible to book the best artists from around the world, it's no longer expected that a principal conductor will effectively carry an entire season. A fallow season allowed the CBSO's extended family of conductors to stretch out. Michael Seal conducted Korngold's Symphony in F sharp, Grainger's *The Warriors* and Beethoven's 'Eroica'; assistant conductor Alpesh Chauhan performed Shostakovich's Fifteenth and Bruckner's Third, and principal guest Edward Gardner conducted a luminous concert performance of Verdi's *Falstaff*.

More important, it gave the orchestra time to think about what they wanted from the future. Well, that was the idea, anyway: three days after Nelsons' farewell didn't exactly seem like an auspicious date for a debut. Bryony Morrison remembers that first rush job of a trial concert – in which, counter-intuitively but, as it turned out, dazzlingly – Gražinytė-Tyla paired music from Tchaikovsky's *Sleeping Beauty* with Samuel Barber's *Knoxville* and Beethoven's Seventh Symphony.

We were all ready to be sad. And then, all of a sudden, there was something so exciting. It was really awesome timing: I remember most of the orchestra going for a drink at Bank in Brindleyplace after the concert, and there was just this real buzz in the bar. Everyone was saying, 'We must email Stephen.' It was almost like we couldn't see past Andris until we'd had to say goodbye, and then suddenly it was really exciting. There were lots of really fresh things about her – she's got an incredible technique; the energy of that Beethoven and its tightness and vibrancy.

'By the time I got home I was already getting emails from members of the orchestra,' recalls Maddock: '"Sorry to bother you now, but we

On a journey: Mirga Gražinytė-Tyla became music director of the CBSO in August 2016.

had the most amazing evening with Mirga";
"Everyone's talking about it in the pub"; "We feel
like we could be on the verge of something really
exciting here."'

Among the critics, Christopher Morley of
the *Birmingham Post* called it first, on 27 July
2015: 'This concert, which seemed to come
out of nowhere, brought an exciting new
name which audiences will surely add to their
shortlist of possible successors to the much-
missed Andris Nelsons.' There were still other
conductors to hear, with the young Israeli Omer
Meir Wellber making a powerful impression, but
rumours about Gražinytė-Tyla bubbled under
in Birmingham throughout the autumn season
– which didn't prevent some London-based
commentators from making predictions, some
of them comically wide of the mark. Gražinytė-
Tyla returned in January 2016 with Sibelius'
Lemminkäinen Legends; and the conductor
search committee felt that it was time to put the
question more formally.

A players' meeting was held. 'It was in no
sense a dance-off,' says Maddock.

> But the mood was very clear. They had
> about an hour and a quarter's very frank
> discussion in which her gender was not
> mentioned once, either as reason to appoint
> or a reason not to appoint. Then there was a
> secret ballot, but with only one name on it –
> the question being, do we invite her now, or
> do we need more time to decide?

'White Smoke at the CBSO' was the headline
on the arts review website *The Arts Desk* on
4 February 2016, when the results were made
public. 'To an audience member, at any rate,
the connection between Gražinytė-Tyla and the
orchestra seemed dazzlingly evident. She's a
musician with energy, intelligence and a bright,
natural musicality,' I wrote at the time.

Gražinytė-Tyla was overseeing a production
of *Carmen* at the Landestheater in Salzburg when
the call came through:

> I had a touch of 'flu, I was in bed, and
> when I saw the phone ringing. I thought
> – 'I can't take that message now.' It was
> the next morning that we talked. I felt
> joy, but also responsibility: taking on the
> whole bunch of those incredible musicians
> and then thinking about the direction
> of the orchestra, its role in the city and
> everything. I thought, 'Wow. This is really a
> huge thing to manage.'

Yet the overwhelming impression of her first
season in Birmingham was one of uninhibited
enjoyment. Her very first concert as music
director in Birmingham was on 26 August 2016:
Mozart's *Magic Flute* overture, Tchaikovsky's
Fourth Symphony and Hans Abrahamsen's song
cycle . . . *let me tell you* . . . And the following
night, it was straight into her first ever BBC Prom
– placing the new relationship on the biggest
stage imaginable, right out of the box. If the
daring was remarkable, so too was the critical
response. 'Everything about this appearance
suggested that the twenty-nine-year-old
Lithuanian has already established a wonderful
rapport with the members of the orchestra,'

wrote Andrew Clements in the *Guardian*. 'It was a "were you there?" kind of event,' said Fiona Maddocks in the *Observer*. An extract from *Sleeping Beauty* was the encore. 'See you in Birmingham!' yelled Gražinytė-Tyla, to a cheering Royal Albert Hall.

And here, in Birmingham, we are. It's hard to write about a work in progress. Gražinytė-Tyla's first season was shaped by the speed with which it was devised. (Most of the 2016–17 concerts had already been fixed by the time she was appointed.) But among the big statements of intent, such as the concert performance of Mozart's *Idomeneo* with which that first season closed, a fresh and idiosyncratic voice was already audible in repertoire choices such as *Fires* by Gražinytė-Tyla's Lithuanian compatriot Raminta Šerkšnytė; in a joyous rediscovery of an early Feeney Trust commission, Tippett's Piano Concerto, and in Haydn's early *Hornsignal* and *Le Matin* symphonies (Gražinytė-Tyla asked the six woodwind players to perform standing up, and conducted them as if they were soloists), as well as an uncompromisingly personal approach to that warhorse of all warhorses, Beethoven's Fifth.

'A gesture from her can change the sound of the orchestra,' says Bryony Morrison. 'That's something that is quite rare. Not all conductors have it. She doesn't just talk about dynamics and speeds. She talks about sound-worlds, and colours, and shows it with energy and clarity.' By mid 2017, there was an unmistakable new energy at Symphony Hall. Gražinytė-Tyla's habit of slipping unexpected but illuminating 'extras' into concerts – the finale of Ligeti's *Concert Românesc* as an encore to Bartók's Concerto for

Orchestra, say, or Purcell's *Funeral Music for Queen Mary* seguing into the thunderous opening motif of Beethoven's Fifth – helped generate a sense of each concert as a special occasion, or what Simon Rattle might have called 'an adventure'.

That bond of trust with the CBSO's Birmingham audience drew big, animated crowds even for her most quirky (some might say quixotic) repertoire choices – works such as Jörg Widmann's sprawling *Babylon-Suite*, Čiurlionis' *The Sea*, or Weinberg's Symphony No.21. Gražinytė-Tyla has used her personal connections with guest artists including Widmann and the violinist Gidon Kremer to stage events – like her 2019 recreation of the Baltic song festivals of her childhood – that feel like they could happen nowhere else but here and now. Parallels are being drawn with another young CBSO music director with a city-wide vision and a taste for the unexpected. 'It just feels so much like the Rattle years,' says David Gregory. 'There are still people – just as with Rattle – who don't like too much new stuff, and she wants to go into new stuff in a big way. But I think they're exciting times.'

What goes unsaid is that – compared with the organisation that Rattle inherited in 1980 – Gražinytė-Tyla's responsibilities are immense. At the end of the 2017–18 season, the orchestra's strength stood at ninety contracted players: with fifteen vacancies under recruitment, the make-up of the orchestra was 46 per cent female, 54 per cent male, with fifteen different nationalities represented. There are some thirty-six management staff. On an annual income of £8.6 million, the orchestra alone gave 123 concerts, reaching an audience in excess of

200,000, and undertook five overseas tours. The CBSO's education work reached 20,000 people; and the CBSO Chorus and Youth Choruses, SO Vocal, CBSO Youth Orchestra and CBSO Centre all have, and continue to develop, their own artistic profiles.

Gražinytė-Tyla understands that she isn't just dealing with an orchestra, but with the artistic embodiment of a whole city – something that goes beyond simply flying the flag on tour, important though that is. (She thinks of a concert at Hamburg's Elbphilharmonie in November 2017 as a moment when their joint interpretation of Debussy's *La Mer* 'really took off'.) Her March 2018 Debussy Festival – as well as cramming eight concerts into two weekends – became more than just a personal sequel to Oramo's *Floof!* It opened out to showcase the entire breadth of the CBSO's extended 'family', with Michael Seal and assistant conductor Jonathan Bloxham sharing the orchestral programmes, violinist Cath Arlidge hosting a family concert, performances by the Chorus and Youth Chorus, slots for BCMG and Simon Halsey's newly formed Birmingham University Singers, solo recitals from students of the Royal Birmingham Conservatoire and a performance of *Images* by the CBSO Youth Orchestra under Gražinytė-Tyla's own baton.

'The diversity of Birmingham is fantastic,' she says.

> In a way, the whole globe is focused in this city. I see it as a really big, very beautiful but huge challenge to reach our people here. My dream is that every kid

in Birmingham would know Symphony Hall, would know how cool and great it is – one of the absolutely top places for music in the world. And maybe I say this too much, but this orchestra has a youthful spirit, in the sense of being open to things: being curious, wanting to discover new repertoire, new ways of playing known repertoire, and new ways of carrying out our role in society. Both the audience and the orchestra are incredibly supportive to their music director – and this is a wonderful privilege because it really gives a feeling we are on a journey together. On a very wonderful journey.

November 2018

Monday 12 November 2018 is in most ways an unremarkable day for the CBSO. Work begins at 8 a.m. at CBSO Centre, as the assistant centre manager Peter Clarke arrives to unlock the building. After deactivating the alarms and checking the doors, his first job is to reset the Justham Auditorium – the Centre's 300-seat main hall – for the orchestral rehearsal, scheduled to begin (as CBSO rehearsals have begun for as long as anyone can remember) on the dot of 10.15 a.m. Every minute – literally – of the orchestra's schedule is governed by strict rules in the players' contract, and is closely monitored. Even ninety seconds' overrun can lead to overtime costs, and the schedule is so busy that every one of those seconds is valuable. For any orchestral administrator, delaying scheduled rehearsal time is an unbreakable taboo.

This morning, the hall is still set up from Saturday night's jazz concert by Sara Colman, part of the regular series promoted at the Centre by Jazzlines. The various acoustic settings of the room – fabric banners and overhead panels – need to be modified too: a full symphony orchestra makes a very different sort of noise from a jazz ensemble and a lively audience. Then it's a matter of re-arranging the portable risers that double for orchestra and audience (each one takes two people to lift, but a couple of casual crew have been booked to help) and putting out music stands ready for the orchestra's own platform crew to go to work.

Platform manager Peter Harris (universally known as 'Rambo') and his assistant Robert Howard have long since moved beyond paper plans. Between them, every possible orchestral seating configuration in a hundred different halls has been committed to memory, along with the intricacies of handling and storing each of the CBSO's percussion instruments. This set-up isn't too big. 'Not this morning,' says Peter. 'I mean, this show is basically just snare drum, cymbals, bells and timps – nothing really. The rest of the equipment you see in there is for the workshop they're doing this afternoon.' The metal door of CBSO Centre's percussion store screeches up, and they get on with it.

But it's true: the afternoon's rehearsal is a bit different, with Michael Seal directing a workshop session for young composers from Cambridge University, part of a new partnership scheme. First, though, comes the morning session with guest conductor Stanislav Kochanovsky – Janáček's *Taras Bulba* and Tchaikovsky's Fifth.

Players start arriving at the Centre around 9.30 a.m., by which time receptionist Sev Kucukogullari has arrived and commissioned the switchboard; coffee and tea has been laid out for the orchestra in the Centre's common room and the piano tuner has given the orchestral piano a touch-up (standard practice before every run of rehearsals). A librarian heaves a trolley down from the first-floor orchestral library and distributes the music folders ('pads') for this morning's programme; they'll gather them in again at lunchtime, to be replaced by entirely new pads for the afternoon session.

The office staff have arrived by now – concerts management showing the guest conductor to his dressing room and briefing him on his orchestra for the week; orchestral management dealing with that morning's crop of queries from the arriving musicians. Mobile phones mean that the orchestra manager Claire Dersley and her assistant Isabel Turienzo are no longer glued to their desks, but the eternal responsibility of the orchestra manager remains the same – to make sure that every single seat in the orchestra is occupied at 10.15, or to know the reason why. At the weekend, the orchestra played two 'Spectacular Classics' galas for the promoter Raymond Gubbay at Symphony Hall: a relatively straightforward day's work. Fortunately no one has gone sick or is running late this morning. 'It's not too bad this week.' says Claire.

Around the building, rooms light up. An extra player, not needed in the Janáček, has booked a rehearsal studio for a spot of private practice. BCMG has an early management team meeting in the Ratcliff Room, where the CBSO's board is also due to meet tonight. By the time Stanislav Kochanovsky gives his downbeat at 10.15 a.m., some 120 people are in the building, every one of them occupied with something necessary. Orchestras these days can't afford passengers.

Now it's the late afternoon. The afternoon orchestral rehearsal is due to finish at 5.30 p.m., and then the Centre has to be turned swiftly around for a BCMG rehearsal. Stephen Maddock and the senior managers are all closeted away with papers for the 4 p.m. CBSO board meeting, and heads throughout the offices are bent before computer screens. Niki Longhurst has been with the CBSO since 1998, and she doubles as CBSO Centre manager and PA to the chief executive. With him off her hands for the next couple of hours, she's double checking the Centre's plans for the week – staff rosters, catering requirements, cleaning schedules and security. 'The counter-terrorism unit of West Midlands Police did a sort of audit on the building, and we've been tightening up on lots of things,' she explains. Professional door staff are one more thing to book and budget for. HR manager Hollie Dunster shares the office; she's currently writing up the outcome of a contingency planning meeting.

In the finance office, Galia Bouhayed is using the accounting software to check that the CBSO's records of recent development income match what the CBSO's bankers (HSBC, successors to the Midland Bank that gave the CBO its first overdraft in 1921) say has been received. 'It's a bit of a beast,' she comments – and as the steward for the staff union, BECTU, she's also had her hands full with pay negotiations. A cash tin

of bar takings from Saturday's jazz concert at the Centre waits to be counted up and returned to the safe. Board meetings generate more work: finance manager Dawn Doherty, at the opposite desk, is preparing the month's management accounts for the next finance subcommittee. 'It takes about a week,' she says. 'Tomorrow I'll work on costs.'

As money goes out, it's the job of the development department to bring it in. In the main office, Eve Vines is juggling several chores:

> I spent the whole morning on GDPR [general data protection regulations] – it's a huge, huge thing – and now I'm looking at how we research and meet prospective donors. We've also got about 1,400 Members, and there's a full event programme that supports their involvement with the orchestra. So we've got two concerts this week and events around both of them: two corporate clients coming in, one on Wednesday – that's a dinner – and then another on Friday.

In marketing – putting it very crudely, the people whose job it is to sell concert tickets – Katie Goldhawk, Rob Corrin and Lucy Dwyer are at their desks and Tom White, the assistant digital manager (a relatively new role) is busy in the hall with a video camera, capturing footage of the composers' workshop for use in social media and on the website. 'We're doing fewer and fewer of the mailings and print or fliers that we used to produce,' he explains. 'This afternoon is just project documentation, really, but next

MIRGA GRAŽINYTĖ-TYLA

Mirga Gražinytė-Tyla grew up with Lithuania's great choral tradition. Her father conducts the Aidija Chamber Choir in Vilnius; her mother is a pianist, and in 1994, at the age of seven, Mirga travelled with them to the International Eisteddfod at Llangollen: the choir won the grand prize. 'Life was not possible without music,' she recalls. She experimented with violin and percussion before focusing on singing, and later choral conducting – studying in Graz, Bologna and Leipzig. 'But you are studying orchestral conducting as your main subject, aren't you?' asked the Austrian conductor Wolfgang Bozic. A masterclass with Herbert Blomstedt encouraged her to enter the 2012 Nestlé and Salzburg Young Conductors Competition – where the judges, impressed by her 'great clarity and determination', awarded her first prize.

That led to opera jobs in Heidelberg and Bern, a Dudamel Fellowship in Los Angeles, and the post of *Kapellmeister* at the Landestheater Salzburg from 2015 to 2017. Opera house positions have been a traditional part of a conductor's training in Central Europe – Andris Nelsons and Rudolf Schwarz followed a similar path. But since coming to Birmingham in 2016 (where she rents an apartment in the Jewellery Quarter) Gražinytė-Tyla has become equally fascinated by the local musical tradition:

'It's already a huge, wonderful heritage of hundreds of years, Birmingham being an industrial city and such an important cultural centre, also, with so many stars of the nineteenth century coming here – Mendelssohn and Bruckner playing in Birmingham; Liszt, Dvořák, Elgar. We must build on that.'

week we're hoping to film the whole of the Roxanna Panufnik premiere – it'll be the first time we've tried to do a concert the whole way.'

But some aspects of the marketing mix are unchanged. 'We've got a mailing landing – quite a big mailing, with our new Christmas leaflet and our new concert guide,' says Lucy. 'I've been looking at details for that, and I've started to put together a plan for our new issue of *Music Stand*.' The CBSO's supporters' magazine is now in its fifth decade. Then there are the concert coaches bringing audiences from Birmingham's wider orbit. 'Lichfield, Sutton Coldfield and Cheltenham,' Rob reels them off. 'We book the coach company, and then we organise a team of volunteers to help us run them, take registers, make sure everyone turns up.' Two devoted long-term CBSO supporters – Anita Davies and Frank North – also organise private concert coaches from communities in rural Shropshire.

With the orchestra rehearsing, and occasional blasts of brass or timpani filtering reassuringly through the walls of the Centre, Claire Dersley is re-examining the routes that the orchestra's three coaches take when returning from concerts outside Birmingham. 'The hallowed routes,' she laughs. They're designed to drop off as many players as possible, as close as possible to home, but it's increasingly clear that one route, agreed back in the 1970s when musicians could still afford homes in Moseley and Kings Heath, is now pretty much redundant. Younger players tend to live in Bearwood, or near the city centre. But the question of modifying an established route has to be thoroughly discussed with the players' committee: this one may run and run.

That's unsurprising, really: huge quantities of orchestral administration time are taken up with logistics. Maddi Belsey-Day, the assistant planning manager, was in early to look after Stanislav Kochanovsky; tomorrow she'll fetch the soloist, Sergei Krylov, from the Hyatt hotel prior to rehearsal – jetlagged soloists, left to their own devices, have an unfortunate habit of getting lost. Her colleague Rachel Lockwood is finalising the next draft of the orchestra's working schedule. She's looking for possible dates for next season's Centre Stage chamber series, and trying not to miss a thing: 'The next schedule goes out this week. The players get the draft schedule for December to March and then also the advance schedule for March to December 2019.'

The CBSO's three librarians, meanwhile, live in a world of paper, pencils and tape: procuring the sheet music for everything the orchestra plays, buying or hiring the pieces it doesn't own, and preparing all the parts required for any given rehearsal or concert. That means pencilling in any cuts or (with certain conductors) discreet alterations to the scoring across all the sixty-odd instrumental parts used for each piece, and adding bowing-marks (usually decided by the string section leaders) in all the string parts. With something like 10,000 individual pieces of sheet music to be marked or checked each season, the library tends to be a busy place. Right now: 'We've got a Classic FM Hall of Fame programme coming up, so we're de-padding Saturday's Gubbay concert and swapping the pieces we need from that into the new folder,' says Jack Lovell. 'Plus, we had this composition workshop today, which we've been helping prepare parts for. We've all been waiting for someone to run upstairs and say they're wrong. But they haven't – so that's cool.'

The day in the learning and participation department, by comparison, has been relatively straightforward: a catch-up session with L&P manager Katie Lucas, newly returned from maternity leave and, for Lauren Craner, the assistant manager, all sorts of odd jobs:

> I came in, sorted out some music for our playalong events, which are in the spring, and tidied away the percussion instruments that we took out to Barchester Cherry Trees Care Home on Friday. And now I'm emailing a guy about a lower woodwind playalong day we're running in the spring – it'll be led by Margaret Cookhorn, Rachael Pankhurst and Mark O'Brien, and they're keen to get some trade stands.

In the chorus department, assistant chorus manager James Rowland is preparing for the evening's Youth Chorus auditions. With CBSO Centre in use by BCMG, he's hired the nearby Birmingham Progressive Synagogue. That's fairly routine now, but it still generates additional work. 'We take music stands, chairs, refreshments – they'll eat as much chocolate as they can get down – we ship the stuff over, sign them all in, keep an eye on things, deal with nosebleeds.' The adult CBSO Chorus is due to rehearse in CBSO Centre on Wednesday, preparing for next week's Panufnik premiere: they'll need registering, supervising and refreshing too, though nosebleeds are less of an issue.

Ten days later: Wednesday 21 November 2018 at Symphony Hall. Mirga Gražinytė-Tyla returned from maternity leave last Friday, and the whole organisation has ratcheted up a gear. Gidon Kremer and Kremerata Baltica flew into Birmingham this afternoon, and have gone straight into rehearsal at CBSO Centre. While the centre team sort them out, the full CBSO, CBSO Chorus and CBSO Children's Chorus have moved 'up the road' for Mirga's first concert since June: the UK premiere of *Faithful Journey*, a full-scale choral work commissioned by the Feeney Trust from Roxanna Panufnik. The retired nonagenarian violinist Stan Smith, who played under Roxanna's father, Andrzej Panufnik, in the 1950s, has expressed a wish to come to the rehearsal and meet her, and bass player Mark Goodchild has arranged a taxi and an intro.

Even for an organisation that puts on over a hundred concerts a year, this feels busy. 'It's definitely the most concerty concert I can remember doing for a while,' says Adele Franghiadi, who's supervising the Children's Chorus, as well as the team of paid chaperones that are required by law when children perform alongside professionals. Children's Chorus members in pink ties and pink blouses mill around by the artists' entrance; with no spare space at Symphony Hall, all the singers – adults and children alike – are warming up at the nearby Birmingham Rep theatre. 'Such a hardship,' jokes learning and engagement director Lucy

OVERLEAF *Mirga Gražinytė-Tyla, soprano Klara Ek, the CBSO and the CBSO Chorus receive applause after a performance of Grieg's* Peer Gynt. *Symphony Hall, 16 February 2019.*

Galliard – the Rep is barely thirty seconds' walk from Symphony Hall. Sophie Adams, who usually runs the CBSO Youth Orchestra, is registering the adult singers as they arrive.

Mirga and the orchestra have been onstage for a while, of course – Rambo and Rob delivered the instruments to Symphony Hall yesterday afternoon and the CBSO's instrument van (nicknamed 'Lilac Lil' for the big purple CBSO 'splat' logo on its side) is parked up in Bay C alongside a BBC outside broadcast van – the concert is going out live on Radio 3. Or possibly not. Producer Chris Wines looks worried, and it turns out that the line to Broadcasting House in London is down. The live relay might not go ahead after all – though, as Claire Dersley points out, 'That's less pressure for us!' She and her team have set up their laptops in Symphony Hall's artists' bar, right in the middle of any off-duty players. Best to be close to any emerging problems, though as 7 p.m. arrives, a text message confirms that the line is back up, and the broadcast is going ahead.

With the rehearsal over, there's a pre-concert talk about to start: Stephen Maddock is to interview Roxanna Panufnik. A couple of lingering players are ushered offstage; Symphony Hall's technicians run out a pair of chairs and some microphones, and the public is admitted. Musicians chat and snack in the artists' bar; an impromptu viola section social unfolds over packed sandwiches while other players make a dash for the Starbucks across the ICC Mall. Tom White checks up on the team of camera operators that he's booked to document the concert; director of concerts Jenny Chadwick

waits to greet the Polish Ambassador and Jack Lovell goes over the evening's surtitles. (He'll be operating them from a cubicle at the back of the auditorium.)

Out in the foyer, director of marketing Maria Howes is in position at the CBSO information desk. Tonight's concert coaches are all safely in; the boxes of programmes – produced by the CBSO's publications manager Helen Tabor from her home in Yorkshire – have arrived from the printers, but Maria's there to handle complimentary tickets for critics and guests, to troubleshoot, and to answer any questions the audience might throw at her: yes, we'll try and re-seat you; no, programmes are for sale over there. Up in the Level Four bar, Megan Bradshaw of the development team is co-hosting a drinks reception for the accountancy firm Smith & Williamson – a major supporter of the CBSO – but there's a separate do planned for Legacy donors in the Green Room, and director of development Simon Fairclough is shuttling between the two.

Symphony Hall's doors have opened. A harpist is tuning on stage, the Chorus is being ushered towards its stalls, the audience are taking their seats and among the instrument boxes, coats, flight cases and empty coffee cups that clutter the cavernous semi-circular space behind the platform at Symphony Hall, the orchestra is returning, now in concert dress. Violin scales and low brass arpeggios fill the air; an oboe plays roulades, and tiny fragments of *The Nutcracker* – the evening's second half – flit about like gnats. A BBC broadcast assistant in a radio headset hovers by the platform door as Symphony Hall technicians glance at the digital

Going on: Symphony Hall, 26 June 2019.

timer next to the main lighting panel. A couple of players examine the portable notice board – nothing much, just updates to the schedule, and a call for claims for the next meeting of the CBSO Benevolent Fund.

Without any visible signal, the backstage area empties as swiftly as if a plug has been pulled. Ninety players move out onto the stage, and Claire Dersley and Peter Harris watch them as they go, making silent ticks on a mental checklist. Tonight's leader Thomas Gould gives the nod to Rainer Gibbons, the principal oboe, to play the 'A', and the orchestra tunes. The soprano soloist Mary Bevan is waiting by the door on the far side of the stage, and Mirga has arrived from her dressing room too – smiling, bouncing up and down on her toes, with a hoodie thrown over her

concert dress. She takes her place at the far-side stage door.

It's hushed out there now. The digital clock says 19.30, and Symphony Hall's stage manager nods confirmation that front-of-house clearance has come through. The door swings open, and we've arrived at the moment towards which every person in the organisation has been working all day, all week, and every season of the ninety-eight years that have brought us to this point: the moment of live performance. For the next two hours, all that matters is the music. The backstage crew starts the applause, the audience ignites, and Mirga Gražinytė-Tyla walks out to where her orchestra, and its city, awaits.

TIMELINE

1760-1909	1910-1919	1920-1929	1930-1949	1950-1959

October 1767
First regular Birmingham Music Meeting – later to become the Triennial Festival.

October 1834
Official opening of **Birmingham Town Hall.**

August 1846
Mendelssohn conducts premiere of his *Elijah* at the Triennial Festival.

December 1873
William Stockley launches his orchestral concerts.

March 1897
Stockley retires and disbands his orchestra.

October 1900
Premiere of Elgar's *The Dream of Gerontius* at the Triennial Festival.

October 1912
Final Birmingham Triennial Festival.

October 1917
Thomas Beecham founds New Birmingham Orchestra.

August 1918
Beecham dissolves New Birmingham Orchestra, citing wartime conditions.

March 1919
Proposals for a publicly-funded City Orchestra submitted to the Lord Mayor of Birmingham.

5 September 1920
Appleby Matthews conducts the first concert of the **City of Birmingham Orchestra.**

10 November 1920
Sir Edward Elgar conducts the CBO's First Symphony Concert.

February 1921
CBO gives its first Children's Concert.

November 1921
First concert of the **City of Birmingham Choir.**

September 1924
Adrian Boult succeeds Appleby Matthews as principal conductor.

January 1925
Boult and the CBO make their first recording – Bantock's *Hebridean Symphony* (now lost).

October 1930
Leslie Heward becomes musical director.

June 1932
Harold Gray appointed deputy conductor (having joined the orchestra's staff in 1924).

December 1940
Heward and the CBO make their first commercial recordings during the Birmingham blitz.

May 1943
Heward dies of tuberculosis at his home in Harborne, aged 45.

October 1943
George Weldon succeeds Heward, initially for one year – but permanently from 1944.

September 1944
CBO relaunched as a permanent, year-round ensemble.

February 1948
CBO renamed City of Birmingham Symphony Orchestra.

October 1951
Rudolf Schwarz becomes chief conductor of the C

May 1955
Schwarz and the C undertake their first overseas tour – to t Netherlands.

December 1955
Premiere of the first Feeney Trust comm Bliss's *Meditations c Theme by John Blo*

January 1957
Midland Youth Orchestra gives its concert.

September 1957
Andrzej Panufnik becomes music director of the CBS(

July 1959
Panufnik steps dow Adrian Boult acts a caretaker conducte for one season.

0-1969	1970-1979	1980-1989	1990-1999	2000-2020

1960
Rignold appointed
incipal conductor.

ay 1962
O gives the world
iere of Britten's *War
iem* in Coventry
edral.

ary 1966
old and the CBSO
their first LP
ding, for Lyrita:
c by Arthur Bliss.

ember 1969
Frémaux
eeds Hugo
old.

31 January 1974
First public performance
of the new **CBSO
Chorus.**

March 1978
General manager
Arthur Baker is ousted
in a musicians' coup:
Frémaux resigns in
sympathy.

July 1979
Harold Gray retires after
55 years of service to
the orchestra.

September 1979
Erich Schmid becomes
the CBSO's first principal
guest conductor.

September 1980
Simon Rattle takes up
his post as principal
conductor.

**June 1987
Birmingham
Contemporary Music
Group** gives its
inaugural concert.

January 1988
The musicians vote
to approve the
Development Plan,
expanding the
orchestra.

September 1989
Mark-Anthony Turnage
becomes Composer in
Association.

May 1991
After 71 years, the CBSO
gives its final regular
concert in Birmingham
Town Hall.

June 1991
Official opening of
Symphony Hall.

May 1995
CBSO Youth Chorus
gives first public
performance.

**August 1998
CBSO Centre** opens.
Rattle gives a series of
farewell concerts.

**September 1998
Sakari Oramo** succeeds
Simon Rattle.

October 2004
CBSO Youth Orchestra
gives its inaugural
concert.

September 2008
Andris Nelsons
succeeds Sakari
Oramo.

September 2016
Mirga Gražinytė-Tyla
succeeds Andris
Nelsons.

February 2019
Mirga Gražinytė-Tyla
signed to Deutsche
Grammophon.

BIBLIOGRAPHY

Bantock, Myrrha, *Granville Bantock: A Personal Portrait* (J. M. Dent & Sons, 1972)

Beecham, Sir Thomas, *A Mingled Chime* (Arrow, 1961)

Blom, Eric (ed.), *Leslie Heward 1897–1943* (J. M. Dent & Sons, 1944)

Boult, Sir Adrian, *My Own Trumpet* (Hamish Hamilton, 1973)

Brett Young, Francis, *The Dark Tower* (Martin Secker, 1915)

——, *The Young Physician* (Collins, 1919)

——, *Portrait of Clare* (Heinemann, 1927)

Colles, H. C., *Walford Davies: A Biography* (OUP, 1942)

Cooper, Jilly, *Appassionata* (Bantam Press, 1996)

Cotton, Maggie, *Wrong Sex, Wrong Instrument* (Apex, 2006)

Downes, Frank, *Around the Horn* (Birmingham City Council, 1994)

Douglas, Alton, *Birmingham at War*, vol. 1 (Streetly Printing, 1982)

Drummond, Pippa, *The Provincial Music Festival in England* (Routledge, 2011)

Elliott, Anne, *The Music Makers* (Birmingham Library Services, 2000)

Elgar, Edward, *A Future for English Music*, edited by P. Young (Dobson, 1968)

Foster, Michael, *The Idea Was Good: The Story of Britten's 'War Requiem'* (Coventry Cathedral, 2012)

Foreman, L., *From Parry to Britten* (Batsford, 1987)

Fraser, F., and L. Jenkins, *Town Hall Birmingham* (Boydell Press, 2007)

Griffiths, Bill, *Northern Sinfonia: A Magic of its Own* (Northumbria University Press, 2004)

Grimley, Terry, *Symphony Hall: A Dream Realised* (Boydell Press, 2011)

Halstead, Jill, *Ruth Gipps: Anti-modernism, Nationalism and Difference in English Music* (Ashgate, 2006)

Handford, Margaret, *Sounds Unlikely: Music in Birmingham* (Brewin, 2006)

Hansard, 22 May 1947, vol. 437

Harman, T., and W. Showell, *Showell's Dictionary of Birmingham* (Cornish Bros, 1885)

Harris, P. (ed.), *Songs of Love: The Letters of Rupert Brooke and Noel Olivier* (Bloomsbury, 1991)

Heighway, John, 'From Belsen to Bournemouth', *Dorset Life*, October 2017

Henley, D., and V. McKernan, *The Original Liverpool Sound* (Liverpool University Press, 2009)

Holst, Imogen, *Gustav Holst* (OUP, 1969)

Howell, Christopher, Forgotten Artists 5: Hugo Rignold [2014], http://www.musicweb-international.com/classrev/2014/Mar14/Forgotten_Rignold.htm

Jenkins, L., and B. King-Smith, *The Birmingham 78s 1925–1947* (CBSO, 1983)

Kay, Robert, *Elgar Society Journal*, vol. 17 no. 3 (December 2011)

Kenyon, Nicholas, *Simon Rattle: The Making of a Conductor* (Faber & Faber, 1987)

——, *Simon Rattle: From Birmingham to Berlin* (Faber & Faber, 2001)

King-Smith, Beresford, *1920–70: The First 50 Years of the CBSO* (CBSO, 1970)

——, *CBSO Diamond Jubilee Yearbook* (CBSO, 1980)

——, *Crescendo! 75 Years of the CBSO* (Methuen, 1995)

Lee-Browne, M. and A. Guinery, *Delius and his Music* (Boydell Press, 2014)

Lloyd, Stephen, *H. Balfour Gardiner* (CUP, 1984)

Mendelssohn-Bartholdy, Felix, *Letters of Felix Mendelssohn-Bartholdy: From 1833 to 1847*, edited by Paul Mendelssohn-Bartholdy and Carl Mendelssohn-Bartholdy (Longman, 1864)

Meredith, P. and P. Harris, *Malcolm Arnold: Rogue Genius* (Thames/Elkin, 2004)

Miller, Geoffrey, *The Bournemouth Symphony Orchestra* (Dorset Publishing, 1970)

Moore, Jerrold Northrop, *Edward Elgar: A Creative Life* (OUP, 1984)

Morley, Christopher, *Royal Birmingham Conservatoire* (Elliott and Thompson, 2017)

Morrison, Richard, *Orchestra: The LSO* (Faber & Faber, 2004)

Orchestral musicians are adept at finding loopholes in official edicts. This 1950s cartoon by second violinist and orchestral humourist Albert 'Rusty' Russell identifies the inevitable oversight in a new orchestral dress code.

Panufnik, Sir Andrzej, *Composing Myself* (Methuen, 1987)

Pevsner, N., and A. Wedgwood, *The Buildings of England: Warwickshire* (Penguin, 1966)

Powell, Mrs R., *Edward Elgar: Memories of a Variation* (OUP, 1937)

Rawle, Phil, *CBSO Chorus History 1974–2014* (Phil Rawle, 2014)

Richards, Steve, *The Luftwaffe over Brum* (Richards Publishing, 2015)

Russell, W. G. A., *The City of Birmingham Choir, 1921–1946* (The Bulletin Press, 1946)

Self, Robert, *Neville Chamberlain: A Biography* (Routledge, 2006)

Sourek, O. (ed.), *Dvořák: Letters and Reminiscences*, translated by R. Samsour (Artia, Prague, 1954)

Stockley, W. C., *Fifty Years of Music in Birmingham* (Hudson & Son, 1913)

Sutcliffe Smith, J., *The Story of Music in Birmingham* (Cornish Bros, 1945)

Tawastjerna, Erik, *Sibelius*, vol. 2: *1904–14*, translated by R. Layton (Faber & Faber, 1986)

——, *Sibelius*, vol. 3: *1914–57*, translated by R. Layton (Faber & Faber, 1997)

Thompson, Brian, *The Disastrous Mrs Weldon* (Broadway, 2001)

Tippett, Sir Michael, *Those Twentieth Century Blues* (Hutchinson, 1991)

Walton, Chris, 'Schoenberg's Alpine Wanderer: Erich Schmid at 100', *Musical Times*, vol. 147 (2006)

Wood, Sir Henry, *My Life of Music* (Gollancz, 1946)

Wright, G. H. von, *A Portrait of Wittgenstein as a Young Man* (Basil Blackwell, 1990)

Young, Percy, *Elgar OM* (Collins, 1955)

"I have never met a group of musicians with a more happily co-operative spirit than the CBSO"

SIR ADRIAN BOULT

1990: the CBSO football team, resplendent in the orchestra's logo and matching malachite green shorts, and recently reinforced by such Rattle-era signings as bass player Mark Goodchild (front left), trumpeter Jon Quirk (front row, second from right) and co-principal cellos Ulrich Heinen (back left) and Eduardo Vassallo (back row, third from right), poses after a pre-concert kick-around at Warwick Arts Centre. Having been knocked out of a pan-European orchestral championship at the 1998 Salzburg Festival, they scored a remarkable (if somewhat irregular) 9-1 victory over the Mahler Chamber Orchestra at Aix-en-Provence in 2000.

OVERLEAF Concerto (1974) by Alexander Walker (1895–1984). The artist was a brother of the Redemptorist community at Erdington Abbey; he dedicated this painting of the CBSO in Birmingham Town Hall 'to Louis Frémaux, with happy memories'.

APPENDIX

Principal Conductors and Music Directors
Appleby Matthews: 1920–24
Adrian Boult: 1924–30
Leslie Heward: 1930–43
George Weldon: 1944–51
Rudolf Schwarz: 1951–57
Sir Andrzej Panufnik: 1957–59
Sir Adrian Boult: 1959–60
Hugo Rignold: 1960–68
Louis Frémaux: 1969–78
Sir Simon Rattle: 1980–98
Sakari Oramo: 1998–2008
Andris Nelsons: 2008–15
Mirga Gražinytė-Tyla: 2016–

Staff Conductors
Richard Wassell: 1920–23
Joseph Lewis: 1924–30
Harold Gray: 1930–79
Meredith Davies: 1957–60
Maurice Handford: 1970–74
Michael Seal: 2005–
Alpesh Chauhan: 2014–16
Jonathan Bloxham: 2016–18
Jaume Santonja Espinós: 2018–

Principal Guest Conductors
Erich Schmid: 1979–82
Neeme Järvi: 1981–84
Okko Kamu: 1985–88
Iona Brown: 1985–88 *(Guest Director)*
Viktor Liberman: 1985–88
(Guest Director)
Mark Elder: 1992–95
Paavo Järvi: 1996–99
Sakari Oramo: 2008–09
Edward Gardner: 2010–16
Kazuki Yamada: 2018–

CBSO Chorus Directors
Gordon Clinton: 1973–79
Richard Greening: 1979
Nicholas Cleobury: 1980–82
Simon Halsey: 1983–

Leaders
Alex Cohen: 1920–21
Paul Beard: 1921–33

Alfred Cave: 1933–42
Norris Stanley: 1942–58
Wilfred Lehmann: 1958–60
Meyer Stolow: 1960–62
John Georgiadis: 1963–65
Felix Kok: 1965–88
John Bradbury: 1970–78 *(co-leader)*
Peter Thomas: 1988–2004
Laurence Jackson: 2006–15

General Secretaries, General Managers and Chief Executives
Appleby Matthews: 1920–21
H S Goodwin: 1922–23
Albert Shephard: 1924–43
Ulric Brunner: 1943–44
Denzil Walker: 1944–52
Kenneth Matchett: 1952–53
Blyth Major: 1953–60
Ernest Edwards: 1960–62
Arthur Baker: 1962–78
Edward Smith: 1978–99
Stephen Maddock: 1999–

Chairs
G. Johnson: 1920–21
R. R. Gelling: 1921–22
G. F. Macdonald: 1922–31

(management committee)
W. Byng Kenrick: 1931–50
Stephen Lloyd: 1950–68
Denis Martineau: 1968–74

(executive sub-committee)
Gerald C. Forty: 1931–49
William G. A. Russell: 1950–63
Denis Martineau: 1963–74

George Jonas: 1974–92
Arthur Knapp: 1992–95
Sir Michael Checkland: 1995–2001
Sir Michael Lyons: 2001–07
Ronnie Bowker: 2007–10
Kumar Muthalagappan: 2010–12
Bridget Blow: 2012–18
David Burbidge: 2018–

INDEX